The Keystone Kid

Mike Furches

Published by:

 **FriesenPress**

Suite 300 – 777 Fort Street
Victoria, BC, Canada V8W 1G9
www.friesenpress.com

For information on bulk orders contact:
info@friesenpress.com or fax 1-888-376-7026

Distributed to the trade by The Ingram Book Company

Table of Contents

The Keystone Kid
Acknowledgments:

There are so many things I could say here, so many people to thank. I could never do it all. This has been a labor of love for many who have gone through similar experiences. Over the long journey of putting this book together I have to give acknowledgment to those who helped over the years. My daughter Marathana Prothro, my wife Mary Jane, my friends William Fosterr, and Debbie Elwood, Mary Taddiken who contributed ideals and thoughts, especially towards the end of the journey with many of those original edits and great advice. I have to also acknowledge though my friend Bill Terrell, we went through life coming so close to touching and knowing each other, yet, it never seemed to happen until The Keystone Kid. For that final edit and sacrifice, I am so grateful. I am also grateful for the cover art provided by Dave Weiss from Amokarts, I appreciate your work, and contribution to this project.

There are others who have been there for the journey, all of those who contributed comments prior to publication. All of that is a part of the work that individuals have done. I also want to acknowledge though Lise Mino my publishing consultant at Friesen Press. I have to also acknowledge the folks at Hollywood Jesus, especially David Bruce, brother, you have no idea how much I value you and how much God has used you to hone my craft which still has a lot to be desired. In that journey, Melinda Ledman and Greg and Jenn Wright, you have and continue to be a part of that process.

I also need to thank a number of people. First, I have been blessed to have found real, personal, human love in my wife Mary Jane. Over the years I have been blessed to have people tell me that my work has touched them. I can in all honesty say had it not been for my wife, I could not have done any of the work I have done. God blessed me with her. I also want to thank my children, Marathana and Nathan, I love you so much. I am so sorry that for so many years you had to live with Anthony, in so many ways you are, outside of Christ and your mother, the greatest gift I have ever been given,

I wish I would have gotten help sooner. I also need to thank those who sacrificially supported this work over the years. I am amazed to this day that God would choose to use me, and beyond that, choose to bless me with the friends I have. I also thank my church, both those at The Virtual Pew, and Mosaic Wichita for your support, we have been on this journey together and I am blessed to share the ride with people I love. To those who struggle with Mental Illness, keep your head up, go for your dreams, I thank you for the way you have inspired me. To all of the victims of abuse, we have been on this journey together, you and in reality, we, are not alone. To those in the music industry I have worked with, thanks for helping me keep my focus, especially my dear friend Rob Cassels. I still say, you are the best, and God has and will continue to use you. I also want to thank the people at Tiroma Films seeing to it that the movie of The Keystone Kid gets made. To Rob Harris, Matthew Lord, Titus Jackson, and Megan Hurley, thanks for believing in me and this story. I could name so many others and I know I have left out people, I am grateful for you all. That said, there is one I am forever grateful for, the one who has become my loving father, my mighty counselor, and the healer of all of my pain, I thank and am grateful for more than any other, the embrace and love of a Savior named Jesus.

Dedication

Many will be amazed by this dedication, but I dedicate this book to my mother, Geneva Lewis. The truth is, in the end I had a mother, a mother that ultimately found a way to see to it that The Keystone Kid got published. It was so easy to judge, but I found out, there is always more to the story, and there is more power in love and forgiveness than in hate and judgment. In the end, I know I'll see you in Heaven.

Quotes on Mike Furches
and The Keystone Kid

"The Keystone Kid is this generation's The Cross .and the Switchblade"
~ **Lisa Baker, Freelance Writer, Contributor to Dr. Charles Stanley's In Touch Magazine**

"I just finished the Keystone Kid. As I finished this book, I had tears in my eyes." ~ **Dr. Jack Alkon**

"Furches is a gutsy guy; he turns his own life inside out, and then dares the Church to look at what years of abuse really do to a person."
~ **Mary Diane Goin, Author,**

'Every person on the planet should read this book, because we need more understanding'. ~ **Deirdre McGuirk, Ireland**

"Mike Furches is truly one of our countries good guys" ~ **Jack Elery, National Radio Talk Show Host**

"The world is full of hurting people. They have been abused, assaulted & cast aside. They are victims. They walk by you every day. Some bury their pain in addictions. Some inflict their pain upon others. But the truth about pain, is that it always leaves scars. In this unsettling, & viscerally honest book, Mike Furches has chosen to tell the story behind every one of his own personal scars. Because sometimes hurting people, just need to know they are not alone..." ~ **Rob Harris, Actor**

"Do not let that "Aw shucks" demeanor fool you. You won't find a sharper wit and keener mind than what Mike has in his repertoire." ~ **Jack Yatsko, International Mental Health Advocate**

I can clearly see God using this story to heal many from the bondage of "false guilt," they have suffered all their lives, even into adulthood. Mike is one of my dearest and truest friends for decades, (we traveled and worked together for many years). I have no question of the integrity of his work. As you read "The Keystone Kid," you will find it hard to put down. The ultimate grace of

God could show up in the next chapter, and surely it does! ~ **Rob Cassels, Christian Music Pioneer**

"I love this guy. The things this blessed soul has seen, experienced and endured have worked a depth and sensitivity into him, such that I can't imagine anyone who would not be profoundly touched and moved by the Lord through Mike Furches. He is living, moving, breathing irrefutable proof that earth has no sorrow that heaven cannot heal." ~ **Burt Rosenberg, Nationally Known Comedian**

"Mike Furches tells his story as raw and riveting as he lived it..." ~ **Mary Diane Goin, National Radio Host**

"... graphic and detailed but real, I was moved and chills ran my skin at times, I've lived a familiar life, just in another darkly crazed way. The courage it took to keep on moving forward and write this book was and is amazing, thank GOD for will power and forgiveness, I loved this Book!" ~ **Chuk Cooley, Rock Musician**

"The Keystone Kid meets everyone's greatest fears and hopes about experiencing abuse. For those who have lived it first hand, this book offers hope - hope that there really is healing, that despite the injustice of the past, there is a better future ahead, and the reality that God genuinely cares about the brokenhearted.

For those who have never lived with abuse and don't want to hear or read about it, The Keystone Kid offers a unique opportunity to address those fears and move beyond them. Seeing God's hand in the author's life reinforces faith in a passionate, loving God rather than points the finger at an uncaring deity who allows evil to exist. It also stretches the breadth and depth of compassion for any Christian who would rather look the other way. The Keystone Kid safely and realistically portrays the life of a victim/abuser in a way that builds bridges, and answers the question of why Christ went to such great lengths to rescue the crushed in spirit." ~ **Melinda Ledman, Senior Writer, Editor, Hollywood Jesus**

"The Keystone Kid is for all the misfits, mavericks, and rogues who think God wrote them off a long time ago. ~ **Mary Diane Goin, Author, National Radio, Television Host**

"The Keystone Kid is an unsettling, face to face journey through the deconstruction of a young man, from sexual abuses, chemical & alcohol addic-

tions, murderous hatred & gang violence to his life changing encounter with honest, unwavering, grace & love, that led him to become one of the most compassionate & genuine men alive today, Pastor Mike Furches."
~ **Rob Harris, Actor**

"While I am not a religious person, I recognize the value of faith in helping many cope with the most challenging circumstances life puts in their way. In the case of the author, the transformation of life caused by his acceptance of Jesus is astounding. It took courage to write this book; the writing of it has proven therapeutic to the author and the reading of it will likewise prove therapeutic to many victims of physical and sexual abuse." ~ **Dr. Jack Alkon**

"Mike, Thank you for being a source of inspiration in the world and for shining light in the darkness." ~ **Angela Shelton, National Advocate, Comedian, Filmmaker**

"One of the best Christian-themed books I have read in a long time."
~ **Lisa Baker, Former Book Editor, Hollywood Jesus**

"Anthony's story is of one boy living in extreme conditions of abuse, neglect, struggle, loss and lack of basic needs all before he was old enough to drive a car. Yet, he had a internal determination to overcome his circumstances. His story is way too common in our American society. Dysfunctional family life destroys the heart and will of so many of our youth. Entangled in drugs, gangs and the occult, The Keystone Kid is an amazing true story of survival and the critical element of finding personal healing." ~ **Becky Volz, Christian Music Pioneer**

"The Keystone Kid vividly represents in the life of one young boy what has been happening to America's young people for decades. While the Church sits in the comfortable pews behind pristine walls, boys and girls are being robbed of their innocence and hope...not by strangers, but by the very ones that are supposed to be their first introduction to God as a caring, loving father." ~ **Mary Diane Goin, Author, National Radio, Television Host**

Mike, I really like the timing with your pending release of the Keystone Kid. I think it is a great contrast with the recent publicity about the movie Precious and the book it is based upon Push, both great works that illustrate surviving horrendous abuse issues. Their graphic nature though can be off-putting for people not understanding the cycle of abuse. Your book pulls the reader in without that aspect. I hope social service and juvenile service agencies make this available to their consumers. God bless ~ **Klint Deere**

"A picture of our young people today, so aptly brought to life in Anthony's story, *The Keystone Kid?*"

"I enjoyed the read, and ask the Father to use it to open the eyes of the Church, and an inspiration for other "Keystone Kids" to break out in Jesus from the past that defines them!" ~ **Mary Diane Goin, Television Host**

"There are few books I've read in my lifetime that have touched my whole mind, heart, and soul the way The Keystone Kid has. In his book, Mike takes you on an unflinchingly honest journey of abuse, recovery, and redemption. He shows how the church can be both a help and a hindrance to those who have suffered outside its doors and sometimes even within. The book reaches out to those whose hearts have been trampled and offers hope and love in a way few others ever have. The Keystone Kid is a must read for both those who have been abused and those who want to help in the healing process." ~ **Jenny Baker, Survivor**

Kudos to Mike Furches for having the bravery to share his very personal, and very painful, story. The Keystone Kid is a book which needed to be written; but it also is a book which needs to be read and discussed. The good news is, that in the midst of our pain, there is healing in God's wings; and we can be sure that in spite of our life circumstances, there is nothing that happens without His notice, nothing, no circumstance and no one which the Lord cannot redeem. ~ **Gary Zanow, Pastor Z**

From the stunning opening pages, The Keystone Kid grabs and shakes the reader in a gripping, powerful manner. This is a story of pain, anguish, and sadness. It is also a story of resiliency, hope, and faith. I found myself rooting for Anthony over and over again despite what he did to others and the activities he engaged in. This is a story reminding of us of our humanity and to also never easily give up on anyone.

The Keystone Kid is the kind of book that offers perspective to our everyday lives and reminds us to tell those that we love, exactly that. The author, Mike Furches, vividly brings this story to life! ~ **Jack Yatsko, MSW LSW**

"This book drew me in and forced me to question that which I believed regarding faith, family, and most of all forgiveness. I thought I understood true love and forgiveness, and then I read The Keystone Kid." ~ **Titus Jackson, Tiroma Films**

"Sometimes we learn best through stories. In The Keystone Kid, Mike Furches weaves a tale of trial and redemption that pricks the conscience with both the harsh light of reality and the unexpected power of love. It will make you re-think what it means to walk alongside someone, enter into the realness of their pain with love and compassion, and see a life transformed. One thing The Keystone Kid won't do is leave you unchanged. It is a call to action." ~ **Maurice Broaddus, author of King Maker.**

"Every once in a while you meet someone who is not concerned with vanity. They speak from the heart and are often ridiculed for it. Mike Furches is one of those unique people. He's one of those that you always look forward to talk to and now he has written it down for the sake of those that say they have no hope. No matter what lies ahead, he will travel the path that nobody else will take. The Bible talks of those that were dead in their sins. From this seemingly insurmountable hole, Mike's life testimony proves the mighty power of God's saving grace. I thank God for this book." ~ **Eric Johnson**

Review of The Keystone Kid
Mary Diane Goin, Christian Author, Radio, TV Host

The Keystone Kid vividly represents in the life of one young boy what has been happening to America's young people for decades. While the Church sits in the comfortable pews behind pristine walls, boys and girls are being robbed of their innocence and hope, not by strangers, but by the very ones that are supposed to be their first introduction to God as a caring, loving father.

Anthony became a waif, as what was to be a safe and nurturing family broke from its moorings with the early death of his father, followed by his mother's revolving door of abusive relationships and the heartbreaking, incestuous seduction of her own son.

The abused will abuse, finding ways to relieve the pain of rejection and secret shame. Anthony embraced drugs, sex, gang violence, and the satanic with a vengeance, each episode releasing the boiling emotional pressure, if only for a little while.

A few people tried to reach him, but mostly they focused on Anthony's acting out and how to punish it without asking "why". I imagine it's like many people today who enjoy pointing out and picking at the bad fruit from a tree, rather than uprooting it to see the hidden damage.

For sure, many may feel ill equipped for such a task, but the fact remains, young people like Anthony are dying all around us; either they succumb hopelessly to their own devices (Anthony came close to suicide on a number of occasions), fall prey to the violence of others or though young in age, just wither away.

Anthony's story reminds me of the classic novel, *Mary Shelley's Frankenstein*. Despite how Hollywood has brought her epic to life, the author's intent was to show that the doctor was the real monster.

Brought to life, but then rejected, the walking dead man externalized his tremendous emotional pain. In the end, he wept, moaning that all he wanted was a father, and for that father to accept him and give him his name.

Is this not a picture of our young people today, so aptly brought to life in Anthony's story, *The Keystone Kid*?

They are given life, only to be rejected and cast aside by those who brought them into the world. These young boys get into trouble, yes; but behind the act, the heart is screaming, "Look at me! Love me! Accept me!"

A man who once worked in the White House during the JFK administration said that only a few days after the President's funeral, a young John-John (JFK, JR.) came walking through the halls. He stopped and looked up to the man.

"Are you a daddy?" he asked.

"Yes, son; I sure am," replied the tall man.

John-John's eyes grew wide. In an excited voice he pled, "Will you pick me up and toss me in the air?"

Anthony was looking for a father figure who would take time out from his own pursuits, bend down, and lift up the little boy.

Anthony finally found such a Man, not in his stepfathers, teachers, coaches, or gang members. But wait; truthfully...the Man found him!

Jesus reached down and saw the broken heart of a little boy inside of a tough-acting teenager's body. Without hesitation, He bent to Anthony's level, joyfully embraced him and lifted him up out of *what was* into *what could be*.

Jesus gave Anthony what years of drugs, illicit sex, gang associations, athletic accolades and the occult could not—the unconditional love of a Father who would never embarrass, abuse or reject him.

Over the years, Anthony learned to walk out his salvation, making many mistakes along the way (as we all do). Nevertheless, it was a joy for him to discover that through it all, God's commitment to him was consistently stronger than any faithfulness to God Anthony could muster up on his own. God *never* removed His grace and goodness from His adopted son.

What Anthony, Frankenstein's creation, and all of us are searching for is available in Jesus Christ. He offers a new start. Through Jesus' perfect sacrifice on the Cross for our imperfections, He opened the way for us to become adopted into a better family. If by faith we accept what He has done for us, then grace does the rest and transfers our identity out of the old man and his failures and into the newness of Christ and His sufficiency. We are even given permission to use His name—Jesus—as *our* legal family name in every spiritual transaction and prayer.

However, there comes a point in everyone's life, including the Christian's, where issues once tucked neatly away inside of an internal compartment don't stay that way. God, in His Wisdom, allows the lock to break and the lid to rise, exposing all those ugly, bitter, hurtful things to us in the glaring, but safe light of His love.

Anthony could no longer pack away what had happened to him as a child. Unable to make the connection at first, his spiritual and relational problems as an adult were freely drawing upon the pain of his childhood, a vast reservoir that had never been drained.

It took tremendous courage for Anthony to reach out to a Christian counselor and face his past, but little by little, memory by memory, the Holy Spirit-working in and through both men, turned on the valves. Finally, Anthony watched as his dammed up, debris filled heart emptied out the bad, and the wondrous Spirit of God poured in fresh, clean, living water!

There's a part in *The Keystone Kid* where Anthony and a friend were walking a hilly area outside of town known for its jagged cliffs. They began to hear cries for help, and discovered two younger boys who had slipped on the slope and landed on a narrow ledge.

Knowing time was of the essence, Anthony made a decision to reach out to the boys himself rather than sending his friend into town for help.

Putting his own safety aside, Anthony and his friend made a chain to reach out to the youngsters and pulled them up.

Are you perched on a narrow ledge that feels as if it could give any moment? Do you wonder how much longer you can hold on? How many people have ignored or misunderstood your cries for help?

Like Anthony, perhaps you've been diagnosed with Post Traumatic Stress Disorder or another mental illness that springs from the tragic events of your past…leaving a pain so intense that it altered the physical functioning of your brain and the way it manufactures and sends chemicals throughout your body.

Well-intentioned, but misinformed people have defined and limited you with their words or worse, cast you aside altogether as incorrigible and hopeless.

I encourage you to read *The Keystone Kid*. I believe Anthony's story can be the hand that reaches down to pull you up to higher, safer ground.

Inspired by his courage, you can then begin to walk away from the cliff of despair toward a future and a hope. Paradoxically, the way to a better future for those who have been abused involves a going back, much like the title of the classic movie, "Back to the Future".

But this time you don't have to travel alone. If you ask, Jesus will not only walk with you, but in the scariest, darkest, and most painful places of your journey, He'll carry you.

I enjoyed the read, and ask the Father to use it to open the eyes of the Church, and an inspiration for other "Keystone Kids" to break out in Jesus from the past that defines them!

Introduction

Rev. Dr. Don Davis, World Impact, Director of the Urban Ministry Institute

"The Keystone Kid is a gripping portrayal, a truly extraordinary work, and to me one of the most transparent, gritty, and gripping stories regarding abuse, neglect, and fractured relationships I have read. It pulls no punches in describing hurtful, horrible events without flourish or sugar-coating. This level of honesty and transparency will make it a must read for those who, like the Keystone Kid, has experienced varieties of sexual and substance abuse, occultism and violence, parental neglect, and ongoing social chaos but with a remarkable turn. In my mind the Keystone Kid is not a never-ending script of horror and abuse, but a real hopeful tale of how the grace of God can in fact penetrate and transform even the most difficult and abusive situation. On the one hand, there is no logic at all that can suggest that such a story should not have ended in tragedy and death, suicide or worse, with nothing redemptive or helpful to be said from perennial neglect and abuse. Yet, this is the twist and the hope of the Keystone Kid; it reveals through the rescue and impact in the life of Anthony that the grace of God is able to keep and save, to heal and provide, and to direct and finally to transform. This grace is embodied in his story, and it is real. Thank God, it is available to all who need the healing that only God through his Son can provide.

Unfortunately, all too often, God's ability to touch and transform the broken and abused is seen in stylized, even hokey ways, as if Christianity is nothing more than a topping off kind of religion for people who are already good, and who needed enough of God to make their calm and tepid lives just a little more respectable. One would think that Christianity is for those already disciplined and moral, merely a kind of decency faith for those already good enough and healed enough for respectableness. Counter to this idea, the Keystone Kid reveals truly how fierce, persistent, and yet tender the grace of Jesus is. This story demonstrates how the grace of Christ can draw even the most unloved, mistreated, and genuinely desperate heart, one in the tragic state of Anthony's, to himself, giving him the courage to face all the horrible abuses of the past, and yet, by God's tenacious power, to face them

1

and overcome them. It has been said that the grace of God functions like water: it goes to the lowest point first, and then rises from that place. The Keystone Kid reveals just how radical and redemptive this gracious work of Christ is, and what God can do in the heart of one who, by anyone's external standards, had little or no chance but to become a forgotten statistic, an abused child who would grow up to be an abuser or something worse. This is a testament to the Good News that the Kingdom offers, and should be read by everyone who needs to hear how Jesus can truly transform and shine his light into the very darkest corners of our most horrible circumstances.'

Foreward

Pastor Bob Beeman

The book you are about to read is "dangerous." If you are easily offended, it has a few "cuss" words. If you have a weak stomach, some of the stories may be a little too much for you. If you have a heart for those who are being abused and mistreated, then reading this book is going to be difficult.

Numerous news stories and documentaries have been done about "latch key" kids all over America. There are many children who silently suffer as they continue to be mistreated and forgotten. Some are rescued, but most are doomed; it seems, to a life of unhappiness and crime. Many will continue the behaviors they have learned and will sexually, physically, emotionally, and mentally abuse those around them. For most, the cycle of abuse continues for many generations.

Anthony was one of those kids. From the time he was born, it seems he didn't have a chance. He was abused, unloved, and largely forgotten. As his story unfolds, it is difficult to believe that one person could experience such trauma. This story chronicles Anthony's struggles to find peace and meaning in a life out of control.

Anthony was born into a little community in Tennessee. If abortion had been legal, he likely would have been easily terminated. But instead, Anthony would be born into a world of alcohol and drug abuse, sexual perversion, physical abuse, gang violence, and witchcraft. He would learn how to "take care of himself." He would learn that most of the religious people around him were simply hypocrites, and chose to ignore his situation. And, sadly, he wouldn't learn about "real" love until later in life.

Anthony was a survivor. He did what he had to do to make it through his young life. He learned to fight, steal, and lie to survive. Soon, his personality was defined by anger and bitterness. He trusted no one, and he didn't really care if anyone trusted him.

At a time when it seemed Anthony was doomed to simply become another statistic, some life-changing things began to happen. A small spark of hope was ignited. And even though Anthony continued to get knocked down again and again, he continued to get back up. Until one day, Anthony was a new man.

If you have a similar story, this may be one of the most therapeutic books you will ever read. You may find yourself here in these pages. You may identify with Anthony and his abuse. If that is the case, keep reading. The end of this story might surprise you! It may be just the ending you are looking for to your personal story as well!

Foreward

David Bruce, Hollywood Jesus

You are about to sit down to one of the finest meals you ever ate. Here is one of the finest of steak dinners, smothered in sautéed mushrooms with greens and everything good. I am referring of course to the book that you hold in your hands. Mike is the chef, and a master one at that. And like all good chiefs he does not skimp on the spices, seasonings, and just the right sauces. I encourage you to sit back relax and take in this book. Enjoy it just like you would the finest gourmet dinner that you could imagine.

My choice for a great meal is a steak. I recognize that red meat is not the healthiest choice for me. Therefore, I enjoy such a feast on those special occasions when I want to treat myself. Mike's book is like that steak dinner, which is served a little on the raw side, a little red. This is not a well done overcooked steak, which you might find in the Christian bookstore. Those books are always generally sanitized, overcooked, homogenized, with lots of added ingredients that are not natural or from life but rather artificial. There is nothing artificial in Mike's cooking. No sir! Mike's cooking is true to life. Real red meat here and all natural trimmings!

I must say, Mike has been around the block a few times. He's not afraid of life and how life happens to people. He's given his life to helping people who struggle within their life journey, and don't we all? This book reflects his heart. He writes with a deep concern for people and their welfare. I once asked Mike, "What kind of church do you pastor?" And he responded by telling me about the people and the community, his church's denominational affiliation, doctrine, and belief system, where the last things he told me about. This says a lot about Mike. Unlike institutional religious organizations, which center on themselves, Mike centers on others, those he's in relationship with. That's where his heart is. Jesus was once asked what the two most important commandments were. Jesus responded by saying, "The greatest commandment is to Love God, and the second is to love others." Love God, Love Others, and that sums up Mike, and every page of this book.

This is a very different book. It is not one that most religious publishers would know how to handle. Their assumed market demographic, they probably imagine, would not appreciate how Mike writes about everyday life, in this fallen world. Too bad! All too often religious books center on a fantasyland masquerading as real life. The market for these books seems to be people who have little connection or concern with the world around them. It is pure sugarcoating. There is no syrup in Mike's cooking, just real choice all natural sauce.

Mike is part of a growing group of Christian writers, who are emerging, that insist on telling it like it is. These writers are connected and real. They are not afraid to use the language that we hear every day in the world. They do not reconstruct the world into some kind of fantasy that doesn't exist. But rather, and again I say, they tell it like it is. That's Mike. That's this book.

As you read the pages you will become aware that this comes out of Mike's life and his journey with others. Much of the book reflects Mike's own struggles. The openness and honesty of this book is refreshing and breathtaking. I count it an honor to know Mike. I have known him for over a decade. And have worked with them on several projects, most especially on HollywoodJesus.com. I have always enjoyed his reviews. Simply put, he connects with life, in which he is well experienced. And all of his writings and reviews reflect that reality.

So sit back, relax, and savor this fine steak dinner. A little on the raw side, and smothered with sautéed mushrooms and all the right seasonings and spices. It is served with all the necessary greens and side dishes. It is delicious so, enjoy! And don't be afraid to smack your lips!

Prologue

The 1954 Ford Mercury, Charles was driving purred like a kitten. The black leather exterior had been well maintained even though the car was 6 years old with 85,000 miles. The chrome bumpers reflected the surrounding lights of Johnson City. The bench seat made it easy for Wanda to sit next to him as they waited at the red light at Market and Roan. At the corner was the John Sevier Hotel, the reported former southern getaway for Al Capone. Johnson City, known by many as Little Chicago, had a history of violence and recklessness that stemmed from the days of speakeasies, prohibition and more. That violence had an unknown impact on many of the residents of the area. This was certainly the case for both Charles and Wanda whose parents and family had seen this history evolve around them in their youth.

The interior of the Mercury was well maintained as Charles even polished the chrome circular horn and the hard formed plastic steering wheel. He took care of his car, and working on cars was something he enjoyed.

Charles and Wanda were returning home from a night on the town. Those nights were few and far between over the last months. During the last months of her pregnancy and since the birth of their son, Anthony, they just didn't have the time to get out. Wanda hoped their relationship would improve, especially since it seemed Charles lost his temper a lot recently.

Charles was in his early to mid 20's, well built and very handsome. He had dark black hair with a slight curve to it. It was cut close and his time in the Air Force had taught him how to dress nicely and stay well groomed. His appearance was one of the things that had women on his elbow for most of his early life. It was one of the things that drew Wanda's attention when she first met him a little over a year ago.

Charles was notorious for his temper; Wanda had seen it first hand. He was quick to lose it and take it out on her with the backside of his hand. He was 60 pounds heavier than Wanda and she was no match for him when the arguments turned physical. She hadn't learned to be argumentative or to voice her opinions to the extent she later would. The fights often resulted in Charles taking advantage of her.

Wanda tried to avoid conflict. She had done this since the time she was a child, and hid as she witnessed both physical and sexual abuse taking place in her family. This was especially true with her twin sister and others. She still cringed at the potential of violence and wanted at times to hide just like she had done when a little girl.

Wanda was an exceptionally beautiful girl. Only 17, she was slim and well built. She weighed less than 110 pounds and her medium length black hair accented her slim build. It was obvious that both had Cherokee blood in them, by their physical features, including their dark skin. This was more evident with Wanda than Charles, although both of them had grandparents who were full-blooded Cherokee Indians.

Both of them had had too much to drink. Alcohol was a popular drink which had been a part of Johnson City from the years dating back to when Al Capone helped popularize the city. Many had turned to drinking, even those who were a part of the rich religious traditions of the region. As was the norm with Charles, his temper worsened during intoxication. Wanda had not yet taken to the bottle as a habit, and she felt the full impact of the arguments, both from a psychological and, when things turned physical, a physical perspective.

Wanda knew the argument they had engaged in at the party could lead to bad things once they got home. She tried to resolve it and make things better by sitting close to him. She had her arm around him as he drove, caressing his left ear and neck. She was concerned when he didn't reciprocate. Charles hardly said a word on the trip home.

It was December and many of the homes had Christmas lights decorating their doors and windows. Wanda had not told Charles of her pregnancy. She knew she would have to eventually do so. She was small but she would start showing soon. The arguments and disagreements were bothering her on various levels. The last thing she wanted was to share the news and have him thinking he had to stay around in a marriage he didn't want to be in.

Angela was a young 17 year old who worked with Wanda at the Trailways bus station in downtown Johnson City. She was a good friend who understood a lot of what Wanda was going through because they had spoken over many cups of coffee on numerous late nights while working. Angela realized Wanda needed some time with Charles so she was eager to volunteer to watch Anthony while Wanda and Charles went to the party. She had as much hope as anyone that they would work out and resolve their problems.

Charles came from a tough but loving family held together by his mother Velma. His father, Oscar and some of his other relatives had been difficult at times. There were some aspects of sexual abuse that had been a part of the family for generations. Charles worked in construction, and while a previous marriage had failed, he had hopes this one would make it. He just wasn't certain because there was a lot of inner turmoil he had to take care of.

Wanda, on the other hand, knew too much abuse as a child. She had longed and hoped for a family where love existed and now the hope of a better future was possible. She had Anthony, but knew the child on the way also needed that love. Wanda was a beautiful young woman who had hopes, dreams and aspirations.

Charles was cautiously quiet as he and Wanda arrived home. After a few kind words between Wanda and Angela, her friend left for home. Wanda was concerned because during the 30 or so minutes Wanda and Angela spoke, Charles had not said a word. Wanda wasn't certain why he was so mad, she just knew he was and the fact that he had had too much to drink didn't help matters.

Charles's temper stewed and you could see in his eyes that he was getting increasingly angry with each passing moment. Wanda walked to the couch after turning on the radio. She was listening to Christmas music in the background and on her way to sit down when Charles came into the living room from the kitchen. He was gritting his teeth, eyes beaming as he forcefully walked to Wanda.

"You fucking slut," he yelled as he backhanded her across the face, busting her lip and knocking her back into the couch. "Don't you know who your man is? How dare you flirt with those assholes at the party? I'll be damned if any woman of mine is going to act like a whore." He proceeded to hit her two more times. He continued yelling, not giving her a chance to respond, "Take off your fucking clothes you bitch, all of them, take them off now!"

Wanda tried to respond, "I didn't flirt with anyone, Oh God I promise I wasn't trying to flirt with anyone."

"Take off your fucking clothes you bitch, I am not telling you again." Charles drew back as if to hit her again but holding his back hand a half an arms length from her face, spewing spit on her now.

Wanda didn't know what was going to happen, was he going to rape her? Why did she have to take her clothes off? Through the tears as she started to undress. "I'm sorry Charles, I promise, I wasn't flirting with anyone, you are my husband."

"Shut up Bitch, take 'em off!" He yelled.

Wanda was now naked, crying with her mascara running down her face from the tears. "I'm sorry Charles, I'm sorry. Please don't hit me again."

"Don't worry bitch, I'm not going to hit you again, but if you are going to act like a whore, I'm going to present you as a whore." He pulled over a kitchen table chair to the front of the living room picture window facing the street. He yelled for Wanda to sit in the chair. "Put your ass in that chair, bitch."

Wanda moved to the chair, still crying, and pleading, "Please, Charles, please."

"Shut the fuck up bitch! Don't say another fucking word." Charles yelled with eyes glaring.

Wanda didn't speak, she simply sobbed as the tears streamed down her face.

Charles got an electrical cord and tied Wanda's hands behind her on the chair. "Don't you fucking move, do you hear me, don't fucking move!" Charles's temper raged.

Through the sobs, Wanda shook her head yes, she heard, she understood.

After she was securely tied to the chair Charles stood there looking at her, fully exposed. He started to laugh, "Look at the whore." He said over and over.

The curtains on the picture window had been shut, but Robert had not fully made his point yet. He opened the curtains so Wanda could be seen by anyone either driving or walking by their home. She was fully exposed and the tears continued to stream down her cheeks. Charles stood to the side of the curtains, laughing, saying, "There is the whore, there is the whore." Meanwhile, the new baby Anthony was in his bassinet on the other side of the living room. He could hear his mother crying, and although only 6 months old, he knew something was wrong as he lay there crying for his momma.

~ Chapter 1 ~

Startin' Hard

As a mental health professional Anthony shouldn't have been sitting in this room. To help others with their psychological problems, he thought he had to be all together. Anthony knew when he was studying 'Procedures and Methods of Psychological Testing' in college he didn't quite understand the results of the tests he had taken. He now felt he understood why the M.M.P.I. showed him to have some schizophrenic tendencies in some aspects of his personality.

Anthony stood at 5' 11", had dark long hair tied back in a pony tail and weighed around 210 pounds. He was athletic and was built quite well from running and working out with weights. While younger and in college Anthony had spoken to his professor and friend, Joe Linn, a Chinese American who was in his late 20's. Joe was slim with dark hair, glasses, and standing in just a hair taller than Anthony. Joe was also athletic and he and Anthony would play basketball together quite often when they were in college. Their relationship had developed beyond just a professor-student relationship. They had become friends.

Anthony and Joe spoke on several occasions about his test scores and Anthony developed a healthy grasp on how to control his temper. Yet, he didn't understand what schizophrenia tendencies were, or understand or accept himself.

After the testing in college Anthony and Joe spent time together because they enjoyed each other's company. Through their involvement in church, basketball, Intercollegiate Peace Fellowship, and other activities at Tabor College in Hillsboro, Kansas their friendship grew.

Joe nominated Anthony as one of North America's Most Outstanding Christian Students through the Extraordinary Christian Students of America organization during Anthony's senior year. Anthony did well in college despite his psychological test scores. He had no reason to think he needed any kind of therapy or counseling, so he had not sought it.

This was all 9 years in Anthony's past and was the farthest thing from his mind. He spoke on occasion to his pastor and coworker worker, Bill Lewis, about the possible need for counseling. Anthony wanted to accept himself and his past but he didn't take the counseling option seriously. He was getting by, and while there were issues, he thought he had control. Then, one night, he rented a movie to watch with his wife.

While walking through the video store Anthony picked out a family movie the family could watch. He was also looking at the new releases and saw the movie, "Prince of Tides" with Barbara Streisand and Nick Nolte. He was hesitant about renting the video because he didn't especially like Barbara Streisand. He didn't know what it was, despite the fact she had been in several movies he did like.

"The Prince of Tides" appealed to Anthony because it was written by one of his favorite authors, Pat Conroy, had one of his favorite actors, Nick Nolte, and was filmed in a state he had just lived, South Carolina. So he overlooked his dislike of Barbara Streisand and rented the video.

Anthony kept putting off watching the movie during the five day rental period. He knew the movie took second place to the Atlanta Braves baseball games being televised. They were in the middle of a pennant race with the Pittsburgh Pirates and Anthony wasn't going to miss it.

It was an off night from the series, so Anthony decided to watch 'The Prince of Tides'. It was not often he watched a video without getting up for breaks; yet, here he was, glued to the TV. Anthony was drawn into the story. He related to the Nick Nolte character. He understood the character's feelings of confusion and hurt due to the abuse he experienced as a child because he had experienced the same types of abuse. The movie brought back memories and forced him to reflect on the pains and confusion he continued to feel as an adult. Anthony understood what Nolte's character had been through. Anthony broke down crying during certain scenes. They were all too real and reminded him of a past he would have just as soon forgotten.

In many ways, 'The Prince of Tides' became an epiphany moment for Anthony. Through understanding and knowing why he related to this character he finally decided to see a counselor. The movie helped him understand that good could come in his life and the nightmares and memories could be explained.

One week after seeing 'The Prince of Tides', Anthony spoke with Pastor Bill Lewis about various counselors to see. Bill, a short, blonde haired man wearing round glasses, in his early 30's was a coworker at Trend Mental Health Center in Hendersonville, North Carolina. He was the pastor of a small Calvary Chapel Church Anthony and his family attended. Anthony knew he wanted to see a Christian counselor because of his faith and how that faith affected his life. Bill recommended a small counseling service that had helped several of his friends.

Anthony called to set the initial appointment. He was impressed with the interest Christ Life Counseling had taken in him. They were not primarily interested in charging a fee to make money. They were willing to apply a sliding scale fee, even saying that money was the least of their concerns. Anthony guessed this was why he was now sitting in their waiting room.

He remembered pulling up to the two story white house and walking from his car through the front door. His appointment was at 4:30 and traffic was pretty heavy on that particular day. Hendersonville was a tourist town, and especially during rush hour, traffic could get that way. Anthony was early though, as was his custom. He couldn't help thinking, would anyone recognize him going in? If they did, what would they think?

Christ Life Counseling was next to a Catholic church. Anthony had assumed it was a mission of the church. Later he learned the house was operated by Naples Baptist Church and not the Catholic Church. Outside was a large white, wooden carved sign that said, "Manna House / An Evangelical Ministry." Upon entering the house, Anthony saw a small reception area, but no one was there. He went to a large room to the right and had a seat. He first sat on a couch in the large sitting room then realized the couch was blind to the entrance / exit way, so he decided to move in order to be seen when someone came in from outside or down the stairs. Anthony moved to a large white wicker chair and sat down.

He was reading an opinion response of political candidates when someone came down the stairs and exited. He was looking at viewpoints of Bill Clinton and George Bush when he heard footsteps coming down the stairs. A man, in his early forties, dark hair, 6' tall, and in pretty good physical shape approached him. He was dressed nicely, wearing dress slacks, a dress shirt, probably an Arrow and standard blue paisley tie accented with a large, warm and friendly smile. The smile wasn't fake but honest, sincere.

"Hello. Are you Anthony Beechup?" the man asked.

"Yes sir," he replied.

"Well, my name is George Wilson. Why don't you come on up and we can get started."

Anthony followed George up the stairs not knowing how to feel or what to expect. He wasn't worried or afraid because it was evident this was a person who was warm and caring, and gave the impression that he would be easy to talk to. So it was that Anthony began one of the most important seasons of his life.

~ Chapter 2 ~

In The Beginning

It took five minutes to work out the details. Anthony would see George for one hour each week, and the cost was far below the standard hourly rate most agencies charged. It was reassuring that he would only pay every two weeks. George told Anthony if he had any problems paying, for any reason, he need not worry. They were there to help people receive help. Most of their support came from Naples Baptist Church. Naples considered the Manna House a mission of the church and made it clear; their concern was helping others, not making a profit. This concept was unusual, especially for an organization that had accredited staff.

"Well, Anthony, I would like to start with the reason you have decided to come here. We could do that in a number of ways, but I believe, well how can I say this? In order to start understanding yourself, in order for me to better understand you, what we need to do is go back as far as we need to, in order to understand your past. We need to go back to the beginnings of where you may have felt stress and hardships beginning in your life."

"Do these need to be areas I remember, or areas where I am sure difficulties began?" Anthony asked.

"If you are aware of problem area or areas where there was stress, then we should start there. Do you have an idea of where to start?" George asked.

Anthony felt comfortable talking to George. He really didn't know why, but he decided to open up anyway. This was unusual because with Anthony's past there was also a strong sense of distrust. Maybe it was that, after years of anguish and struggle that he had gone through, he was now ready to do something about it. Being able to talk in confidence was certainly a positive, so Anthony responded, "I think so, but it's going to go a long ways back."

"That's fine. Start from where you need and we'll go from there." George answered with reassurance.

Anthony began to talk in detail for the first time in his thirty three years about the circumstances of his life. He started sharing aspects that had held him, his marriage, and family captive for that period of time. It was here, through the discussions that Anthony began to experience the true joys of freedom, his salvation, for the first time on a regular basis.

Anthony realized the sins of his father and prior generations had followed him throughout his life. He didn't understand many of the old time Biblical concepts, yet he knew the abuse, confusion, temperament, and hurt had been with his relatives for generations. In the words of the late president Harry Truman, Anthony decided the buck was going to stop with him. He decided that, if at all possible, his children would never know the horrors he had experienced while growing up, and he certainly wasn't going to be the one to transfer those nightmares to his children. He would do everything possible to ensure the horrors of his past would never occur with his children. His children would experience the true and loving parents God intends for all.

Anthony knew in his heart, he was going to be honest for the first time. He didn't need to lie to impress George. He needed to be honest and learn to accept himself for who he was, despite what he had done and been. Anthony started with his earliest memories in talking with George.

Problems began early for Anthony, even before he was born. He had never known why his mother quit high school in her junior year. He often thought it was due to her being pregnant. He also knew she had grown up in a large family and had experienced many difficulties in her life. His dad had been married once before but after the birth of a daughter and a difficult divorce, he had as much as he could take. He had grown up in a large family and came from a rough background. He was the oldest of seven children and had an older half brother. Charles had been in trouble numerous times for fights, on one occasion killing a man in a fight that had been determined by the courts to be self defense. Charles had learned to settle down some, especially with his temper from his service in the Air Force, but his quick temper would still get him into trouble on occasion.

Wanda and Charles seemed to be looking for an escape from their past. After Wanda got pregnant she knew there weren't many options but marriage. In the late 1950's abortion wasn't an acceptable option. There was also criticism of unwed mothers. There were also difficulties in accepting fathers who did not take care of either the women they got pregnant or the child they were responsible for. This concept encouraged marriage but sometimes for the wrong reasons. Then again, with Charles coming from a strong religious family, he knew he had a commitment to fulfill to his child and future wife.

Anthony was born June 9th, 1959 in Kingsport, Tennessee. This is where the stress and difficulties began. Anthony believed even the smallest of children, even those still in their mother's womb, were aware of difficulties and pressures around them.

It was almost as if Charles and Wanda were fighting a losing battle. They had some understanding of how to build a marriage even though they didn't have the helps, seminars, and assistance many couples have. They even went to church where Wanda worked as a church secretary. Yet the honesty of their faith and relationship with God had never been real. Building a marriage and family for them was like a carpenter trying to build a house using only a ruler. It was next to impossible for Wanda and Charles to build their marriage on love. They almost made it through the year with each other before things fell apart.

Wanda never talked about the early days of her marriage to Charles. Charles wasn't around after the birth of Anthony. He either traveled to find metal lathe construction jobs or stayed away to keep from arguing and fighting with Wanda. She was on her own to fend for herself and her baby boy, Anthony.

Due to the difficulty, Wanda began to rely on her in-laws, Oscar and Velma Beechup, to help raise Anthony. Wanda worked at textile mills, factories, or wherever she could find a job. She did this to help make ends meet to take care of Anthony.

It was hard for women to find good paying jobs, especially 17 year old high school drop outs. Wanda did the best she could. She used this situation in her life to develop a long and lasting relationship with Charles's family.

Anthony was almost a year old, and Wanda was pregnant again. Charles had had enough, and divorced Wanda. He was working in Washington DC. Wanda was seven months pregnant and had been separated from Charles for 5 months. She still had a good relationship with her in-laws, Velma and Oscar. They were there to offer support and help in various ways. Wanda relied on them to keep Anthony while she was at work. She also lived with them at times.

Over a period of time during the pregnancy, Velma and Oscar spoke with Charles and tried to get him to come home to work things out in his marriage. Wanda and Charles spoke to each other on the phone and started to write back and forth. Velma and Oscar finally got through and convinced him to come home to work things out.

After much soul searching Charles decided to come home and get back with Wanda. It was May of 1960 when Charles made the decision to give the marriage another shot. He packed his car with gifts for Wanda, Anthony, and his new child who would be arriving soon. He left Washington after work and made the effort to drive straight through. He didn't think the drive would be any trouble. It was, after all, only a nine hour drive through the back roads of Virginia.

Wanda, Velma and Oscar knew something was wrong when Charles had not arrived by 2:00 a.m. They were worried and it was difficult going to sleep. Wanda spent the night with Velma and Oscar and waited to see Charles when he got home. After all, Charles had not spent much time with his son, and Wanda hoped he would be glad to see him. They all finally decided to go to bed shortly after 2:00 a.m. They had so anticipated Charles's arrival through the day, that it took them about 45 minutes to get to sleep.

It was about 3:00 a.m. when Velma was awakened by someone knocking at the door. Wanda awoke as well after just falling asleep, thinking Charles had gotten home. To the surprise of both women, they were greeted at the door by a policeman who had a solemn look on his face. He spoke calmly and in a caring voice to the two women. "Mrs. Beechup, I am sorry to notify you that a Charles Wilson Beechup was killed instantly a few hours ago outside of Richmond, Virginia. We believe he fell asleep at the wheel, crossed over into the lane of on-coming traffic and had a head on collision with a tractor trailer truck. We believe he was asleep at the time of the collision and that he died instantly."

Anthony realized he was speaking to George in his office. "I have seen the pictures of the funeral many times. For some reason I never felt any emotion from looking at those pictures. I guess some of that comes from never having known my father, and some of it is from him not looking anything like the few pictures I have of him. I've heard a lot of my family say the casket should never have been opened because it didn't look anything like my dad. He was thrown through the windshield into the semi-truck, so I can see how it didn't look anything like him."

"Have you ever regretted not knowing your father, Anthony?" George asked.

"Yeah a lot of times," he replied in a monotone and uncaring voice. "I've often thought about how things could have been different. Would he and my mom have stayed together? Would Father's Day mean anything? I don't even know what I would have called him, Dad, Pops, Daddy or what. Can you imagine that? Never knowing what it was like to have a dad or even what you would call him? I've just always felt that things would have been a lot better than they have been. I guess I've always blamed my father's death for all of the tough things that happened in my life."

"Most people seem to overlook what it is like to have a dad." Anthony continued, "I've always resented that. What has really been bad though is that I have some of the minor details about my dad, and that is it. I've tried many times to get people to tell me about him so I would know something about my roots, about what might have been. Yet my own family has not even been willing to help in this area. They don't understand that it makes me feel worthless, almost like I was just an accident."

Anthony began tearing up and let the emotion of what he was saying get to him. Having a father or mother is something many people take for granted. Anthony was in a situation where he never knew the experience. What he did know was confusing and disturbing, not having or knowing a father complicated things.

Anthony often had people respond, "Yeah, I lost my dad too when I was young." While a reply with good intentions, it always made Anthony somewhat angry. They knew what it was like to have a dad, to have some knowledge of him. Anthony would never know.

George responded to Anthony's hurts and anger. He tried to be reassuring, stating that what Anthony had had to go through was not ok. No child should be put in the situations he had. George tried to reassure Anthony and let him know he was there to listen and help in any way that he could.

George spoke to Anthony for another 15 minutes trying to provide the reassurance and caring he needed at the moment. After doing this George realized they had gone overtime. It was obvious to Anthony that the issue of time wasn't George's concern. However, there were other people for George to see. George reassured Anthony in this regard, and he changed the times of future meetings to the last appointment of the day so that when need be, it would be ok to run overtime. It would have been easy for Anthony to feel he was being taken advantage of, but it was obvious that George cared.

George closed the meeting, looking at several areas he wanted Anthony to study. "Well, Anthony, what I want you to do this week is to read these passages of Scripture. They talk about how God intended the family to be, as well as how valuable you are as an individual."

Anthony took the passages and spent the next week looking over them. He saw God's Word as he had never seen it before. Anthony could tell that he had made the right decision about going to Manna House. It was going to be worth it, help was on the way. George handed Anthony a list he had made out as they were talking. The passages in the Bible George wanted Anthony to read were: John 1:12 , 1 Peter 1:23, Ephesians 1:7, Romans 8:1, Colossians 3:4, Romans 3:22, 2 Corinthians 5:21, Romans 8:31, Romans 8:17, 1 Corinthians 3:16, Colossians 1:13, Philippians 3:20, Ephesians 2:6, Romans 6:14, John 16:24, Hebrews 4:16, 2 Corinthians 5:8, and Philippians 1:21.

~ Chapter 3 ~

William Smith?

The week went by quickly for Anthony and he once again found himself back at Manna House to meet with George. He spoke to George in a relaxed tone, "I don't know how long it was after my father was killed when my mother met William Smith. He was her second husband and she was married to him for around a year and a half. I've often wondered about him and have asked my mom many times about my dad and William. She has told me little about my father but never anything about William. She has never shared anything about his personality, his looks, how they met, nothing. Whenever I asked questions she would get upset and not answer. It was obvious from her response that she seemed to care about him. I don't know, because of her unwillingness to talk about him, but she was never willing to talk about my father either."

George asked, "How old were you, Anthony, when your mother and William married and do you have any memories of him at all?"

"Well, let's see, I must have been around three, and my sister around two. I think it was William, but I have never been sure. I have a memory of my mother being with a man who was really nice to both my sister and me. I also remember that my mother was happy with this man. He was kind of tall, and if my memory is correct, he had blondish brown hair. I've talked to my sister, and she has the same memories."

"How long was your mother with him?" George asked.

"I'm not really sure. I recall her being with him for around a year or so, but it's hard to say. I do know these are some of my earliest memories." Anthony answered George and seemed to be in a good mood. He didn't show much expression except an occasional smile. This was a reflection of how he felt talking to George more than a sense of feeling good about what he was sharing with him.

George asked, "What ever happened to William Smith?"

"I've never been sure as to the circumstances, but I know he was killed. It was in or around Chicago. I know a train was involved. He was a hobo catching trains when he fell and was run over."

George turned the question around, "How did your mom respond and how did you respond?"

"I'm sure my mom took it really hard, that has to be why she never talked about it. She must have been hurt so badly that she just didn't want to bring up the hurt again. I don't know how she felt from the aspect of losing two husbands. It had to be difficult knowing she had the responsibility of raising my sister and me. She was around my grandparents a lot. It seems like they have always been around."

"How did you and your sister feel?" George asked.

"I don't know, to be honest. I've never known how to feel or how she felt. I do know that one of the only pleasant memories I have as a child involved who I think was William. I don't really remember much about him though. I guess I've never come to grips with that. It's like my dad. I don't know why people hold back information. I can accept that neither may have been decent men. I just have trouble handling and coping with the fact that I don't have the answers. Here are two men who were vital parts of my life, two men who had an important part in developing my personality, and I have heard that most of one's personality is developed by the age of three, and I don't know squat about them. They would have been the ones to play the part of a father in my early years. Even though William wasn't my birth father, I was so young when my mother and he got together that I would never have known the difference."

Anthony began getting upset in discussing these things with George. He started showing signs of anger, not at George but at the story. Anthony realized, as he had many times before, he had been given the shaft by so many people in his family. Even if the family's actions were not intended in a negative way, the unwillingness to share information with him about his past was received that way.

"How does that make you feel?" George asked.

"Well to be honest, it makes me feel as if I don't matter, or at least didn't matter. I mean, what am I, a toy for people to play with? Why aren't my feelings important? I never asked to be brought into this world. It seems like if people were going to make that decision, then they would at least have the courtesy to answer my questions. Even if the answers to those questions are bad, that would be easier to deal with than not knowing anything, especially about my father, my own flesh and blood, where my genetics and very makeup came from. It's like a kid who is adopted who wants answers about his past. He wants to know about his birth mother and father. He searches and searches for answers and he doesn't quit until he finds the answers. Well, I've found and know the people with the answers about my father and what he was like, what he did, how he acted. The problem is that they will give me very few if any answers to those questions."

Anthony, even more upset now, "How do I feel? I feel like a piece of shit!"

✼ ✼ ✼ ✼ ✼ ✼ ✼

After William's death the difficulties were only just beginning for Anthony and his sister. It wasn't long before Wanda started to lose hope as a mother and for her future. She started to believe she was not capable of raising Anthony and his sister Madeline.

Shortly after the death of William, Wanda put Anthony and Madeline into foster care. No one ever spoke to Anthony and Madeline about this and it was almost 25 years later when another member of the family told them about it. Anthony had vague memories of staying with someone he was not related to. He just assumed these people were friends of the family. On occasion he still saw his mother and other relatives. It was an experience that had to have some bearing on him. He had a few vivid memories taking place before being placed in a foster home but very few during the time he was in foster care.

Anthony never knew or understood why he had blocked out many of the memories during this period of life. He didn't even know how long he and Madeline spent in foster care. He did know how his grandparents, Velma and Oscar, his dad's parents, felt.

The Beechup family had always been a tight, close knit family. Not every aspect of the family was good. Later on both Anthony and Madeline would find out there was a lot to be desired. Yet, they were close and seemed to want to care for each other.

Oscar was the father in the family and the obvious head of the family. Oscar was a strong leader, which was the way it was supposed to be in the early 1960's. That was especially the case in a Southern or Missionary Baptist Church family.

Oscar was small in stature and had dark wavy hair. He was 5' 9" and weighed 142 pounds most of his adult life. He was in good physical shape and stayed healthy, never smoking or drinking. He had a deeply squared chin much like Burt Lancaster's and a temper that was liable to go off at any moment for almost any reason. His temper could go off around his children, his wife, or especially when driving or being challenged by strangers in any way. The temper had been in the Beechup family for generations.

There was a good side to Oscar that was easy to see for those around him long enough, or those considered friends of the family. He was a caring and giving individual. While uneducated in some ways, he only completed the third grade; he was as educated as anyone you would ever meet. Throughout his life, Oscar continued to read and learn as much as possible, especially in basic knowledge and Biblical knowledge. He had more common sense than anyone you might ever meet. He learned and gained knowledge from working and living in the real world. He quit school early in life to help take care of his family. He worked as many odd jobs as he could find. He did this despite his youth and small stature. This was not unusual for the time.

Oscar grew up in Erwin and Embreville Tennessee, before moving to Johnson City. He was a religious man who took his family to church on a regular basis. To go three or four times a week was not unusual for the family. He was in the Navy, where he was the Naval Lightweight Boxing Champion. The toughness it took to acquire this honor was not lost, even after leaving the Navy. He stayed in good physical shape, lifting weights throughout his life.

Oscar married early in life, having two children, but divorcing his first wife. He met Velma Man, formerly Velma Tinson who had also gone through a divorce. Velma had one child from her former marriage, who lived with her. Oscar worked in construction and carpentry. He acquired the reputation for being a skilled, hard worker at these trades and had little difficulty finding work. He took pride in his work and instilled in those around him that they should take pride in what they did. He felt it important that one should leave their mark on this world. One of the best ways to do that was doing what they did to the best of their abilities.

Velma was a large framed woman who came from a large framed family. She stood 5' 8" tall and weighed 175 pounds. She had shoulder length wavy hair and while she was light skinned she had the physical features of her Cherokee ancestors.

Velma grew up in the coal mining towns of Virginia and lost a brother in a mining accident while in her early teens. Velma fit the traditional mold of a submissive wife. She was a strong and prominent feature in the family that few people could find any fault in. She was the glue that held the family together. She was someone who Anthony could never remember anything negative about. Of all the influences on Anthony, she would be the most dramatic. Even when times were bad in the future and he made excuses, Anthony knew he could look at his grandmother and see a positive person. She was one of the truest Christians he ever knew. She worked as a maid, and occasionally folded clothes at a Laundromat in order to get extra cash to help the family finances. Due to Oscar's job and the need to travel, Wanda took care of the children at home for months at a time. She did whatever it took to keep the family together.

Velma's eldest son from her first marriage was Bill, or Jerry, as everyone called him. He spent some time in the military and was married. He had a family in Nashville, Tennessee, where he flew a helicopter for the Tennessee Valley Authority. Charles, Anthony's dad, was the next oldest and after him was Jarvis.

Jarvis lived with Velma and Oscar. While in the army and serving in Germany, he was thrown off a train. He had suffered some brain damage and lost most of his eye sight. He was legally blind. He came in and out of the V.A. centers due to violent episodes and extreme religious beliefs he experienced. Jarvis experienced hallucinations and heard voices most the time. Schizophrenic characteristics were present along with the brain damage. He had to be cared for the rest of his life. Jarvis was married with two children, but separated from his wife since the incident in Germany. After Jarvis was the oldest daughter, Sarah.

Sarah was married and lived in Washington, DC. She looked a lot like Velma, but Anthony wasn't around her much when he was younger. She ran a successful beauty shop in DC, and was mother to several step children from her husband's prior marriage. Even though Anthony wasn't around Sarah much, he came to know her better in the years to come. After Sarah was Leo.

Leo was also married and had served in the military. He lived in Washington State with his wife, Barbara. Anthony and Leo had many of the same physical characteristics. They had large body frames and a tendency to carry too much weight. In the early years Leo had the same temper as the rest of the Beechup's. It could explode at any time and on more than one occasion got him in trouble with family and others around him.

Next in line were the twins Frank and Mary. Both still lived at home, but not for long. Frank joined the Army and served two terms in Vietnam as a helicopter gunner. Anthony remembered the horror of that war because before Frank went to serve he was a practical kidder who was fun to be around. Frank was easy to get along with and always seemed to have a smile. After Vietnam he served in the National Guard, but seemed too sad and had difficulty getting along with others. Years later, after his second marriage, Frank began showing signs of happiness again and began to enjoy life.

Mary was still in school and dated quite a bit. She was very attractive, and had no trouble getting dates. On occasion she got into trouble with her parents for staying out too late. Anthony didn't know what the deal was with Mary. She was somewhat wild in her youth, even as a child. Anthony could tell she wanted to get out on her own as soon as possible. This was a characteristic many young girls had during the early days of the Vietnam War.

Jeremiah was next in the family tree. He also lived at home. He was small in stature like his father. He was built almost exactly like Oscar. Jeremiah went through a period where he stayed at home as a child due to hepatitis. He was quiet and in some ways quite odd and different. He also had a temper just as the others in the family; and like the others, it would on occasion get him into trouble. This was especially true after Jeremiah entered the Army. There were several occasions where he was disciplined due to the fights he got in, including those with superiors.

The youngest child of Velma and Oscar was Bill. All of the children were tall except for Jeremiah. Bill was close to 6' 7". He was almost ten years older than Anthony but Bill was loved a great deal by Velma and Oscar. Anthony noticed this at an early age.

Bill was recruited out of Junior High to go to an elite high school in Johnson City to play basketball. Velma and Oscar always took pride in this. Bill received much of the attention the other children deserved but seldom got.

Anthony looked up to Bill in his early years. He followed him as a mentor and admired Bill. As Bill moved out of elementary school Anthony started to spend most of his time with the Beechup family. Eventually the time he spent with them began to increase.

Velma and Oscar had a rough time seeing Anthony and Madeline in a foster home. Anthony and Madeline were family, their own flesh and blood. Anthony wasn't able to find out the legalities involved with him and his sister staying with Velma and Oscar. It was certain. Velma and Oscar would not accept any of the Beechup children being raised by someone outside the family!

* * * * * * *

"I don't know what happened," Anthony said. "There must have been some type of agreement where they would take us out of foster care and be responsible for raising us. I don't remember. I was maybe four or five at the time. I do remember they either lived on, or had just moved to Cherokee Lane in Johnson City just off the campus of East Tennessee State University. My grandfather had a brother who had two houses on Cherokee Lane and a place where he raised chickens. Anyway Paps and Mamaw moved into one house and right down from there was another house where my mother moved to. I saw her all of the time but stayed with my Grandparents most of the time. I always thought it was kind of strange to live in a situation like this. Then again, it couldn't have been too strange because it was something that was already a norm, that is, to move around and not be around a set family for any consistent period of time."

"Did things seem to improve for you at this point?" George asked.

"Well, at first they did, but that didn't seem to last long." Anthony answered.

"Exactly what do you mean?" George asked.

"Well it is a long story and would take a lot of time." Anthony answered while at the same time giving clear indication he really didn't want to talk about things right now.

"That's O.K. We have time. Do you want to talk about it?" George asked.

Anthony began to choke back tears. After waiting for what seemed like five minutes of silence he answered, "I just don't think I'm ready for this. I'd rather not talk about it right now."

"That's O.K. then. Let's spend some time in prayer and ask the Lord to give you the strength and ability to talk about this the next time you come in." They prayed for about five or ten minutes, Anthony didn't remember exactly how long. He was thinking about whether or not he wanted to share this part of his life with anybody.

Anthony had been married for 13 years and never shared what George wanted him to, not with his wife or anyone. He was concerned about what people would think of his family. He felt he knew what George and others would think. If they ever found out, many of their impressions would change. Anthony was convinced he deserved much of the blame for his past. He knew he was just as guilty for the things which had taken place as were the people and circumstances surrounding those events. He knew that if he started to share about his life and those in his family who were responsible, he would have to share the things about his own life that he felt responsible for. Anthony had undeservedly blamed himself for years. It was blame he didn't understand. He made excuses for his actions and knew he was responsible for those actions. The last thing Anthony wanted was to share things about his family. It was bad enough to experience rejection that had come about but to take the chance of bringing on more rejection, especially from those he was supposed to love and be loved by, was another story altogether.

Anthony felt there would be misunderstanding, even doubts as to whether the story was true. He didn't want to tell his story to hurt others, but to help himself. Anthony was confused as to whether this was going to help him or hurt him. Anthony struggled for the next week.

Anthony spent time in prayer and fought against his feelings regarding what he was going to do, and what he was going to share with George at their next meeting. "Oh God, give me wisdom, knowledge and understanding. Give me patience, honesty, truth and love. Help me know what to do. Help me to learn to accept myself as I am. Help me learn to share the truth so I may be helped, but also so I may help others in letting them know of your love. God, I ask these things so you may be glorified in the name of Jesus, my Lord and Savior I pray. Amen."

~ Chapter 4 ~

Cherokee Lane

Cherokee Lane was a small two-lane gravel road. It was barely wide enough for two cars to pass without one pulling over to the side of the road and stopping. It had steep hills that ran its length on both sides of the road. Going down Cherokee Lane on the left were fields used to grow hay. Along the right side was a steep hill and houses with woods behind them. The first house on the right after turning onto Cherokee Lane was the only nice house on the street. After passing that house you went up one hill, down another and up another before coming to any other houses. This covered approximately a half a mile. Then the road leveled off and down on the right you saw three small houses. They were all small, shabby, wood framed houses with the backs of the houses on a steep hill. The back yard went into the woods after about 60 yards. Even in the early 1960's these houses were shacks. They were all heated by either coal or electric heat. Most people living like this used cotton blankets and wool sweaters to keep warm in the winter.

In the summer the houses were cooled by nature's air conditioning, not the electrical kind but the kind which comes about from opening the windows and hopefully having a breeze. If a family was doing well financially they had a fan to put in front of one of the screen doors to blow air through the house. This wasn't too bad. It all depended on which way the wind was blowing.

Right behind the houses in the woods was a chicken shed where several hundred chickens were raised for meat and eggs. If the wind blew from that direction you kept the windows shut. It was impossible to get used to the smell of hot chickens and the odors they produced.

The chicken houses belonged to Holland Beechup, Oscar's older brother. Holland also owned the houses. He used the third house to store junk and supplies. He was someone who had the knack for finding the good junk, the kind you looked at for hours wondering what it was for. Holland and Oscar always knew what the junk was for. It was often things they had seen when they were children and had to have, because who knew when they might have to use it for something. It was often things they said they needed and would use to either improve the properties or one of the cars around the house.

There were the building supplies they gathered and collected with their treasures to help with the repairs and building they planned to do. Anthony seldom saw Holland or Oscar use any of the materials from the third house for any of the plans.

Holland rented the other two houses to provide additional income. It wasn't much income because he was renting to family, and one thing the Beechup family would not do was take advantage of another family member. The middle house was rented to Oscar and Velma. The house next to Oscar and Velma was rented to Wanda who was living alone. Mary, Jeremiah, and Billy would often stay with Wanda as would Anthony and Madeline.

To Anthony, Holland seemed to be a hard working, kind man. He had a full head of thick, wavy white hair. Holland almost always had a cigar stub in his mouth that he occasionally lit up and smoked. Anthony never knew if they were good cigars or the cheap kind. They always had the same aroma, a cross between sweet and stale.

Holland's most noticeable and distinguishing mark was his missing left arm. He shot it off in a hunting accident when he was younger, after tripping on a log. Holland was one, though, who never let this handicap him. He could do all of the things he wanted and certainly everything he was able to do before he lost his arm. Even though Holland only had one arm, he still enjoyed hunting and the outdoor life he had enjoyed in his youth. It was funny seeing Holland drive his old Chevy Impala around with one arm. Imagine a one-armed man driving a car that was not an automatic. It was a straight shift with the gear shift on the right side of the steering column. He took his hand off of the steering wheel and, while using his right knee to steer, he would change the gear shift on the column with his right hand, while pushing the clutch in with his left foot, then after releasing the clutch, would catch the steering wheel with his arm. He even learned to master this while coming to a stop and going up a hill. He never came to a complete stop but instead took the hill slowly. On occasion if he did come to a complete stop you could hear him start mumbling something, almost like cursing but Holland never cursed in front of children, if at all. The mumbling with the cigar in his mouth was enough to get the point across that he was reacting to his poor judgment of the driving conditions.

Anthony looked back at Holland in a positive light, which was far different from when he was alive. Anthony remembered hating for Holland to come around because his grandparents and mother had Anthony go out to help Holland with various things. He helped gather eggs, pick blackberries or chestnuts, or go to turkey shoots (which was one of the few fun things Anthony did with Holland). Turkey shoots were competitions where individuals took their guns, normally shotguns, and would shoot at a paper target. The person getting a bead of the gun shot closest to the center of the target won a turkey. It normally cost $1 per shot and there were as many as 15 – 20 shooters at a time, shooting at their own individual targets.

Anthony remembered Holland pounding a piece of 2 X 4 wood into the ground and resting the barrel of his 'long tom' double barreled 12 gauge shotgun with one hand on the top of the 2 X 4. He took aim with his sight eye resting against the wood shoulder stock of the gun, then shooting at the paper target. It was easy for Anthony to remember because Holland got a lot of attention from the other competitors. He always won 3 or 4 turkeys at the turkey shoots after only shooting a total of 4 or 5 times. This was even more of an accomplishment when considering that old 'long tom' shotgun had a hair trigger. On the trigger for the left barrel you hardly touched it and the gun would fire. This made it incredibly difficult to shoot, but Holland wasn't afraid and had learned the right way to shoot the gun. That was saying a lot more than for most people who shot the gun on occasion. Holland realized an advantage, and the long barrel on the shotgun was a definite advantage at the turkey shoots.

This was all fun for Anthony and provided some positive input and guidance for a few years of his early life, but at the time, he didn't appreciate or understand it. He had a positive role model and learned a different lifestyle than he would have, had Holland not been around. Holland was largely responsible for Anthony's love of the outdoors. Anthony, like many others, realized he had taken for granted some of the best times of his youth.

* * * * *

"Peddle, you've got to peddle," Billy laughingly rebuked and told Anthony.

"I'm trying," Anthony responded while wiping his tears.

"Well we're going to the top of the hill again and we're going to keep going until you get it." Billy stated.

So they pushed the bicycle to the top of the gravel road on Cherokee Lane for what seemed like the hundredth time. This time Billy pushed Anthony even harder down the hill trying to get up enough speed for the bike to carry its own weight and keep balance. Anthony made it a little further down the hill than the times before. This time Anthony ran off the side of the road and down the grass bank. It wasn't so bad though, the grass and branches didn't hurt like wrecking on the gravel. His legs were already bruised and bleeding from wrecking so many times on the gravel.

"Let's go. Now bring the bike back up the hill," Billy yelled at Anthony. "Now that was better, but if you pedal and think about what you're doing you won't wreck. Now push the bicycle up the hill again," Billy yelled, keeping a smug look.

Anthony pushed the bike up the bank, crying and ready to give up. He finally got to the top of the hill and took off one more time. It might not have been so hard, except Anthony wasn't even in the first grade and was riding Billy's old bike, which had a banana style seat and was 2 sizes too big. Even when Anthony rode it, the only way to stop it was to either wreck or keep peddling and swing his leg over the bike on one of the pedals and jump off. This was not something a new rider like Anthony could accomplish. His feet couldn't reach the ground and he barely reached the pedals. After several more tries that lasted almost half a day, Anthony finally got the hang of it. He even mastered a dismount swinging his leg over the seat, balancing on one of the pedals before jumping off. He could brake, stand on one of the pedals, and dismount all in the same motion, while jumping off, running beside the bike, and holding the handlebars until the bike came to a stop. Anthony learned that this was a credit to his Uncle Billy's teaching ability and his own ability to either learn fast or wreck. It was like the sink or swim method many used when learning to swim.

It was easy for Anthony to get over the anger towards his uncle Billy for having him learn to ride in such difficult circumstances. He didn't look at his bleeding and bruised body on that day either. Anthony saw in himself the ability to ride a bicycle, and Billy was the reason he could. On occasion that bicycle allowed Anthony to escape the difficulties he faced on Cherokee Lane.

Anthony soon started school at Cherokee Elementary School just a few miles away from Narrow Lane. Wanda took Anthony to school. He would attend early kindergarten. It seems like all Anthony did that first day was cry. All he had known was life on Cherokee Lane. It was a little easier because his uncle Billy was in eighth grade at Cherokee and Anthony saw him on a regular basis. This helped make the year easier. While at school Anthony learned to make friends on his own. It wasn't too hard and later that year Anthony was elected the kindergarten king by his class. It didn't mean much except he would be presented as king at the school's Fall Festival. This wasn't too bad except when Wanda took him into the ladies' bathroom to change into his clothes while at the Fall Festival.

The clothes Anthony wore were embarrassing to him. It was one of the few times he wore a suit. This suit had dark blue slacks and a deep, candy-apple red blazer with blue insignia on the left breast. Red was a color that didn't look especially good on a dark haired, freckle faced little boy. Even at an early age this was embarrassing and something he wouldn't forget. Anthony was embarrassed and upset that the women in the restroom where Wanda was changing him could see him in his underwear. None of this embarrassment was addressed or felt by Wanda. It was Anthony's first feelings of noticing his own sexuality that he could remember. It was an event where he was aware of his body and was in a situation where he was embarrassed by others around him looking at him and laughing. They were not laughing at Anthony as much as they were laughing and trying to keep a little kid from being upset. Anthony didn't understand this and was upset by the episode, no matter what the intent.

The rest of the year was not eventful. Only one other event happened that left a lasting impression.

While outside playing during recess, Anthony often made new friends and played with other kids. Once while out on the playground Anthony noticed an older red headed little girl. Anthony tried to get her to play, and on occasion she did. Even when she didn't, she was nice and courteous in her rejection. She would become the first love in Anthony's life.

In Anthony's classroom the teacher had an aquarium filled with gold fish. Anthony sat next to the aquarium and had a favorite fish. One day when coming in from lunch, Anthony noticed the fish had died. The teacher was more than willing to let Anthony scoop the fish out of the tank, thinking he was going to take it to flush down the toilet. Anthony went to the break room with the fish, but didn't flush it. Instead, he put the fish in a brown paper towel and placed the towel into his pocket.

It was another hour until recess and Anthony hoped to see the girl of his dreams on the play ground. Sure enough, there she was. It didn't take long for Anthony to go over to her.

"Hey Anthony, how are you doing?" Alicia asked.

"O.K., Here I have something that's important that I want to give you," Anthony said reaching into his pocket for the towel.

It would have been easy to be offended and upset by what she was about to receive but Alicia saw that Anthony was giving her something important to him. She took the paper towel, slowly opened it up and saw the dead fish. She had a strange look on her face when she saw the dead fish. It was what Alicia did that provided a life long lasting memory. Alicia simply said, "Thank you," she then bent down and gave Anthony a kiss on the lips.

This was Anthony's first kiss from someone outside his family and one he would never forget. Often, looking back on this episode, Anthony saw it with humor and confusion. He believed the story was humorous, but he was thoroughly confused as to why someone so young was aroused by this kiss.

Anthony didn't have thoughts of sex entering his mind, but he thoroughly enjoyed the kiss in a way that attracted him even more to Alicia.

Anthony and Alicia carried on their friendship through the rest of the year despite the fact that she was older than Anthony. On occasion she gave him a kiss on the cheek before they went back into the classroom, but it was never as enjoyable as the kiss on the mouth. At the end of the year, they both went their separate ways, never seeing each other again.

Anthony got along well with the kids at school, and things seemed to be going well. At home was another matter. Anthony seldom saw his mother anymore. She was either at work or out on dates with men she met at work or other places. Anthony recalled there were very few of these men he liked or cared for. Often when his mom was out on dates, she wouldn't come home and sometimes stayed away days at a time. During this period Anthony and Madeline spent a great deal of time with their grandparents, Oscar and Velma. During this time a series of events began to occur which was not within the ability of a 6 year old to understand.

These events continued on until Anthony was 11 or 12. It impacted Anthony's behavior for the rest of his life. These events were responsible for Anthony having to see a therapist as an adult. He never knew or understood how these events impacted him until he was 33. Even then Anthony didn't have a complete understanding of how these events had impacted him. He realized though, that they had. This was a major step in starting to get his life back together.

~ Chapter 5 ~

Be My Friend

Anthony was in George's office talking in a monotone voice. He was aware of what he was saying but not aware of much else. Anthony spoke using body movements indicating he was reliving the episodes he was telling. There were the facial expressions and on occasion body flinches indicating fear. George looked into Anthony's eyes and saw the stare. Anthony rarely blinked and was staring off into space. Anthony remained in this state for most of the meeting on this particular day.

* * * * * * *

"Let's go out and play down in the woods," Uncle Jeremiah said to Anthony and Madeline.

"We don't want to," Anthony answered.

"Oh come on, I just want you to be my friend. We can have a lot of fun down there. We can play on the grapevines or play with the chickens; there are all sorts of things we can do."

"Well, O.K., but can we go and play at the grape vine?" Anthony responded, getting a little excited.

"Sure, let's go," Jeremiah responded grabbing their hands as he led them down to the woods behind the house.

Anthony and Madeline were skipping into the woods. Anthony was 5 and Madeline was 4. Jeremiah was quite a bit older, and about ready to finish high school.

On the way into the woods, Jeremiah asked Anthony and Madeline to go by an old shed which was on the way to a grape vine. "Let's go in the shed for a while," Jeremiah said.

Anthony and Madeline didn't think much of this because they had gone into the shed many times to play cowboys and Indians or various other games like hide and seek. It was with no hesitation the two of them skipped into the shed.

The old log and wood-shingled shed was surrounded by woods and was away from the houses. There were no furnishings and no one was sure what the shed had been built or used for. There was only one door at the shed and it had a lock on the inside. Jeremiah locked it after entering.

* * * * * *

There was a long time of silence in George's office. "What happened next?" George asked Anthony.

Anthony sat in the chair staring at the floor. He spoke in an almost unemotional tone and manner never taking his stare off the floor. "Jeremiah had me and my sister take our pants off, and had sex with us," Anthony answered. "He took turns with us. He had sex with me for a while and then my sister. We didn't know what was going on, or what he was doing. It didn't seem right. We tried to get him to stop, but it didn't do any good. He just kept saying it's all right; it's something grownups do and keep a secret about. We can pretend we're grownups. When you get older you can do it to. He said this as he was having sex with us from behind. We didn't know what to do. We believed him. It didn't seem right though, he was so manipulative. I feel like shit about this even until this day."

"How far or how long would this go on?" George asked.

"I don't remember exactly; it seemed like a long time. I do remember it went until he reached orgasm. It was disgusting. I can't think back on it without wanting to puke."

"Did he penetrate either you or your sister?" George asked in a caring and reassuring voice.

"Not that I can remember, at least not the first time he did this to us," Anthony answered with embarrassment.

"So, there were other times?" George asked, wanting to put a hand on Anthony's shoulder to reassure him but knowing that during this point of the conversation, Anthony didn't want any physical contact.

After a long pause Anthony answered "Yes."

"How many?" George wanted to be careful and not push Anthony.

"Quite a few more, later on there was penetration, there were many more times he did this to us, sometimes alone, sometimes the two of us together. I wanted to tell, I am sure my sister wanted to tell. We had heard adults talk, we were supposed to trust them. Our family had people with tempers and sometimes when kids questioned them they got spankings. How was I to know?" Anthony responded.

* * * * * *

Anthony was still sitting in the office staring at the floor, not showing any emotion or changing the tone of his voice, still, emotionless. He continued telling his story to George.

After spending time in the shed and doing what he had intended from the very start, Jeremiah took Anthony and Madeline down to the grape vine. They spent what seemed like several hours playing, swinging and holding on to the grape vine, playing like Tarzan as they swung over a small ravine.

When they were tired, they headed back up the hill out of the woods to the house. While walking up the hill Jeremiah started singing, 'Michael Row the Boat Ashore,' Anthony and Madeline started singing, thinking not so much about what had happened at the shed, but playing at the grape vine.

~ Chapter 6 ~

Robert

Wanda had been dating on a regular basis for some time. She left Anthony and Madeline with their grandparents when she went out. As far as she knew they would be ok. She didn't know the sexual abuse took place for years, which was a result of Anthony and Madeline being left with their grandparents.

Anthony and Madeline went out with Wanda several times and met several of the men she dated. They remembered one man in particular, a musician who played a piano quite well. This man was one Anthony remembered as one who was kind and friendly. He joked around with the children and Anthony was amazed that he could make music come out of a piano the way he did. Anthony remembered him because he visited Wanda shortly after Anthony broke his arm. Anthony was pretending that he and Madeline had joined a circus and were performing various acts. While doing a balancing act Anthony fell off two cinder blocks balanced on top of each other. The full force of his fall caused his arm to hit the corner of one of the cinder blocks. Anthony entered the second grade with a broken right arm.

The relationships Wanda had were creating some confusion for Anthony. This, along with his broken arm contributed to him becoming difficult to deal with. The ongoing sexual activity and abuse contributed to Anthony having bad grades in school.

Wanda continued seeing a number of men but became more serious with Robert Gerrard. Robert was 6' 1" and in his early thirties. He was tanned with blondish brown hair. He was in good shape and took care of his body. He seemed nice and was pleasant and kind to Anthony and Madeline, at least at first. They developed a sense of trust with Robert. He took the time to play with the children when he was with them. This was something they enjoyed, and was new for them. Robert was one of the first male figures that the two had clear memories of. Most of those early memories were pleasant. Anthony and Madeline continued to spend most of their time with their grandparents, Velma and Oscar. Some sexual contact started with another uncle, but it was limited contact for Anthony, and eventually stopped before too long. While contact with that uncle stopped, it still continued with Jeremiah. Unfortunately for Madeline, the contact with the other uncle increased. During the time Wanda was seeing other men, Anthony and Madeline started spending more time with their grandparents and less with their mother. There were occasional visits with their mother and Robert.

When Anthony was halfway through the second grade Wanda, married Robert. She let Anthony and Madeline live with their grandparents until they finished the school year at Cherokee. Anthony occasionally saw his mother, but going back and forth led in part to low grades. Having a broken arm didn't help matters. He passed at the end of the school year but was very far behind the other students in his work. He spent much of the next few years behind in school, always trying to catch up. It took a great deal of time and effort for Anthony to get on the same grade level as his classmates. He even spent time in remedial classes with the slower students.

Wanda and Robert's first house was small, where they lived for a short time. After Anthony and Madeline stayed with their mother and Robert, Wanda decided to take them to live with her and Robert most of the time. This seemed appropriate because Velma and Oscar moved across town, and Anthony and Madeline needed to change schools anyway. Wanda felt the time was appropriate and it wouldn't create many problems for the two children.

Shortly after Anthony and Madeline moved in with their mother, Jeremiah joined the Army. During this time they were not involved in sexual activities for some time. Anthony's opinions and views regarding sexuality had already been formed, and would take years to change. There was a period of time before Jeremiah joined the Army that Anthony learned to say no to Jeremiah's attempts at making him a submissive sex partner.

As early as third and fourth grade, Anthony changed his attitudes from being submissive, to becoming an aggressor. He started forcing sex on others and participating in various sexual activities.

As an adult when reflecting back on his life Anthony realized he wasn't involved in sex for enjoyment. He was too young to enjoy the act. It was the power and acceptance that came about as a result of the act. It was one of the few times he was in control. It was possible at this age to find willing partners, both male and female who gave into the notion of showing affection.

Anthony always had questions about his sister's participation in sexual activities with Jeremiah. He didn't know if Jeremiah continued to force himself on her or not. Later on in adulthood he discovered the more aggressive nature and involvement with another uncle. Anthony was suspicious that Jeremiah continued to make advances on her even when she was older and in high school. Anthony became more aggressive in telling Jeremiah no, and was not around him as much. As a result the sexual activity diminished and didn't take place as regularly.

Wanda and Robert only lived in their new house for a short period of time when they moved to the north side community of Johnson City. They moved into an apartment directly across from where Anthony and Madeline ended up going to school, North Side Elementary School. The apartment was one of the nicest in the complex, but that wasn't saying much. The apartments were primarily for short term tenants. Many of the tenants were students at East Tennessee State University who lived in them for short periods of time and moved on when school was out. Robert and Wanda moved into one facing the street and elementary school.

The apartment complex was two older houses converted into seven apartment units. Robert and Wanda's was the largest on the lower level, facing the street and the only one of the seven taking up over half of the original house.

Wanda's mother, Marilyn Martin, lived in an apartment in the same complex. This was how Robert and Wanda became aware of the complex. It so happened that the apartment that became available was in the same house where Wanda's mother lived.

From this move Anthony and Madeline got to know their Grandmother Martin better. They also got to better know their uncles, aunts and cousins on their mother's side of the family. They were still around and felt closer to Velma and Oscar but they had a good relationship with their Grandmother Martin who they called Mamaw Martin.

Mamaw Martin was kind and loving to her grandchildren, and Anthony and Madeline appreciated her love. She was a small woman, not quite standing 5' tall. She was a little heavy, weighing 150 pounds and had high cheek bone features consistent with her Native American heritage.

The children's new stepfather Robert was someone who at first seemed to be nice and he made a good impression on Anthony. Anthony and Madeline had been spending the majority of time on weekends with Velma and Oscar, but this soon changed. Wanda decided that Anthony and Madeline should live with her. She made plans for them to start school at Northside the next school year.

The children spent more time with their mother and Robert. They gradually saw another side of the two. The picture of what they saw was not a good one for Anthony. Wanda was never around her children much but she seemed at times to care for them and on occasion even gave them a hug or kiss. She didn't seem like a mother in a traditional way, because she wasn't. She certainly didn't fit the role of a mother as portrayed on television shows or movies at the time. The reality of it was Wanda had likely never had good examples either. She had had a bad string of luck with men and in such ways that most any woman would be confused. The closest thing to a traditional mother for Anthony and Madeline was their grandmother Velma. Wanda took them out to buy clothes and other items which they needed, but other than the basic needs, there wasn't much of a mother present. Anthony tried to see Wanda as a mother, but even early on had difficulty in seeing her this way. He knew she couldn't be the mother their Grandmother Velma had been. He made the effort though, which led to more confusion. There were many things that made this issue confusing for Anthony.

Anthony and Madeline were used to having meals prepared by their grandmother. Breakfast was usually eggs, toast, cereal and/or pancakes. Lunch consisted of soup, a sandwich and a dessert, usually a Little Debbie Cake. This was everyday with the exception of Sunday when all of the family showed up for a cooked meal, then either watched a ball game on T.V. or went out to play ball in one of the fields next to where they lived. Velma made supper every day, a large meal fit for a king. The exception was on Sunday when the family had leftovers from lunch. She was the best cook Anthony ever experienced and her meals were in his memory long after her death.

This was one of the many ways Velma filled the traditional role of mother. It was a role which gave a sense of stability and support. Anthony never knew if this was a role she liked or not. He wondered what it would have been like if she had been born later, when it was acceptable for married women with families to have a career outside the home.

Wanda never was one for doing a lot of cooking and wasn't about learning a new behavior. It is not that she never cooked; it was just unusual when she did. Wanda was actually a good cook. She would fix simple meals, and they were good. To go from Mamaw Velma's masterpieces to where now, if he got anything for breakfast, it was likely a bowl of cereal, was a let down for Anthony. Now, more often than not, lunch was a do-your-own sandwich, and for supper Wanda would say, "Here is a dollar go out and buy you something."

Anthony and Madeline learned how to manage and get by. On numerous occasions, the two managed all sorts of original recipes. They made cereal sandwiches, put steak sauce on tomato sandwiches. With the dollar their mother gave them, they could buy two hot dogs at the local Dairy Queen and a pack of Kool-Aid at the local thrift store. When they got a meal they couldn't believe how good it was! It was amazing how good a meal could taste, and it was a rarity like it was now.

Neither Anthony nor Madeline was lazy. Both of them became excellent cooks due to coming up with so many unusual recipes. Their problem was they were learning these skills in the fourth and fifth grade. Robert and Wanda always did quite well, however. They were seldom at home and went out almost nightly. They ate well and Robert gave most of his time to Wanda. He was married to her, not the kids. From the time Wanda and Robert got off of work until bed time they were out doing something. Meanwhile, the kids were at home fending for themselves.

Anthony never remembered having a baby sitter during this, and rarely before. Robert occasionally worked second or third shifts. When working the later shifts he usually slept through the day until Wanda got home. Anthony and Madeline learned to be careful and not wake him. They became fearful of making noises for fear of waking him up. It was after waking him a few times they learned about his temper.

From an early age, before entering fifth grade Anthony learned to do for himself. He learned along with Madeline, that neither Wanda nor Robert was adults you wanted upset. Neither Robert nor Wanda had control of their tempers and it usually showed if someone upset them. Both were aggressive towards their children. When getting into arguments with each other they also became physical, they often got into fights when going out.

Robert liked to take Wanda to pool halls to play pool. He was a decent player but got into fights at the pool halls on a regular basis. He bought pool cues on a frequent basis due to his breaking them in fights.

Wanda was not any better than Robert with her temper. She challenged women to fight all of the time. After drinking, she became even more aggressive. She ended up in just as many fights, if not more than Robert.

From early in the marriage Robert and Wanda had Anthony and Madeline go into one of the bedrooms when the need for discipline arose. They had Anthony and Madeline take off their pants and lay across a bed with their bottoms exposed. Robert took a belt and whipped them until they couldn't cry tears anymore. The belt he used was more than a common belt. It was 2" wide and 36" to 38" long. It was leather and every 1" or 2" had a metal braid. The whippings lasted for far too long and it wasn't unusual to bring blood. If something happened around the house, and unless someone confessed to whatever the situation was, then both children were whipped. Whippings often took place over things neither Anthony nor Madeline had anything to do with. Sometimes Wanda or Robert might misplace something, or they forgot what had happened, due to being drunk or high, and then blamed the children.

Anthony and Madeline learned more about alcohol consumption than they ever wanted to know. Wanda and Robert spent a great deal of time drinking, especially after work and on weekends. Rum and Coke was their drink of choice but they showed no hesitation in drinking beer or any other kind of alcohol, mixed or not.

Anthony was in the 3rd or 4th grade when he first became intoxicated. Robert went to a party with a group of friends but left Wanda at home. He decided it would be a good idea to take Anthony with him. At the party Robert and some of his friends thought it would be fun to give Anthony several vodka and orange juice screwdrivers. Anthony drank these until he passed out. From this experience Anthony developed a taste for alcohol and started to sneak drinks when left in the house.

Anthony could steal and drink alcohol and never be suspected of doing it. Robert and Wanda assumed the other was getting the drinks. This was early in Anthony's life and continued for the duration of time he lived at home. There was a period of time after he left home when he would sneak into the house and steal a six pack of beer or a partial bottle of whiskey knowing he would never be suspect.

There was one specific incident Anthony remembered which caused him to learn not to trust adults, especially Wanda or Robert. As usual, they went out and didn't come home until late, in this case after 1:00 a.m. As they came in, they were arguing and fighting as usual. They were drunk and went to play a tape in the tape player. Anthony was a light sleeper and was easily awakened, and once awake, he had trouble going back to sleep. Wanda or Robert did something to tear up the tape player. Anthony saw them arguing about it. They argued for a long time, cursing and fighting. Eventually they went to bed and Anthony finally went back to sleep.

The next day Wanda and Robert were both waiting for Anthony and Madeline at home for them when they returned from school. "What did you do to the fucking tape player last night?" Wanda yelled.

"Nothing, we promise, nothing," Anthony and Madeline answered apologetically. They both saw them like this before and they knew the harm they could do.

"Well, we'll find out who in the hell tore it up." Wanda yelled. "Now both of you get your ass into the bedroom and pull your pants down," she yelled as she grabbed Madeline by the hair and pulled her into the room. Robert grabbed and pulled Anthony by the arm. Both children were crying, knowing what was about to take place.

It was bad enough knowing what was about to take place. It was much worse for Anthony and Madeline knowing they had done nothing wrong. Robert beat both of them so bad they cried until they could cry no more; the tears had all dried up. This was not just a whipping limited to the buttocks. The back of the legs as well as the lower backs of both children were bruised, marked, and bloodied from the belt.

The whipping was not the extent of the punishment for the children. Madeline was slapped over and over by Wanda and Anthony grew angrier with each strike. Robert and Wanda never laid a hand on Anthony like this, but this was the first of many times Madeline was slapped and hit, never deserving it a single, solitary time that Anthony remembered. It was the first time Anthony learned the regretful behavior of hitting his sister when he was mad at her. This beating lasted for what seemed like 30 minutes. The more Robert and Wanda beat the children the angrier they got. Constantly yelling, "Who tore up the damn tape player?"

Anthony finally responded, "We were both playing with it when it broke," knowing it wasn't true, but it would probably stop the beating. During this episode Anthony learned and developed behaviors which he would carry for years. He couldn't trust anyone, especially adults. He started to feel like he was a piece of meat for adults to do with as they wanted. They raped him, beat him, changed their minds on where he lived and moved him from place to place. They used him for their advantage. Anthony couldn't trust, love or care for anyone except his sister. He would to do unto them as they did unto him. He would take advantage of others and live his own life. He would do this to his advantage, not giving a rip what others thought or felt. He would manipulate and use others just as he had been taught. Anthony now knew anyone who was good to him was only doing it to meet their own needs, not because they actually cared for him. It was now his turn, and Anthony's focus was going to be on himself.

After the beatings Wanda and Robert sent the children to their rooms and went out again for another night of partying. Later on Anthony and Madeline came out of their rooms and realized Robert and Wanda were gone. It took a few minutes for Madeline to call out, "Hey Anthony, come and look."

Anthony walked into the kitchen and saw the note Madeline was pointing at, a note they had seen many times. A note which Madeline stood, staring at, and one Anthony looked at and thought of in an almost comical way. The smile wasn't from it being funny though, it was the irony of the whole thing. It was a note he saw as a joke. It was one Anthony knew he would see again in the future. The note read:

Anthony and Madeline here is $1 to get you something to eat for supper. Leave the change on the table. ~ Love, Mom

~ Chapter 7 ~

Northside

Northside Elementary School was a large brick school on the corner of North Roan Street and Chilhowee Avenue in Johnson City. It was an older school consisting of two stories and a large number of class rooms. The school had grades from kindergarten through sixth grade. Over 1,000 students attended the school. Anthony was now in the third grade. There were four 3rd grade classrooms with approximately 25 students per class.

The neighborhood was primarily residential but also near a number of commercial properties. Roan Street was one of the major roads in the city and used to access the busy and rapidly growing north side of town. Northside was unique and new for Anthony and Madeline in various ways. Going north on Roan Street was a large residential neighborhood that was a predominantly Caucasian community. It also included several dozen blocks of housing which consisted of predominantly poorer housing for whites. This is where the family lived. Their apartment was almost directly across from the school on Chilhowee Street. Just north of that, in either direction was a neighborhood consisting of wealthy, well-to-do homes with predominantly white families. As far as Anthony knew, no Blacks lived in this area for whatever reason.

To the west of Roan Street was poorer housing, primarily all Black families. While some Whites lived there, there weren't many. Anthony had been around Blacks at Cherokee but not to the extent he now was at Northside. It seemed as if the majority of students at Northside were Black. There was certainly much more housing where the Blacks lived than there was for Whites. There also seemed to be larger families within the Black community.

Anthony's primary experience around Blacks or concerning Blacks was hearing his Grandfather Oscar, cursing them or calling them Niggers. Anthony vividly recalled his grandfather saying, "It's about time somebody killed that Nigger," when Martin Luther King Jr. was killed in Memphis Tennessee. It was a side of his grandfather he was glad to see change later in life, not just in tone but to the point to where Oscar ended up having many Black friends and expressed openly about being sorry for the feelings and comments in his past.

This was an era when many Whites, including Wanda and Robert, openly supported and campaigned for George Wallace, the Governor of Alabama, when he ran for President of the United States. They supported him for his views on labor and the poor, as opposed to his views of separation. This was a time when a Democrat supported the nominee simply because he was a Democrat. This was the beginning of the end of what some called the era of the Dixiecrat.

Even at an early age, Anthony never understood the bitterness and hatred many Whites had towards Blacks. To him, they were just people working hard and having to put up with the same difficulties other people did. If anything, the difficulty of the time, the prejudice, the difficulty of racism, made what accomplishments that were obtained even more incredible.

Anthony knew there was more to a person than the color of their skin. It was almost instinctive to Anthony in realizing this. If Blacks were people that his family harbored bitterness, hatred or misunderstanding towards, then he would do his best to get along with them. Anthony had had it with his mother and life in general, even at this early of an age. He couldn't figure his mother out, how she could support George Wallace for President and not support his racist views. To Anthony, if you support the man, you support his policies, especially his racist views.

To Anthony, Blacks were people who were abused just because they were Black. Anthony saw a group of people who loved their children, worked hard on their jobs, and believed in a God. He saw them making the efforts to improve their lives yet lived with some of the worst prejudice one could imagine. Anthony saw their situation as not much different than the one he was in. It wasn't the racism, but it was the fact of being taken advantage of and not understood. Anthony realized as he got older that it was much different than this for the Black community. He later learned more and developed even more respect for the African American culture and their history.

While in the third grade there were two specific events which helped Anthony develop relationships with, and an understanding of Blacks. One occurred when Oscar took Anthony to see his Uncle Bill play high school basketball. It would have been easy for Anthony to draw a conclusion about Blacks based on the time and what he had seen in the examples of some in his family.

Uncle Bill was in the news on a regular basis starting early his freshman year in high school. He was seen as one of the best, if not the best, high school basketball players in upper East Tennessee. Bill was already breaking scoring records in high school basketball, some of which still stand. It was while going to many of these games that Anthony saw Blacks from a different perspective. Instead of focusing just on Bill, Anthony noticed the confidence and pride that many of the Blacks played the game with. The confidence and pride started when they hit the floor for warm ups. While their confidence and pride was obvious, it spilled out to the other players on their teams. It was obvious to Anthony, the pride was enhanced from the music used during pre-game warm ups, usually music by Black artists. Anthony saw this pride beaming from the players, and the confidence develop among each player due to the way their culture was influencing everyone on the team, but beyond that, even the fans in the stands. Most of this recognition came from players from other teams because University High's didn't have many Black players. This change of acceptance, and understanding, due in part from basketball and sports in general, was taking place in society despite many of the negative and racist comments from many in the stands. This was something Anthony respected and admired in the young men playing the game. Later on when involved in sports he knew a player could hear the comments. How someone continued to play the game, not losing their temper or getting in fights, was inspirational to Anthony. It would be so for others and the inspiration these sporting events provided helped change a society's racist views.

There was another incident which helped develop Anthony's respect for blacks. It was his going trick-or-treating on Halloween. Wanda took Anthony across Roan Street into the Black community to trick-or-treat. This particular Halloween, Wanda dressed Anthony up as a girl. He had the wig, dress, makeup, and balloons for breasts, the full works. While trick-or-treating at one house, an elderly Black lady took Anthony into her house bragging about how good he looked. "Honey, you look just like a little girl. Everybody come in here and look at this little boy," she said. This was one of the first times someone made a big deal of any kind in a positive manner towards Anthony. He wouldn't forget, he felt this family saw something good when no one else did. He realized this was an incident that was not as big a deal as he thought at first. It was a situation where he was so used to nothing positive being said, that when something good was said, it left a lasting impression. Anthony knew, especially when older, it would have been rare for a White family to have said anything good about a little Black boy. The Black lady did not possess this prejudice.

Nothing else eventful happened to Anthony during his first year at Northside. There were occasional beatings with the belt from Robert or Wanda, but that was common. Anthony and Madeline adjusted accordingly to their moods and learned how and when to stay away from them. This resulted in fewer beatings and less direct intervention and contact with adults.

The other aspect which continued to develop was their sexual contact with others. Anthony was petting and attempting intercourse with two female cousins and one friend of the family in the 3rd, 4th, and 5th grades. The sexual contact developed to the point where Anthony and Madeline were involved in minor sexual petting with each other. This was a situation Anthony regretted. There was some resolution because he realized his view of sexual activity had already been skewed.

The only explanation to sex that Anthony had was from what had been taught by those around him. He realized later this was not the best type of education. Neither he nor Madeline understood the sexual activity they carried out and were involved in.

Early in the 3rd grade Anthony started initiating sexual activity with others. Even at an early age he felt he could control others. Anthony also knew he was getting attention whether it was appropriate or not. He hadn't gone through puberty and wasn't capable of orgasm during intercourse. It was attention he wanted and felt he could get from others. Anthony knew this was something that had been done to him by adults taking advantage of him. They were responsible for teaching him this behavior which he was now involved in. Anthony's thought, at least with the people he was involved with, is that they were willing participants. Anthony hated the adults who had used him.

That summer Anthony and Madeline spent most of their time with their grandparents, Velma and Oscar. Wanda and Robert were arguing and fighting on a regular basis. The fighting involved physical contact and one of them always ended up hurt. Anthony and Madeline appreciated the time with their grandparents away from the fighting.

The summer months were difficult because Oscar still got easily upset and frequently yelled at his sons and/or hit them with a belt or stick. It was easier for Anthony and Madeline to deal with because this didn't occur on a nightly basis like it did at home with Wanda and Robert.

One night that summer Wanda and Robert got into such a severe fight that Wanda went to stay with Velma and Oscar for the weekend. She was badly bruised and had a black eye from Robert's beating. Velma, Oscar and Billy were taking care of her and trying to talk her into getting a divorce. Wanda wasn't interested in this though. She knew Robert would come around and get back to his old self. As Anthony grew older he knew she stayed with Robert due to her thinking that Anthony and Madeline needed a dad.

One night Velma and Oscar were watching television with Wanda when they heard a knock at the door. "Who is it?" Velma asked.

"It's me Robert. Is Wanda here?" He asked, obviously drunk.

"Billy and Oscar, come in here quick, it's Robert!" Velma yelled. Billy and Oscar were there in seconds.

"She's here but you just best get your ass out of here and leave her alone!" Oscar yelled back, turning red from anger.

"If she's here I want to see her, and I mean now!" Robert yelled.

"I said to get the hell out of here! She'll talk to you when she wants to. Now leave before we call the law!" Oscar shouted.

About then Robert kicked in the door and ran into the house. "Where the hell is Wanda? I'm going to kick her no good ass, now tell me or I'll kick yours too."

Wanda came running up the stairs yelling at Robert, "Get out of here you no good piece of shit." She continued to curse him as she ran towards him. Robert drew back and slapped her as she got close enough for him to strike her. Wanda fell back and hit the floor. She let out a sick sounding "ugh" as she was hit. She didn't lose consciousness, but Anthony saw his mother sitting there on the floor, dazed.

Immediately after Robert hit Wanda, Uncle Billy had seen enough so he started towards Robert. Robert realized how big Billy was, he had spent time with the Beechups. Robert thought Billy would be easy to deal with because of his age. Bill was still in high school in his junior year.

Bill was also close to 6' 7" tall and 200 pounds. He worked out, participated in athletics and was seeking a college athletic scholarship so he worked hard to maintain his shape. Robert was tall at 6' 1" and in good shape himself. He had several disadvantages though. While he was in good physical shape, he wasn't in nearly as good of shape as Bill who was also a younger, trained athlete, which was a distinct advantage.

The problem for Robert was Bill was not drunk, and Bill was really upset. He hit Robert hard with a right and then a left knocking him down. Bill picked Robert up and threw him several feet onto the couch. Bill was on top of Robert before Robert had time to feel the pain of the blows he had taken. Billy hit Robert several more times, one punch busting a vessel in Robert's eye and another breaking his nose. "Now get the shit out of here before I kill you!" Billy yelled point blank in Robert's face, spitting and cursing in his face as he yelled at him.

"You may think you can hit on a woman, but I'll be dammed if you'll hit Wanda again. You sure as hell won't threaten me. Now get out!" Billy yelled, getting angrier and drawing back to hit Robert again but holding it back.

There were a few more words exchanged before Robert left. Each time words were exchanged Bill would hit Robert in the face with no resistance from Robert. Bill started to slap him instead of hitting him with a closed fist to humiliate him.

Robert was so drunk, the only reason he took this punishment was he didn't know better. Later on not much was said of this to Billy, Wanda or Anthony who had been in the room the whole time. The only thing said was the family telling Wanda of the need to leave Robert. She agreed for a day or two but decided to go back to Robert, and take the kids with her.

As much as Wanda seemed to hate Robert at times, she seemed happy at others. She didn't mind the abuse and learned to live with it. She appreciated the recognition and attention she received from Robert. There were the fights which occurred at the apartment on Chilhowee, however there was no one for Robert to answer to like he had to do with Billy.

Anthony hated what was going on but he was much smaller than Robert. All he could do was sit back and watch or go into his bedroom and shut the door, listening to what was happening outside. Robert slapped or beat Wanda at will and there was nothing he could do. Wanda fought back sometimes holding her own.

On one occasion Wanda grabbed a steak knife and stabbed Robert on the arm. Anthony and Madeline witnessed this and another fight where Robert grabbed Wanda's finger and broke it while yanking it back. After Wanda fell down in pain, Robert stomped and kicked her. Many nights, more nights than Anthony could count, he and Madeline went to bed crying while one of these fights was going on. They went to bed not knowing if the physical abuse would carry over to them or not. As they got older, Anthony and Madeline felt they were lucky that this level of violence never carried over to them.

✶ ✶ ✶ ✶ ✶ ✶

The 4th grade started out as an exciting time for Anthony. He tried out for the 5th and 6th grade football team at school. He became the first fourth grader to try out for and make the team at this level in Johnson City. This was an area where Anthony excelled. He got positive attention from others in football, but hardly any place else. Anthony was a good sized boy and it was easy for him to make the team and play. He continued to develop strong relationships with the Blacks at school. It was easy for the kids on the team and neighborhood to pick on Anthony because he always hung around with older kids and he was much smaller. Whether on the basketball courts at school, the play grounds, or in his yard, Anthony was always around other kids. He was hanging out with these older kids on a regular basis.

It was one of the older Black kids who on one occasion took up for Anthony and told some other kids picking on Anthony to leave him alone. They were playing basketball on the playground and the other kids listened to the young man taking up for Anthony. He took up for Anthony because he knew about Anthony playing football and the effort he made at practice. This young man was respected because he was one of the better football players in Johnson City and eventually played pro football in the NFL.

Anthony also tried out for the basketball team in the 4th grade. He made the team but seldom played. Football was the sport Anthony could excel at. Yet, the situation at home hindered his chances of excelling to the fullest in any sport or activity. The year went by quickly. Anthony was involved in various activities and developed friendships which took him outside of the house and into the community. When not in the home he wouldn't have to be around the arguing and fighting taking place between Robert and Wanda.

Anthony developed a friendship with an older boy named Randy. Randy lived two blocks from him in a large three story house. He wasn't a good example for Anthony. Randy was more aware of the world around him in an adult way. This was obvious in his attitudes, thoughts, and conversations. Randy and Anthony began new adventures that continued for the next year and a half.

He went home with Randy and spent a few hours after school each day. Anthony started getting into fights with other kids at Randy's initiative. Usually they picked fights with younger kids, or a single person the same age as Anthony. They ganged up on the kid and beat him up. They never beat the kid up bad, just enough to cry and run home.

This was not the only new experience for Anthony with Randy. When at Randy's, they watched "Dark Shadows," the television show. After the show Randy and Anthony begin experimenting with drugs and mutual sexual activity with each other. From these early experiments Anthony also formed a fascination with the Occult. He started studying the subject in any way he found. There were books from the library and he sought out others with an interest in the Occult, devil worship and witchcraft. It was a game at first but became serious later on.

Anthony and Randy used Randy's room to experiment with the Occult and Witchcraft. They made up potions, and used them in their neighborhood and school. The boys used these potions on friends, relatives and people they didn't like. Anthony never knew if the potions actually worked but he knew they gave them a sense of power which felt good.

Anthony was bitter and felt negativity towards all of his family and the Church, for what he felt was a lack of concern and legitimacy. The Occult was a way to get back at the Church and Christianity. It was a journey and battle that lasted for some time.

* * * * * *

Anthony and Randy increased their sexual activity and involvement with the Occult and Witchcraft. They started involving other young boys who had shown an interest. Many of the boys were from families where they didn't get along with their parents. On rare occasions the boys would find girls to be involved in the activities.

The boys formed a club where they occasionally got together and became involved in several of activities. Those activities were illegal and a number of the boys got into trouble with various people, including businesses and the police.

They often met in an old, abandoned, two-story garage with an empty upstairs apartment. The apartment was vacant except for some old couches and a couple of lamps. The downstairs garage was empty but for old abandoned barrels and scrap wood. The boys climbed over the junk to get to the stairwell that went upstairs to the apartment. This is where they met. The apartment was on the property which also had a house. There was an older couple who lived in the house but never used the garage. Anthony and his friends figured out the times someone was home and the times when they were away. They knew anytime between noon and 8 p.m. they wouldn't get caught.

The meeting house was also located next to an eye hospital and doctor's office. There was always traffic, both foot traffic and traffic from motor vehicles. It was easy for the boys to occupy the building without getting caught. The noise of the community kept the boys and their activities hidden. The boys met over the next year and got together on a regular basis without getting caught. No one ever knew they were meeting there.

During the late 1960's and early 1970's a popular New York City gang named The Mau Mau's, was making inroads into getting recognized for the trouble they were getting into. Some of the boys read about this gang and were aware of a gang that had formed in one of the roughest parts of Johnson City. Some of its members patterned themselves after the Mau Mau's. The spread of gangs was not taking place here the way it would a few years later. Many of those in gangs wouldn't refer to their gangs by any particular name. The leaders in these groups made alliances for themselves and their benefits, more than promoting the name of any particular national group. The Keystone group for example, became known more for being from Keystone than any association with the national group the Mau Mau's. This was also true for the group where Anthony lived, Northside. They always referred to the gang as a club, as opposed to a gang.

To join the boys' club, one sat in one of the chairs in the upstairs apartment. Another lit a cigarette placing it in the hand of the person sitting in the chair. The inductee had to let it go out on the palm of their hand. Refusal to do this or the inability to make it through the pain resulted in not being accepted in the club or being beat in. In getting beat in, all of the boys in the club fought the prospective member until he couldn't fight or they thought he had had enough. There were always several boys in the room during the initiations.

When doing the cigarette initiation, if at any time the person in the chair flinched his hand or threw the cigarette out of his hand the rest of the boys in the room pounced on the person beating him until he could barely move or defend himself. After this it was up to the other boys as to accept him in or not. In most all cases anyone who wanted in eventually got in.

Anthony did this just like everyone else, except he did both parts of the initiation. This helped put Anthony close to a leadership role. He was willing to do both parts of the initiation. During the beating part, the person could fight back. Anthony thought he would enjoy this aspect of the group, as he felt he had a decent chance if fighting. He was wrong and learned a valuable lesson from this experience. It took an event later on, requiring encouragement from his mother to toughen Anthony up.

As the year went on more activities took place which helped develop Anthony's personality for years to come. The boys were experimenting with drugs and other illegal activities more. They stole cigarettes, marijuana, alcohol or other things from their parents. After a while they developed enough courage to break into peoples houses. As far as Anthony knew nothing was ever stolen. It was the excitement of breaking into a home and not getting caught. The thrill was in not getting caught, while at the same time knowing they had violated someone's privacy. They looked through the drawers, dressers and cabinets. They looked at the women's underwear and night garments, jewelry and other personal items. Along with the breaking and entering and using drugs, the boys became more violent. Anthony reached the point where fighting was a regular occurrence. It was something he felt comfortable with as long as he was either one-on-one or with friends fighting against others. In addition to these things each boy tried to out do each other.

Anthony tried several times to set fire to the apartment next door to his house on Chilhowee Avenue. Each time Anthony tried to set the fire someone was at home. Luckily for Anthony he tried starting the fire by lighting exposed insulation on the outside of the building. He didn't know at his age that insulation did not burn. Anthony was successful at burning trash dumpsters. He made this a regular activity with some of the boys in the group. This was easy to do. All one had to do was fill a bottle up about three-fourths full with gasoline and stick a rag down the top of the bottle, pour gas on the rag, light it, throw it into the dumpster, and take off running. The boys called the Fire Department, and sometimes hung around to show them which dumpster was on fire. None of them ever got caught setting the fires.

The incidents with fire ended when Anthony and Randy took gasoline and poured it across their apartment club house. They set the building on fire by lighting a book of matches and throwing it onto the gasoline soaked inside of the building. They ran away never looking back. They didn't need to; they saw the building immediately go up in flames. They felt the heat and heard the roar of the flames as they ran away. They knew the flames spread quickly, and their effort was successful. Before making it home they heard the sirens of several fire trucks.

* * * * * * * * *

One day Anthony was playing on the playground, by himself. His mother, Wanda sent him out of the house which was something he didn't mind. Anthony knew this was a chance to get away from the headaches that took place at home. It was also a chance to make more friends. Playing on the play ground was something he enjoyed. He didn't realize it, but it was one of the times he could be a kid. That was after all what he was, a kid. Anthony was forced to grow up too fast; he didn't have a chance to be a kid. On this day, however, he was enjoying some of those lost times.

Anthony was playing on the play ground for about 30 minutes when two boys several years older than he came onto the playground. He didn't think much of it because even though one of the boys was much older, he was about the same size. The other boy was about a foot taller than Anthony but again, he didn't think anything of it. For all Anthony knew they were just two guys either walking through or deciding to play on the playground.

"Hey punk, get off of our playground!" one of the boys yelled at Anthony.

"I don't think this is your playground. I go to school here and I live across the street," Anthony responded in an angry tone.

"I think we're going to have to show this boy who this playground belongs to," the smaller boy said to the other.

"Yeah," said the larger boy.

The older and bigger boy grabbed Anthony from behind. They started beating him with their fists. They got Anthony to his knees and started kicking him in the ribs and legs. This was the first time Anthony could recall getting beat up, especially this bad. Once he was beaten up by a girl, but that was because he wouldn't hit her back. These were boys though, and for whatever reason, they whipped him pretty good without a lot of resistance from Anthony.

After the boys had beaten him up, Anthony ran to his house. He was crying because he was hurting, and his pride was hurt. He would surely lose some of the reputation he had developed. As Anthony reached the house, Wanda met him on the front porch.

"What the hell is the matter with you now?" His mother asked.

"Two boys from across the street beat me up," Anthony responded still crying."Are they still over there?" Wanda angrily asked.

"I think so," Anthony responded as Wanda walked towards the front yard, cursing under her breath the whole way where she could see around the trees to the playground across the street.

"Damn it Anthony, they're not that much bigger than you. Now, damn it! I don't want to hear your whimpering anymore. Now get your ass over there right now and kick their ass. If you don't then I'm going to kick yours when you get back home. Do you understand?" Wanda was angry now, yelling and cursing at Anthony, the whole time not taking a breath.

"Yes ma'am," Anthony said as he went back over across the street to confront the two boys again.

Anthony knew he didn't want to answer to his mother when he got back home. It didn't take any time for him to get across the street. He didn't say anything to either of the boys, when he saw the smaller one he ran towards him. Anthony tore into the smaller boy, fists flying.

Anthony was yelling, cursing, spitting, biting and kicking. He grabbed the boy by his hair and any other way he could. It wasn't long before the smaller boy was in a state of shock, not knowing what had happened to Anthony to cause him to be so violent. The larger of the boys jumped on Anthony's back. Anthony went to the ground and grabbed the larger boy by the ankles. Anthony yanked as hard as he could, pulling the larger of the two boys down to the ground. As the larger boy hit the ground Anthony was on top of him, hitting him in the face as hard as he could. He whipped both boys, one at a time, while his mother, Wanda looked on. Anthony was sure he had done what he had to do so he wouldn't have to face her when he went home.

Anthony didn't know why the older boy waited to jump him when he was beating up the smaller boy. All Anthony could figure was that maybe he was afraid that Anthony's mother was watching. This was the only time Anthony ever encountered these boys so he never had the chance to ask him why he waited. As far as Anthony was concerned that was O.K., these were two boys who obviously didn't belong in Northside.After this fight Anthony developed more self reliance and confidence in his ability to take care of himself. Mostly because he knew his mother would advocate and allow him to fight. Not only did she advocate it, she expected Anthony would do what was necessary to win the fight. With this type of support and encouragement from Wanda he enjoyed the fighting more. It was an attitude which at times had him fighting for fun, never getting hurt but fighting none the less.

Anthony was going into the fifth grade and getting into several fights a week, some for fun and others out of anger. He was smart enough not to have those fights on school property due to the consequences of having to answer to his teachers if he did. He followed kids as they walked home. At someone's yard or a street corner, out of the view of the school Anthony started the fights. A church corner at the end of the block down from the school was a favorite place. He didn't start fights just for the fun of it very often though. Usually someone said something at school which got him angry and he ignored it until school was out and then took care of it in his own way.

There was one kid named Tommy whom Anthony never liked. He was in Anthony's class and was a wealthy blond headed child. Tommy was the type that always had parties and invited all of the rich kids over but seldom the poorer kids like Anthony. Most of the girls in the class thought Tommy was the cutest in the class. He was proud of his reputation and used his parents and their reputation as a means of getting other kids into trouble.

The trouble with Tommy was more with the school staff and parents. After a month of school, Anthony had enough of Tommy. He was tired of trying to figure him out and of taking bull from him at school. Anthony was confused because Tommy was a master at deceiving others and Anthony could see, as could most of the other children, exactly what Tommy was like. For the kids who were poor like Anthony, it was a personality trait they didn't appreciate. For the other kids, those coming from wealthier families, it was a part of their make up and culture.

Tommy pretended to be Anthony's friend, yet at times put him down in front of others. Anthony knew Tommy had heard enough stories about him, so the only thing he could figure was that maybe Tommy was trying to impress the other kids by trying to be tougher than him. After coming to this conclusion Anthony decided to settle the score after school.

"Hey Tommy, wait up for me!" Anthony yelled while chasing him down the side walk toward the Methodist Church on the corner.

"What do you want?" Tommy responded sarcastically, not in an impressive mood. "I'll tell you what I want," Anthony responded as he grabbed Tommy by the upper body around the scruff of his shirt throwing him up against a chain link fence separating the school from the sidewalk near the street.

He yelled and pointed his finger at Tommy. "If you ever smart off to me in class or in front of others again I'll beat the shit out of you. Do you understand that?"

"You can't do a thing to hurt me, and you had best stay away from me and let me go or I'll tell my parents and the principal on you," Tommy responded, still smug in a better-than-you attitude.

Anthony hit him hard in the stomach and slapped him across the face. He didn't know why he slapped Tommy; this was the first time he recalled ever slapping someone in a fight except for the two boys he had fought previously. As he aged and got into more fights he realized he often slapped people to humiliate them. Maybe this was the time in life his attitude was coming out. It wasn't enough to beat them up. He had to humiliate them. As

Anthony was getting ready to slap Tommy again he felt something grab him across the shoulder and yank him away.

"Come on boys. You're both going with me." Anthony looked up and saw that now holding them both by the neck was Mr. Stern, the principal of Northside.

Mr. Stern was a tall rather thin man. He had a reputation for being tough and quick to swing a paddle. Anthony thought his name fit his reputation. Mr. Stern was balding with tufts of hair on the sides and back of his head. He didn't have enough to comb over the top and had apparently given up on growing it back. He spoke in a tone of that seemed to fit the stereotype of most principals. Mr. Stern took the boys into his office in a dark, dingy part of the school. Most of the students and teachers had already left the school with only a few people left walking the hallways. It was at the completion of the school day.

"What do you boys think you were doing?" Mr. Stern asked.

Tommy didn't respond, but Anthony did without hesitation. "I'm tired of Tommy acting better than everyone else and then treating me and others like dirt. So I decided to do something about it."

"So are you the one to start this ruckus?" Mr. Stern asked, still in a calm but confrontational voice.

"Yeah, I did, but so what? It was after school and off of school property. There is not a thing you can do about it." Anthony responded with bitterness and anger.

Anthony was also showing an attitude towards Mr. Stern he really didn't deserve. Mr. Stern had been kind, not raising his voice to the two.

"Well I'm afraid that is where you're wrong." Mr. Stern said, now getting angry at Anthony's attitude. He turned towards Tommy. "Tommy you can go on home. As far as I'm concerned you didn't have anything to do with this."

"Yes Sir," Tommy responded, smiling at Anthony on his way out the office.

"All right now, Beechup, I want you to turn around and bend over and put both of your hands on the desk over there." Mr. Stern said roughly as he turned Anthony around with one hand while reaching for a long oak paddle with the other. The paddle was about 26 inches long, one inch thick with holes drilled all over the paddle. As Mr. Stern went to paddle Anthony, he whipped around and looked him straight in the eye. "If you touch me with that thing, I'll kill you, you stupid son of a bitch." Anthony said this, cursing and angry as he spoke. His voice did not quiver or break. He said it as if he meant it, and there were no guarantees he didn't.

Mr. Stern couldn't believe what he heard. He stood frozen for what seemed like minutes. It was the first time he heard this type of assault coming from someone so young. Mr. Stern didn't know what to make of the confrontation and after a while decided he better involve someone else in this episode.

"Let's go get your mother, boy," Mr. Stern finally said as he walked towards the exit. Anthony, unafraid, followed him out the doorway.

Mr. Stern addressed Anthony's mother when she came to the door. "Mrs. Gerrard, we have a problem with Anthony."

Answering Mr. Stern while looking at Anthony, Wanda asked, "What's going on here?"

Mr. Stern explained the situation. Anthony still showed no sign of emotion, even though Mr. Stern told Wanda the whole story. Anthony was surprised at the response of his mother. Anthony expected his mother to fully support Mr. Stern and she would allow the paddling. He was at the point to where he didn't care. If the paddling was to take place, then he would get even with both Mr. Stern and his mother.

"Let me ask you a question, Mr. Stern. When you broke up the fight was Anthony on school property?" Wanda asked.

"Well, no, not technically, but I don't see that that has anything to do with it," Mr. Stern responded, somewhat confused by the question.

"Well let me ask you this question, was it during school hours?" Wanda asked.

"No, but then again I don't think that has anything to do with the situation," responded Mr. Stern. This time he was getting frustrated.

"Well as I see it, it has everything to do with the situation. If it wasn't on school property, didn't take place during school hours, then as I see it, you're the one out of line here. You have no right to take on the role of mother or father for my son. So let me see if you understand this. If you ever lay a hand on Anthony again under these circumstances, then I'll sue the shit out of you. Now do you understand that, Mr. Stern?" Wanda asked, looking Mr. Stern squarely in the eyes without blinking.

"Yes, I understand, Mrs. Gerrard, but you need to understand that if this takes place on school property in the future then I do have the right to take action," responded Mr. Stern in a defeated tone, clearly frustrated by the events that had occurred.

"You'll deal with it in an appropriate way or you'll have to answer to me and my attorneys. Now I think I've heard enough, Mr. Stern. I think it's time you get your ass off of my front porch," Wanda told him. Mr. Stern turned and walked away without saying another word.

Anthony thought the situation was over and he didn't have anything to worry about. As he was watching Mr. Stern walk away, his mother said in a calm collected voice, "Anthony, go to the bedroom, pull your pants down and lay across the bed. I'll be dammed if you're going to embarrass me like that again."

Anthony went and did as he was told. Wanda proceeded to get the belt and give Anthony a whipping. It was a whipping Anthony recalled where his mother didn't lose her temper. It was a whipping that hurt none the less, but after hearing his mother take up for him the way she did Anthony was not so angry. This was, as far as Anthony was concerned, one whipping that was worth it.

The rest of the school year continued until spring without much event. The only exception was Anthony getting to meet Colonel Sanders at a nearby Kentucky Fried Chicken during a promotional visit. Wanda and Robert were still fighting on a frequent basis, but Anthony and Madeline had become as used to them as they possibly could. Anthony was developing more confidence and continued to learn how to manipulate others to get his way. He was making friendships at school. All of this changed in the spring.

Wanda and Robert were looking at buying a house. They finally found one in the Keystone area of Johnson City. Keystone was an area of town with a reputation known all over the state of Tennessee, especially Upper East Tennessee. It was in the news on a daily basis. There was a legitimate, affiliated, authentic gang with drugs, murders and more which most everyone in Johnson City was aware of. Moving was a problem for Anthony because he knew he would have to reestablish himself and his reputation. Moving wasn't something he had a say about though. He was moving to Keystone, whether he liked it or not.

~ Chapter 8 ~

Welcome to Keystone

The house the family moved into was on East Main Street in Johnson City. It was a nice, white, one story house facing Main Street from the south side. It was on East Main and two blocks from the Keystone Housing Projects and Keystone Elementary School. Keystone covered an area 2 miles square. Within those 2 miles was a community recreation center, simply known as The Rec. There were several small community stores, a Dairy Queen, Steve Spurrier Little League Baseball Park, The Johnson City Cardinals professional baseball field, Johnson City Memorial Football Field, several hundred lower income smaller homes like Robert and Wanda had bought and two housing projects, one just to the south-east and one to the south-west. These two projects were separated by some small houses that covered 5 square blocks and Keystone Elementary School directly between the housing projects.

Keystone was one of the largest elementary schools in Johnson City. It was the roughest in terms of the attitudes of the students and their disciplinary problems. Keystone was also the most run down in terms of the upkeep of the school. The northern border of Keystone was a small mountain owned by a local mining company. The company had "no trespassing" signs all along the border, but all of the kids ignored them and went into the wooded areas anyway. The hills were deserted most of the time with the exception of an occasional drug addict, bum, or kids causing trouble. They were so vast they also bordered part of the eastern side of Keystone. The rest of the eastern side was bordered by what was known as Snob Hill.

Snob Hill was a region of hills and low income houses which separated Johnson City from another town called Elizabethton. Elizabethton was a small town of around 30,000 people. Snob Hill was known for the poorer Whites who lived there and the trouble which usually came out of the area.

There was an almost nightly shooting, and the area was so rough that police avoided both Snob Hill and Keystone when possible. These hills were fairly barren from the mining.

On the southern border of Keystone was another group of hills. There wasn't much on the other side of those hills except a small community known as Warriors Path. The drawing attraction here for the residents of Keystone was an old cave rock quarry filled with water. It would be a place of daring and crime for many of the local residents. Anthony suspected the quarry which was hidden from the main roads had dead bodies at the bottom of the water pit.

The western side of Keystone was bordered by downtown Johnson City and numerous small abandoned businesses. These businesses were used by locals who were homeless and drug dealers, drug users and homosexuals. Anthony knew this to be true due to the number of times he not only heard of the activities but also the number of times homosexual adults tried to get him to go there. Even though Anthony had been involved in a number of homosexual relationships, he considered himself a heterosexual. He looked at the activities he was involved in as a mere chance to get off with someone and experiment sexually to enjoy the perversions. He always preferred women.

Anthony was living two blocks from school, one block from the northern hills, and one block from the main projects. Living next door was a family named the Johnsons. The Johnsons were a family with three kids about the same age as Anthony and two more who were older. The two Anthony grew to know were Gerald and Judith. Gerald was a year or so older than Anthony. He was aggressive in his relationships with others and was full of self confidence. Gerald seldom bathed or washed his hair. His hair was always dirty and long and ungroomed.

Judith was the opposite of Gerald. It wasn't that she bathed on a frequent basis; she lived in a home where she had a difficult time getting to the bathtub. She made more of an effort than Gerald and, with her medium length blonde hair, was a rather attractive girl who Anthony developed a crush on.

Across the street was the Patterson family. Anthony became well acquainted with them. They had a son his age named Vincent. The Pattersons lived in a home that wasn't bad as far as looks from the outside but was dirty on the inside. The Pattersons seldom washed clothes or put anything up. Anthony doubted if the floors had ever been swept. The house was littered with beer cans and whiskey bottles strewn throughout.

Vincent was a boy you would never guess lived in such a dirty house. He was one of the boys Anthony got to know who took care of himself by bathing and wearing nice clean clothes. Vincent had long medium length black hair to match his small, but well developed frame. While he was attractive and clean in appearance, he had a tongue laced with constant bad language.

He was manipulative and was careful who he trusted in the relationships he developed.

Anthony was surprised at the relationship Gerald Johnson had with his parents. It wasn't unusual for his parents to give him a beer, or smoke a joint with him. They seldom got mad unless Gerald stole money from them, which he did on occasion. Gerald cussed them out, which wasn't unusual because most everyone in Keystone was always around bad language. Gerald would get into trouble with his family, laughing as he ran from his dad who chased him around the yard to punish him. Gerald's dad didn't use a belt but literally fought Gerald if he caught him. Neither of them were ever seriously hurt and seemed to enjoy the fights. On occasion Gerald's dad was so drunk Gerald beat him in the fight

Vincent Patterson, on the other hand, lived in a home which was taken care of on the outside but could have been nicer on the inside. Vincent's parents were always pleasant and Vincent almost always asked permission before going out. While he had a difficult time with the relationships he developed on the outside of his home, he obviously respected his parents. This was something new to Anthony. He had not seen good family relationships before, and while it was difficult to figure out Vincent and his family, it was obvious there was something different.

Anthony had lived in Keystone for a short time when he went out and made friends in the community. He went down to the school two blocks away to play basketball.

The weather in Johnson City is nice year round but especially so in the summer. The temperature was in the mid 80's, and not many people were out playing basketball. While Anthony was on the court, more people showed up at the school playground and either played basketball, football or just congregated and talked. The playground was also a popular area for people to buy and/or sell drugs. There was always an abundance of drug activity involving people of all ages.

While playing basketball, Anthony noticed several boys playing and talking at the other end of the court. They looked like they were about the same age as Anthony, maybe two or three years older. It was obvious the boys were brothers, and one was about a head taller than the other. They both had red hair, freckles and short cropped hair. Anthony decided to ask if they wanted to play some full court basketball. They agreed and the action started. The boys had been playing for about 15 minuets when Anthony went in for a lay up. As he went in for the shot he got hit on the arm, causing him to miss the shot and he called out, "Foul."

"Foul, you're full of shit," one of the guys responded to Anthony's accusation. "That's right: foul! You hit my damn arm," Anthony responded.

"Like hell, I did," the smaller of the two, yelled back raising his voice.

"Oh, come on, man, don't be a punk," Anthony said smartly as a matter of fact."Hey, new boy, don't jerk around with me or I'll have to kick the shit out of you," the boy retorted with a raised voice in the same tone. Almost immediately before Anthony had a chance to respond, the other said, "Hey man don't mess with my brother. He'll kick your ass."

"If you want to try and whip me, then let's go for it," Anthony yelled, throwing the basketball at the older of the two boys.

They stepped off of the court onto the grass. Anthony went to put his fist up as if they were going to fight. The larger of the two brothers started to say something to Anthony, "Hey man, it's not that big of a..." Before he finished his sentence he hit Anthony in the face 5 times. Anthony responded and may have hit the guy a few times, but for every hit Anthony got in, the other guy got in several more, always showing control and confidence as he hit Anthony.

"Man, that's enough," Anthony said, giving up after what couldn't have been more than three minutes.

"I told you he would kick your ass" said the smaller of the two brothers.

"I'd say. Man, where did you learn to fight like that?" Anthony asked in a respectful manner, not showing anger.

"Man, you learn it here on the streets. I box at The Rec too. By the way you're new around here. What's your name?" The older of the two who had just whipped Anthony was now a different person. He was even friendly.

"It's Anthony Beechup. I just moved here from Northside," responded Anthony, now holding out his hand for a hand shake.

"I'm David Jansen. This is my little brother; everybody calls him Charlie. Welcome to Keystone." David held out his hand for the hand shake. Anthony shook the hands of the two brothers.

This started a friendship that lasted for a couple of years. Anthony respected David, knowing this was the only fight he ever lost and not try to get revenge. At least it was the only one he would remember losing. Anthony became friends with Charlie, too, but didn't have the respect for him he had for David. He was not upset about losing the fight that had taken place. In Keystone, David had the reputation for being the toughest kid in the projects.

Anthony knew he could learn more in Keystone than he ever thought of learning at Northside. It would be difficult, but Anthony had just been officially welcomed to Keystone and everything looked and felt good. Even though he lost the fight, he met new friends who were going to be able to teach him a lot in regards to making it on the streets. Not only could they teach Anthony, they were the toughest, meanest people in the projects. He could not learn from anyone better.

~ Chapter 9 ~

The Keystone Kid

For Anthony school was, in many ways, a bad joke. He really didn't care about his grades and his attitude was just as bad. His grades continued to go down since the 2nd grade. He was passing most classes with D's. On a rare occasion He got a C but seldom any grade higher than that. In the 5th grade Anthony started laying out of school and playing hooky. Now that he was in the 6th grade that habit didn't change. He missed as many as 20 days a year and for no reason other than wanting something to do through the day besides going to school.

When at school Anthony was constantly getting on the nerves of his teachers. Teachers sent notes home on a regular basis, although most of those notes never made it home. While at school he had almost daily detentions. They were for all sorts of reasons. One of the things he got into trouble for was calling his 6th grade teacher an "Old Bitch," in front of a large group of students and teachers in the hallway one day while waiting in the lunch line. Anthony never liked his new teacher. He despised and disliked her since the time she made him stay after school one day for "walking funny." He was angry and bitter over this incident and never forgot it. Anthony insisted he wasn't trying to be funny; he was walking like he always did to the pencil sharpener. His 6th grade teacher never liked some of her students and especially didn't like Anthony. She had taught school for far too long and it was obvious to Anthony and the rest of the class room that she should have retired years earlier. The rest of the students couldn't believe he was made to stay after school for the way he walked to the pencil sharpener.

Anthony made a number of friends with whom he spent a great deal of time. There were David and Charlie Jansen, Gerald Johnson, Vincent Patterson, and two new friends, brothers named Jerry and Joseph Smith. They were around the same age as the other boys. Jerry had medium length brown hair and was in good shape. His brother Joseph was about the same size as Jerry, although a year younger. His hair was about the same color as Jerry's but it was cut much closer.

Jerry and Joseph had a strict mother and father, much like the parents of Vincent Patterson. It was easy for them to go out, and they didn't get into trouble like the other boys. They were respected in the community because they were both good at sports. All of the other boys, except these two, took drugs and drank together on a regular basis. Jerry and Joseph on occasion had a drink with the rest of the guys but nothing like the abuse taking place with them. They were not immune from the trouble the other boys got into. It was not unusual for them to be involved in vandalism. There were times the boys went out and destroyed property or got into fights. When these things occurred Jerry and Joseph were often in the middle of it.

As Anthony got older he spent less time at home. He saw his sister, Madeline, hit one too many times by his mother and had no desire to be at home and see this any more than he had to. He started spending many nights out at various places instead of staying home. Among those places were some of his friends' houses, but he and some of them started spending some nights at Steve Spurrier Little League Park. The boys were often high and didn't go home in this condition. Most of the boys preferred not going home. When at the park the boys slept in the baseball dugouts. They also had other places to spend the night when not at home. There was the press box at Johnson City Memorial Football Field, bridges, and old abandoned houses. For all practical purposes the boys preferred to be homeless and on the streets as opposed to being in their homes. Most had good reasons not to go home or to want to be there. They knew what awaited them when they got there and while the outside world wouldn't understand they each had their own unique reasons. It was different for each one, but one couldn't escape the fact that they felt the way they did.

Each of the boys became more involved with drugs as they grew older, a sad fact considering how young they were. Each of them protected the events in the life of each other but for a different reason. They had their own set of problems and didn't have the time or ability to help anyone but themselves. They would be the first to tell you they were not boys but young men, learning to be men.

The vandalism, drugs, sex, and other activities they were involved in would shock most of middle class America but it was a unique reality for many who were poor and lived in places like Keystone. Each boy had their own story to tell, and would gladly tell you, the life they chose to live on the streets was better than the life they lived at home. This was a hard fact many living outside of the projects did not understand.

The boys, with the exception of Jerry and Joseph, were heavily involved with drugs. They used some type of drug on an almost daily basis. This was a way to get a quick fix and help them forget how they lived. Keystone introduced Anthony to drugs other than marijuana and alcohol. New drugs that became accessible included LSD, heroine, PCP, and limited amounts of cocaine. There were also pills of all kinds including, ups, downs, reds, yellow jackets, blue bombers, pink ladies and a variety of other street drugs. However, the most common drugs in Keystone were glue, paint, and aerosol sprays. Even though cocaine was readily available in Johnson City, there was not a large market for it in Keystone due to the cost and Keystone's being primarily a lower income housing project. There were not many dealers in Keystone and even if there were, there weren't that many people with the money to buy the top line drugs. This was the primary reason glue, paint and aerosols were so popular, they were easily accessible and inexpensive.

Keystone had an extremely high unemployment rate, so there was little money available to buy drugs. For a group of boys in the 6th, 7th and 8th grades it was a treat to have the two dollars it took to buy a hit of acid. The acid hits were like a weekend party. After a hard week and working at saving up the money, it was party time. A little acid, black lights and lit candles gave them all the party they needed. To have a weekend party on acid was a treat but it didn't happen often because of the difficulty in getting enough money to party. However, it was easy for two or three guys to come up with a dollar to buy two tubes of glue. Two tubes kept two or three guys high for several hours. The high from glue was not as good as that of acid, but you could easily get high and stay that way for awhile. Anthony learned to enjoy the high from glue and other street drugs but he also experienced the dreams or hallucinations that came from them. Those dreams and hallucinations helped in escaping the reality of the environment he was in. While the escape may not have been positive, it was an escape.

Getting high was not always pleasurable, it was just an escape. It helped in forgetting the problems and poverty. It was a way of gaining respect and acceptance from others in the community. Anyone having a way to get high could always find new friends. It seemed everyone was looking for a way to escape the projects, and drugs and alcohol was the number one way of doing this. Word of a party would spread quickly around the circles in Keystone and its surrounding area. Anthony recalled going to a variety of parties with the other guys, to new places and with people he never met before. Most of them only wanted a return favor in the future.

The parties took place at places where it was easy to pick up girls. Anthony was amazed at the number of girls in Keystone who willingly got high and did whatever the party host wanted for more drugs. He recalled an older girl willing to give oral sex to two guys in order to get more drugs. She complained about being forced to do it, and the host told her, "No Honey, you don't have to do it, but it sure would make it easier to give you more smack if you would do it." The girl proceeded to give the guy and his friend what they asked for. This took place in the host's back yard around an old burning burn-barrel and an abandoned car, in open view of 15 to 20 people, including Anthony and his friends.

Anthony and his friends begin to experiment in other areas, mostly while using drugs. They talked about and contemplated various forms of religion. Each of them had had a bad experience with the Christian Church, and most all of them despised it. For most of them the hate came from hearing so much about religion at home from relatives, yet having to live like they did. They never saw the church or Christians show compassion. This was bad enough but seeing the constant hypocrisy and hatred didn't help convince them that religion and the beliefs of those around them was of value. They never disputed the reality of God, but each had serious issues with the ways people carried out their faith. In Keystone most everyone could tell who the preachers were when they came into the neighborhood. The preachers, while doing visitations, wore suits, had sweet smelling cologne, and always seemed to be better than everyone else they met with. The preachers and their cohorts had a stupid looking, fake, and deceptive smile on their faces. To most of the people in Keystone the preachers and Christians seemed to be miserable and boring. They knew everything about what you couldn't do and nothing about what you could. If there were any areas in which they experienced joy and pleasure they never let anyone know it. While there were churches in Keystone, they did little outreach and virtually no service to their neighbors. This was evident in their lack of growth.

The people in Keystone ran from these Christians and preachers when they did their visitations. Some residents talked to the preachers, but Anthony and the rest of the gang confronted, cursed, and vandalized the Christians and their property when they had the chance. As far as they were concerned, the preachers and Christians came onto their turf and were not welcome. Anthony was involved in these acts, and it didn't bother him at all.

Anthony did these things, especially the vandalism, without feeling remorse. Occasionally Anthony saw a glimpse of concern from the people coming into Keystone to share their message. It appeared as if some of them really cared about helping the people they met with. Anthony didn't share these feelings with the rest of the group. He thought it was a sign of his own weakness. He had experiences with Christians he could never forget.

While spending time with his grandparents, Velma and Oscar on weekends they made the kids go to church. Anthony always felt like an outcast at church. He listened and appreciated many of the concepts of God and Jesus which were shared in the church. He heard some ideas about church which reaffirmed some of what he wanted in his own life. On several occasions Anthony went up front during the altar call to try and find God. Unfortunately, Anthony never felt good enough in the eyes of the church and it was one of the reasons he disliked the church and God so much. Anthony didn't just dislike the people in the church but he formed a sincere bitterness and hatred towards God. Anthony heard one message from the preacher in the little church, but saw another message displayed in the actions of the people when it came to living their faith. Anthony saw them talk about love, yet many in the church were openly racist towards blacks and minorities, and their actions were nothing like the actions of Jesus towards those outside their faith. Anthony could have some respect for Jesus. His actions were admirable. The people he had witnessed, on the other hand, were nothing like Jesus.

Occasionally Anthony saw how he would like to be involved in the church; yet the church, he felt, put him on the back pew and wouldn't let him be involved in any way. Parents didn't want their children to associate with Anthony and it was obvious they had a genuine dislike for him. He felt that people attending church had allowed the rapes of him and his sister. Maybe they didn't know about it, but they didn't see the hurting inside that he and his sister went through either. If they saw it they didn't address it. So in Anthony's thinking, they allowed it.

Anthony wondered how Christians could talk about love and be so callused towards the poor and needy. He took this personally. They were blinded to the needs of others. They refused to help those around them who needed help. They talked about Jesus and His love yet refused to be the instruments of that love, not fake, mushy or make-believe love Anthony saw so many times before, but real love. Anthony wanted so much to see and experience genuine and sincere love, love like the Jesus they spoke about in the Bible. If Anthony saw this type of love, then maybe he and his friends wouldn't have looked at Christians the way they did. Anthony knew most people in Keystone had similar experiences.

Anthony and his friends decided to take their bitterness and hatred towards God to the next level. They chose to look to Satan and his demons for their leadership and guidance. Anthony was a good leader by example and he had some experience with Satanism when living in Northside.

The guys knew the Bible spoke about how God would defeat Satan in the end; but from the evidence they saw, they didn't know why that had to be. They decided to join forces with Satan and wanted to win that final battle against God. These boys had no love or compassion towards the followers of Jesus. They were in agreement: much of what they did and how they behaved would be directed toward the Church and anything that appeared to be good within the Church. They believed that whatever the Church did was not really for good but to benefit itself.Anthony concealed from others this belief and desired actions towards others. Many people, even family members were not aware of what he and the other boys were involved in. Much of what each boy did came from the decisions they made in discussions and a few select friends. There was not an official Satanic Church the boys joined; they picked up bits and pieces of their belief from various sources. Vincent had a copy of the Satanic Bible, but it was never taken seriously. Occasionally they tried to cast spells using witchcraft which they learned about. They used the drugs they had, such as pills, LSD or others when praying to Satan and tried to experience first hand his demons and their powers. The boys sought power, yet they only satisfied their own desires and nothing else.

* * * * * *

Anthony had been in the house alone for some time. He only had five more pills, but didn't know exactly what they all were. People often gave Anthony pills and had him try them out. "Give it to Anthony. He'll take it; he'll eat anything," friends often said while handing him new drugs to try out.

Anthony was feeling upset and depressed. He didn't require a reason; sometimes it just happened. Living in the surroundings he did, spending what little time he did at home, did not help. Anthony was happy one moment and would start thinking about almost anything and feeling sorry for himself and what little he had in life the next.

Anthony decided, just as he had many times before, to take all of the pills at once. Through the tears Anthony shouted, "I don't give a damn. I don't care if it fucking kills me." He popped all five pills into his mouth and chased them down with water cursing more towards himself and God.

Anthony finally felt the effects of the pills. It was obvious that LSD was one of the pills among the five. He saw something, not knowing what it was. It looked like a large green fly, but it looked like a dragon too. Whatever it was weighed 250 pounds or more. It was flying all around him, just looking at Anthony, trying to talk but not able to. "What in the world do you want? Tell me, you no good son of a bitch."

Anthony was speaking to the wind now, swatting with his arms as he spoke. "I know this is from you God; get the hell away from me; get away." The tone of his voice was changing now. Anthony thought he was seeing something sent to him from God. "I said to get the hell away from me," Anthony yelled.

"I don't care for you, God. Jesus is dead, and you failed. Your people have failed. You can't have me. Get the shit away." Anthony waved his arms and imagined grabbing a sword and swung at the giant fly as it flew. It did no good, the fly just avoided the sword.

Anthony chased the fly out of the house. He was out the back door and standing in the middle of the street. He watched as the fly flew off into the sky. He lost sight of it when it headed towards the sun. He continued yelling, ranting and raving, swinging his arms the whole time. He carried on a conversation, "I serve you Lucifer; did you hear that, God? I serve Lucifer. We'll kick your ass, and there is nothing you can do about it. Did you hear that? There is nothing you can do about it!" Anthony yelled at the top of his voice.

Anthony didn't recall much after this; he started to wake up but didn't know where he was. "Man, are you O.K.?" Anthony heard but didn't know who was speaking.

"Yeah, where am I, and who are you?" Anthony asked.

"It's me man, Gerald Johnson. You're at my house. We're in the basement." "How did I get here?" Anthony asked, still not all together.

"Me and Vincent were coming home from his place and saw you out in the street. Man, there were a couple of cars stopped. The people were looking at you, didn't know what the hell was going on. You must have got some bad shit or something. We pulled you into the basement before your ol' lady or ol' man got home," Gerald said expressing concern.

"Thanks Ger. Man, she would've died if she would've seen me out there trippin," Anthony said gratefully.

"Yeah, I know. Ya want to stay here or go home?" Gerald asked.

"I think I'm going to go on home," Anthony answered.

"That's fine, man. Be cool. You're just the Keystone Kid," Gerald said as Anthony took off across the street.

Anthony climbed in through his bedroom window. That way, if his mom or Robert were still up they wouldn't see him. He was feeling woozy and didn't want to make something up about where he had been.

Anthony crawled into bed. He wondered what tomorrow had in store for him. He felt better now. He was glad he had good friends who accepted him for who he was, not what they wanted him to be.

~ Chapter 10 ~

Living?

Anthony was at the age where sexual activity for him increased. He was involved with a variety of partners and types of sex. There were different cousins and friends who were willingly involved in sexual activities with him. On occasion Anthony forced himself on his cousins. This took place when they didn't want to be involved in any sexual activity for a variety of reasons. Each person had been willing at some previous time to have sex with him. The problem for him was he knew they were willing before and would be willing again. He had learned to get what he wanted, when he wanted it. Anthony had several friends of the family who were always willing to have sex. He thought it was amazing how easy it was to convince people to have sex. As he grew older he believed his sexually active cousins on both sides of his family were sexually active for the same reasons he was. They had developed the wrong attitudes for the same reasons Anthony had.

The sexual partners outside the family were the ones that surprised Anthony. He didn't know if they had developed misconceived views on sex for the same reasons or not. The reality was Anthony almost always found sexual partners, many much older then he was and others around the same age.

As Anthony read and studied more about Satanic worship and Witchcraft, he involved aspects of those practices in his sexual activities. It wasn't unusual to have sex with multiple partners, both male and female. Anthony involved many of these partners in aspects of satanic communion, sometimes willingly, sometimes not. Some of them knew what they were involved in or the extent of their involvement.

Satanic Communion involved a number of things. Before engaging in sex, Anthony and his partners drank urine, usually mixed with another drink like Kool-Aid, Rum, Coke or any other. Then the partners engaged in violent sexual activity with each other. Anthony mixed the urine and drink in the privacy of the bathroom. He seldom let the person drinking the substance know what was being consumed. He usually would say something like, "Go ahead and have a drink of this, I made it up, it'll help us." Then they drank the substance not knowing what it was.

Anthony had a little ceremony for himself and on occasion a few friends who knew what was going on. There were times Anthony knew some partners had figured out what he was doing and what was in the drink. During one incident, one person figured out what was in the drink and refused to drink it. He grabbed her by the throat, forced her down on the ground and poured the drink into her mouth as she was gasping for air. After he forced the drink down her throat he ripped her pants off and had sex. After he started having sex with her, it was as if she forgot what Anthony had just made her do and enjoyed the sex.

Anthony was not bothered by this because many of his partners were often involved in the same type of sexual activity. The sex often went beyond the point of enjoyment; it reached the point where someone was bruised and bleeding at the conclusion of the act. For the sexual partners who were not willing participants, the act became even more violent. This happened in rare situations. Anthony even struck others in the stomach and head to force submission. He reasoned, "They always knew what they were getting into before we started."

This type of sexual activity went on for four and one-half years. Anthony engaged in sex at least two times a week for this period of time. The sexual acts became more perverted and involved a large number of participants. As the participants grew, the willingness of those participants also grew. Rarely would there be problems due to the unwillingness of others in one on one sex and even rarer for group sex.

* * * * * * * *

Anthony, Gerald, Vincent, David and Charlie were riding their bikes in the woods near Keystone. They had just come from the Jiffy-Mart where they purchased 4 tubes of glue. Gerald and Vincent had brought along a hit of acid for each of the boys to take. They enjoyed going into the woods because they were secluded, and no one was ever there unless having sex or doing drugs themselves.

The boys pushed their bikes 100 yards through a narrow path to get into the woods, but once there they could ride to most any place they wanted.

"Hey guys, over here's a place!" Gerald called out, pointing to an area surrounded by large rocks. They weaved in and out of the rocks to get to the center of the pit.

"Yeah, looks good to me." David yelled back.

Everyone else yelled back, "All right!"

Vincent spoke calmly, "O.K. Tony, pass out the bags." Anthony reached into his shirt and grabbed a handful of small lunch sized brown paper bags. He passed two sacks to each person.

"All right, do we want to do the 'cid before we do the glue or after?" Gerald asked.

Charlie said. "Man, if we do it before we won't remember the glue. I'll do the cid after the glue. Doesn't that make sense to the rest of you guys?" They all responded it did.

It only took the boys about 45 minutes to dispose of the glue. They squeezed a small amount of glue into a sack and took the sack and place it over their nostrils and mouth and breathed in the vapors, only occasionally taking their face away from the bag to breathe fresh air. They breathed in until the vapors ceased and then squeezed in more of the glue and started the procedure all over. By the time they got through the first half of the tube they didn't know if they smelled the vapors or not.

As the boys smelled the glue, they were looser in their conversation and actions. David was talking, almost spiritually about suicide. "Man I don't know what the purpose is in living. You know what I mean. After all, maybe after this life there is something better on the other side. You know, it's not just me thinking while I'm high, I think about death all of the time."

Vincent responded, "Yeah, man, I think about it too. You know, I believe that there are different dimensions and shit like that."

"Yeah," responded Anthony, "Like on Star Trek or something. You know, like where do all of the UFO's and all that kinds of shit come from?"

David went back to his original point knowing Anthony got weird after getting high. "Man, one of these days I'm going to find out. I don't have nothin' to live here for anyway." David's speech was slurring due to the glue working on the brain.

"Oh, come on man, enough of that serious shit," Gerald comically said, trying to change the conversation and using more expletives as he spoke. "Let's get some booty before we hit up on this acid. All right, everybody drop your drawers."

Without hesitation the boys took their pants off and started having sex with each other. Each of them forgot about the conversation. They proceeded to have sex with each other. After each boy finished they took a hit of acid. None of them remembered much after the acid. All they remembered was eventually coming to, and it being almost dark. They had been in the woods, spaced out and high for close to ten hours. They were finally sober enough to ride their bikes around in the woods some. They rode their bikes around, playing in the woods, sobering up, until an hour or so after the sun went down.

The boys went their separate ways after leaving the woods. Anthony went to Gerald's house instead of going home. While at Gerald's house he talked Judith into going into the basement with the hope of getting her to have sex. While in the basement they spoke about a variety of things but he failed to talk her into having sex.

Anthony tried many times to have sex with her but was never successful. He was sure Judith took pleasure in getting him excited and teasing him into thinking they were going to make out, yet never did. Anthony respected Judith enough that he never tried to force sex on her as he had others.

He went home after failing to get any place with Judith. It was early for him before 11:00 p.m. This meant Anthony had to hear the garbage from his mom. He never took pleasure in hearing all the things he had to hear at home. He resented that, and it was one of the reasons he seldom stayed at home. If not for all the activity or the day he had experienced, Anthony wouldn't have gone home so soon. He was tired though, and needed a bed to sleep in.

Wanda and Robert were fighting more, and this was one of the reasons Anthony didn't like staying at home. When possible, Wanda was seeing other men when Robert was away or at work. She would get upset and fight Robert's accusations that she was bringing men home to sleep with her. Even though this was true and Anthony knew it, she denied it and got into violent arguments with Robert.

Fortunately this was a night Anthony didn't have to listen to the fighting. Robert wasn't there and wasn't going to be there for some time. Robert was now working a 3rd shift job and was never at home late at night.

Anthony went to bed, relieved that Robert was working late. He heard his mother call, "Anthony, come here." Anthony got out of bed and walked to her bedroom at the rear of the house.

"Yes ma'm," he answered politely.

"I'm cold. Why don't you sleep with me tonight?" Wanda asked Anthony calmly."O.K.," Anthony responded innocently, not knowing what was about to happen.

He climbed into bed laying on the outside edge, facing away from his mother. He was ready to go to sleep when his mother moved next to him and put her arm around him. Anthony didn't say anything; he acted like he was asleep. Wanda started to move her hand down towards his penis. He could feel his heart beating harder and harder. He knew it wasn't right. He lay there acting like he was asleep thinking, "Oh God, no. Oh dear God, no." He prayed and prayed trying to stop what was happening, but it didn't do any good.

* * * * * *

Anthony was shaking and crying. He was at Manna House talking to George Wilson. "That's O.K., Anthony go ahead and let it out." George said while putting his arm on Anthony's shoulder. George knew a hand on a shoulder could reassure Anthony and give some comfort.

In a concerned voice George asked, "How far did it go that night Anthony?"

"All the way, I still can't believe it; she made me have sex with her," Anthony said barely able to get it out, sobbing and crying.

"Did this ever happen again?" George asked still trying to reassure Anthony."Yeah, at least two or three times I can think of. I really just didn't want to talk about this part of my life. This is the first time I've ever shared this with anybody. I've not shared it with my wife, my pastor, friends or anybody."

Then becoming angrier and still crying Anthony questioned, "What right did she have to do that to me? I was her son. As much as I hated her at times and as bad as I was, I was still her son. What right did she have to do what she did to me?"

George answered calmly and in a caring voice, "She had no right, Anthony. She was your mother, and what she did was very wrong. That is not how God intended for the family to be. Satan continually attacked you in a variety of ways. He never seemed to let up on you. He must have known that God had something special planned for your life and therefore wanted to destroy as much of you as he could. That is how he works sometimes. Satan hurts and tears apart all that he can in order to hurt God as well as God's creation, and you are a valuable part of that creation. Maybe Satan knows of something important that you were going to do for God's Kingdom, and he wanted to do everything possible to tear you down and break you. If Satan knows that he can do permanent scarring, then that is what he will try to do. The good news though is that that scarring doesn't have to be permanent. It is scarring that God can heal if you let Him."

George continued talking to Anthony but decided to go along another path. "You see Anthony, God is our Father, and it is important that we have an understanding of what real fatherly love is all about. God has established things the way they are for a reason. It is as if we in the Christian faith are a family. The way you were violated was not only sexual, but in a way which makes it harder for you to understand what real fatherly love is. The love you should have experienced would never have allowed this to happen. But sometimes people, even parents who are controlled and living outside of God's will do things that hurt not only the people around them but also God."

George continued talking to Anthony about what he had experienced and how it was not what God wanted for any of his children. "You had to overcome years and years of abuse and neglect, and have had to learn on your own what God's love is all about and how you, Anthony Beechup, can benefit from it despite the abuse that you encountered. Yet the reality of it is, God wants to love you in a real and perfect way. God wants you to understand the love He has for you. I want to discuss more of your background, to talk about you getting older. Before we get into much of that though, it is going to be important that we work our way up to that point in the progression of your life. Is that O.K. with you if we progress in that way?" George asked with his hand still on Anthony's shoulder, reassuring him.

Anthony, still crying, shook his head yes.

"Let's pray then," George said as he kept his hand on Anthony's shoulder where it gave reassurance. It didn't help Anthony feel better but it was obvious there was someone who cared. As he bowed his head, George prayed a simple but reassuring prayer. It was a prayer that Anthony was glad for, because it helped provide reassurance and helped him get his mind off of what he had been talking about.

For Anthony to get his mind off the discussion with George was important. He had difficulty sharing that information for the first time and he needed a break from it. It wasn't as if Anthony could not process that information later in the weeks or months ahead. He would, but his life had not been easy up to this point, and this aspect of his life would be a struggle for the rest of his life, outside the grace of God.

Sharing this information with someone for the first time allowed Anthony to feel more comfortable about sharing his life with people who cared. Sharing it with George helped provide an understanding of himself, which helped him feel better about himself and the fact that God had not desired evil things to happen to him. He never fully understood himself, but the ability to know more than what he had known in the past was reassuring. To have this level of understanding at least helped him in knowing the problems, hurt, loneliness and anger he felt for so long was not his fault. The memories were never totally gone from his life but now he understood those memories, feelings and hurts more.

~ Chapter 11 ~

University School

Anthony experienced more than he should have in the summer of 1972. He was still young, only 12 or 13 and grew up way too fast for even his own satisfaction. He was ready to enter the 7th grade and faced the predicament of going to yet another school. He spent more time with his grandparents, Velma and Oscar's. They had moved and lived close to the high school their youngest son Bill had attended.

Anthony's uncle had gone to college on a basketball scholarship in West Tennessee at The University of Tennessee at Martin. During high school Bill attended one of the most prestigious schools in Johnson City, University School, to play basketball. University School was a small private elementary, middle and high school on the campus of East Tennessee State University. The overwhelming majority of students came from wealthier families, many of whom were faculty members at East Tennessee State University and University School. The students came from the families of prominent lawyers, teachers and other business people from across Johnson City.

The academic standards at University School's where superior to most any school in the state. It had such a good reputation in academics that many called the school as soon as their child was born in order to put them on a waiting list. They did this to get their child into the school as soon as the child was old enough to attend. Most of the students went on to college upon graduation and entered fields similar to their parents.

Bill had the privilege of going to University School due to his basketball abilities and the grades he earned through 8th grade. He was recruited by the basketball coach at University School prior to entering the 9th grade. He started playing basketball for the varsity basketball team upon entering the 9th grade and started for the varsity for each of the four years he attended University School. Over the four years Bill established most of the scoring records at the school. As a standout athlete he not only excelled on an athletic level but also on an academic level. He became a virtual legend at the school. Many of the family, as well as others, talked about the quality of student and athlete that he was. Living up to the legend and talk was hard, but Bill was able to do it.

Anthony spent a lot of time with his grandparents, on weekends and throughout the summer. During that time Anthony established a better relationship with his grandparents, aunts, and uncles who were still at home or who visited on a regular basis. Bill was Anthony's favorite uncle and in many ways was more like a brother. This was the case of several aunts and uncles on his father's side.

During that summer Wanda also spent time with Velma and Oscar. In the summer of 1972 Wanda agreed with Velma, Oscar, and Bill, that they would arrange for Anthony and Madeline to attend University School in the next school year. Anthony agreed, he knew he could get out of the house and away from Robert and Wanda. He could spend more time with his grandparents. He had the chance to establish himself athletically at University School like his uncle Bill had done.

The disadvantage was he would not be able to play football for University School because it didn't have a team. This was difficult because he had excelled in football like Bill had excelled in basketball. He loved the game of football but he was still young, and although he grew up fast in some ways, he was immature in others. Anthony didn't realize the disadvantages of going to a school where he couldn't play football and the hurt from not doing something he loved. He thought to himself, "After all I am a decent basketball player."

As good of a basketball player as Anthony was, he knew he was good enough in football to possibly receive a college scholarship someday. This dream of playing college sports was not much different than the dream of most inner city kids. He dreamed of someday playing professional football for the Buffalo Bills. The Bills were one of Anthony's favorite NFL teams along with the Kansas City Chiefs and Dallas Cowboys. O.J. Simpson played for the Bills, but it wasn't O.J. Simpson Anthony admired the most. His favorite player was always Jim Braxton. Braxton was the man responsible for opening up many of the holes O.J. Simpson ran through. Anthony was enough of a student of the game that he realized this and saw the value of a player like Jim Braxton. He respected Braxton enough that he went through a time of sorrow years later when Braxton died of cancer.

Football had to end temporarily for Anthony if he attended University School. It was something he was willing to temporarily give up for a variety of reasons. One was he was convinced he wouldn't need to develop his football skills each year to someday play in high school or even later on in college.

He was too good for that. Others told him how good he was. If he had any weakness it was that he sometimes believed too much in himself.

Anthony's uncle Bill made all the arrangements for him to attend University School at the start of the school year. The summer before school started, Bill took Anthony to meet with Vernon Alexander, the principal at University School.

Mr. Alexander was a short man, no more than 5'2". He was small framed, weighed less than 130 pounds, and was balding. He had a little tuft of hair that stuck out near the front of his forehead and had a close cropped hair cut around the rest of his head. He wore glasses which gave him the look of an academician. He also had a small growth near the bottom of his nose like a large wart.

When Bill took him to meet Mr. Alexander, Anthony was surprised at how short Mr. Alexander was. He was someone Anthony had heard positive things about. Bill, his mom and dad never had anything negative to say about Mr. Alexander. He had earned comments like, "He is caring and special, a real man, supportive, successful," and other positive attributes.

Anthony wanted to meet Mr. Alexander because he always assumed people like him were nonexistent. Anthony never met a role model such as Mr. Alexander was supposed to be. Even Bill, as well as the rest of his uncles, aunts and grandparents had some baggage; Anthony had some negative feelings about most of them. It had been several years since abuse from his uncles took place, and he subconsciously blocked out many of the events when considering that he would be living again with his grandparents.

Mr. Alexander was a man who seemed to be without baggage. Anthony had the chance to learn something positive from this man. With the difficulty he had in life, Anthony was looking for a man like this to learn from. He just didn't know if a man like this could really exist.

Bill pulled up to the front of the school in his little Chevrolet Nova. Anthony stepped out of the car and walked into the school with Bill. He was surprised at how dead the campus of East Tennessee State University and University School was. He didn't think about the school attendance being down due to summer school. It was amazing; here was a high school on the campus of a large university. Anthony noticed the few older college students on campus. He also noticed the older attractive girls. Right away, this was something Anthony liked about the school.

"Mr. Alexander will just want to meet you today and ask you a few questions," Bill said as the two walked up the sidewalk to the school. On both sides of the walkway were large magnolia trees, loaded with leaves and blooms. As Anthony and Bill were walking, Anthony didn't say much. It was one of the few times he was nervous.

When entering the main entrance of University School, Mr. Alexander's office was on the immediate right on the ground floor of the three story building. Mr. Alexander greeted Bill and Anthony immediately at the doorway. "Hey Bill, this must be Anthony," Mr. Alexander said in a joyful tone as he put out his hand to shake hands with them. Anthony was surprised at the strength of Mr. Alexander's grip.

Mr. Alexander looked even smaller next to Bill who was 6' 7". Anthony was a good 4" or 5" inches taller than Mr. Alexander, and he wasn't even in 7th grade yet.

"Hey, Mr. Alexander, this is Anthony all right," Bill answered in a good mood, glad to see him.

"Well, why don't the two of you come on into my office and have a seat and we'll get started," Mr. Alexander replied as he pointed to two chairs directly in front of his desk in the office.

Mr. Alexander asked Bill a few questions about college and spoke to him about how the basketball team had done at University School the year before. After a few minutes of conversation Mr. Alexander took a seat, and he changed the conversation.

Anthony expected Mr. Alexander to sit behind his desk but was surprised when he pulled his chair out from behind the desk and placed it next to the ones near Bill and himself. He wanted to sit close to them without having anything between them. "Well, Anthony, tell me something about yourself and why you want to come to school here," Mr. Alexander asked in a friendly and caring tone.

Anthony was impressed. He was asking him and gave him his full attention. "Well, I've just heard a lot about it from Billy and all. I know it's a good school," Anthony answered with not much enthusiasm.

"Well, we are a good school. I feel as if we are one of the best schools in the state, especially in the area of academics. We are so good that people often call when they have a baby in order to have their child put on the waiting list to go here." Mr. Alexander then asked Anthony a question which threw him for a surprise.

"Why do you think we should put you ahead of those on the waiting list to come here, Anthony?" He wasn't threatening, he simply asked the question.

Anthony was surprised at the question but more so that the question was asked in a nonthreatening way. He thought about it and made an attempt to respond but didn't know exactly how to answer it. "Well, I don't know why I should be put in front of anybody else. I guess I'd just like the chance to come here. I've not heard anything but good stuff about the school. I guess I would just like a chance."

"Well, Bill was an outstanding student while he was here, and sometimes we feel we can afford to give some people priority over others who may be on our waiting list. If you have any of the same capabilities and possibilities of Bill, I don't feel as if we would be making any mistakes," Mr. Alexander said to Anthony. Anthony didn't know how to respond, and as he was trying to think of what to say. Mr. Alexander asked another question in a pleasant kind manner which threw Anthony for another loop. "Would you like to see the school that you'll be starting in September?"

"Sure." Anthony answered quietly and certainly surprised.

"Well, come on along and welcome to University School," Mr. Alexander said while standing from his chair and extending his hand to Anthony welcoming him to his new school. Anthony responded and was again surprised at what seemed to be an even stronger hand shake than the first one he received from Mr. Alexander. After a tour of the three storied school and basement, Mr. Alexander walked Anthony and Bill to the Nova parked out front. "I'll see you the first of September. Make sure you come by to see me when you arrive so I can introduce you to everybody. I'll see you then," Mr. Alexander said before Bill and Anthony got into the small Nova.

"Thanks, and I'll see ya then," Anthony replied still in a state of shock that things had gone as they had in the meeting with Mr. Alexander. As they drove off, Bill started up a conversation.

"Anthony, Mr. Alexander is taking a big chance on you. You're going to need to straighten up a lot and start taking school a little more seriously. Mr. Alexander is giving you a chance that a lot of folks would give anything to get. Do you understand what I'm talking about?" Bill spoke in a sincere and straight forward way.

"Yeah," Anthony answered. He heard the question but didn't let on to the seriousness of it as he looked out the car window to his right, away from Bill.

"Well, Mr. Alexander will know everything about you if he doesn't already. He'll get the information from school records at the other schools you have gone to. You're going to have to work your tail off in order to get your grades up. University School is tough and you're going to have to work in order to make it there," Bill stated in a stern and honest way directly to Anthony.

"Yeah, ok. I'll work at it," Anthony responded sarcastically. He answered this way, knowing not to cross the line too far with his uncle. Anthony didn't talk to Bill much on the ride home to his grandparents. He was thinking about how he was going to be getting out of his house, away from Robert and Wanda, and be able to live with his grandparents Velma and Oscar.

* * * * * *

"What do you mean I'm not going to be living with Mamaw and Grand-daddy?" Anthony asked almost yelling now.

"Just what I said, you're my child and you're going to live here at home with me and Robert," Wanda responded raising her voice.

"Well, how am I supposed to get to school now? They don't have a bus or anything and it is all the way across town from here," Anthony responded, knowing it was at least three or four miles to University School.

"Well, I guess you'll either walk or catch the city bus; and on the days I can, I'll pick you up after school when I'm off work. Now that's enough of it, I don't want to discuss it any more," Wanda answered sternly.

Anthony walked back into his bedroom and slammed the door. He plopped down on his bed and started crying. This was something he normally didn't do unless he was trying to get something. This time, he was genuinely crying because his hopes had once again been shattered. Not only was he going to be going to a new school, but he was going to be staying at home. This meant Anthony had to walk to and from school. He knew his mom said she would pick him up when she could, but he also knew she was as dependable as the local weather man, which in the mountains of East Tennessee was not very reliable. Anthony knew he had the burden of making new friends at University School. He didn't mind this as much when he thought he would be living with his grandparents. He knew that with the burden of walking to and from school, he wouldn't be the happiest of students. He also knew the other students would eventually find out he lived in Keystone.

This created a sense of prejudice Anthony didn't expect. One thing was certain, he had no reason to dream of getting out of this never ending hole with Robert and Wanda. After all, when had anything gone right for him? It hadn't gone right before, and he was now convinced that something on the surface that looked to be good was usually a curse and heartbreak in disguise.

~ Chapter 12 ~

The New Kid

Summer was almost over, and Anthony had a rougher time than usual at home over the last weeks. Some of the guys in Keystone had not been hanging out as much. There was a lot of turmoil, and three incidents had Anthony and his friends confused. The first incident in the projects involved someone Anthony didn't know. Two people were riding on a motorcycle near Keystone's Recreation Center. While driving by the Recreation Center, someone randomly shot a rifle and instantly killed the passenger on the motorcycle hitting them in the head. There was talk over who did the shooting, but neither Anthony nor any one else he knew was sure who it was.

The second incident was near the recreation center in the housing projects. This was not the larger Rec Center, but the smaller one which was actually a part of the projects. Only a few people took advantage of the facilities. There wasn't much available for people to do but they went anyway. It had a boxing ring inside along with ping pong tables and basketball courts outside. The basketball courts were seldom used because every time the center put up goals, someone tore them down. One of Anthony's acquaintances, Cherry, got into an argument with a rival gang member from across town. That gang member didn't have any business in Keystone because this turf belonged to the Keystone Kids. Cherry was a large black kid who was 6' 1" tall, and weighed 200 pounds. No one knew for sure if drugs had anything to do with the fight Cherry got into, but some guessed it did. The two got into a shouting match when someone heard Cherry yell, "Listen you son of a bitch. If you pull that knife, you had better damn well use it!"

People on the outdoor basketball court who were slap boxing turned to look after hearing this. Anthony was among those slap boxing and saw Cherry take off after the guy. No one thought much about the incident until

Cherry collapsed in the field while chasing the guy. Cherry yelled out, "Help, somebody help!"

A group of people ran over to see what was up with Cherry. As they got closer they saw he had been stabbed in the stomach with a large knife. It was still in his stomach with blood seeping out around the blade. Anthony yelled, "Somebody call the Rescue Squad." As some stood around he clarified, "Now, damn it! He's been stabbed!"

The Rescue Squad arrived in a few minutes. Cherry had passed out from the loss of blood and injuries. The paramedics loaded him into the ambulance while doing CPR and attending to the wound. It appeared as if they had stopped the bleeding by applying pressure to the wound.

Later that night, Anthony and others found out Cherry had died at the hospital as a result of the injuries. It took a few days, but the police caught the guy who stabbed Cherry and charged him with manslaughter. It was to his benefit the police found him because if the kids from Keystone had found him, they would have killed him. They were already planning an ambush on rival gang members' territory. The guy who killed Cherry pled guilty and served 2 years in jail. Anthony wasn't sure but believed Cherry's killer would be killed after getting out of jail. No one really knew who it was that killed him, but Anthony thought it was someone from Keystone close to Cherry who possibly moved to the Tyler Apartment complex.

The last incident occurred at the end of summer. It shook up Anthony and a number others. No one was sure why David Jansen killed himself. His body was found up in the woods where a lot of kids did drugs. It was near the same place he told Anthony and some of his other friends that he often thought of killing himself to find out what was on the other side. No one was sure if it was David at first because the body was not easily identifiable due to being in the woods and exposed to decay. David took a shot gun, stuck the barrel in his mouth and pulled the trigger. There was not much left of David to identify. It took a while for Anthony and the others to get over this. They recalled the conversations they had with David. They reflected on the drugs and the good times they had. It was almost a year later when Charlie, David's little brother, died from a drug overdose. These were the first of several deaths of Anthony's friends from Keystone. These two boys introduced Anthony to Keystone with the fight near the basketball court and they were both dead.

Anthony had 7 close friends die. Some died after leaving Keystone, but they died before having the opportunity to turn 20 years of age. There were others that died after 20. Some were homeless and others spent their lives in prison.

The effect of having had so many friends die stayed with Anthony for the rest of his life. He realized later on that he made it out of Keystone and was able to achieve some respect, dignity and success that few from Keystone achieved. He was grateful for the friends he had from Keystone; yet due to so many of them dying, he had a hard time developing close friendships for the rest of his life. He had a tattoo on his arm that said Keystone with 7 blood drops, to remind him of his past and friends that had died.

Those three deaths in Keystone that summer stayed with Anthony for some time, especially those involving close friends. David taught him about survival. They were lessons Anthony never forgot. Because of David, he was never afraid of anyone again. David's lessons gave Anthony confidence that, in almost any situation, he could take care of himself.

With David gone, Anthony felt he should be one of those who carried on David's ways. He had most of the respect in Keystone due to his street smarts and toughness. In these areas, Anthony tried taking over. He became a leader and the one others looked up to. This impressed some while making enemies of others. The enemies made going out alone rare for Anthony, especially at night.

Anthony took time over the summer to learn how to use the bus system in Johnson City. He learned the bus systems in order to learn the routes he needed to use for school. It didn't take long to learn the routes around town, and occasionally he took the bus to get away from Keystone to be alone. He didn't realize that this learning experience wouldn't be worth much. Neither Wanda nor Robert gave him money to buy the tokens he needed. It wasn't much more than two weeks before he started walking to and from school, just like he had expected.

***** **

Anthony entered the school and went directly to Mr. Alexander's' office as he was asked to do earlier in the summer when there with his Uncle Bill. He was surprised that Mr. Alexander remembered him, and that he was friendly when he saw him. "Well, Mr. Anthony Beechup. Welcome to your first day at your new school. I owe you a visit to your new home room here as well as an introduction to your new teachers." Mr. Alexander said with a big smile.

Mr. Alexander turned his attention to his secretary. "Margaret, if anyone comes by, let them know I'm showing Anthony around." He said as he started out of the office with Anthony. "Come on, Anthony, it's time to get you acquainted with a few folks." Mr. Alexander took him down the hallway to show him the school. As they walked down the hall, he introduced Anthony to other people in the school.

Mr. Alexander impressed Anthony with his genuine friendliness as he walked him down the hall. He noticed how much Mr. Alexander was liked by the majority of students and teachers at University School. Mr. Alexander would stop and welcome people back for the new school year, each by name, and occasionally gave those he met a hug. The hugs were for faculty and students. Anthony was impressed that Mr. Alexander stopped what he was doing to help him get acquainted with his new teachers. This was attention Anthony was not accustomed to, especially from someone in a leadership position like Mr. Alexander.

One of the first things Anthony noticed about University School was that most all younger kids were on the first floor. University School had grades from kindergarten on up through 12th grade. The first floor was for kids in grades K - 6. Mr. Alexander took Anthony to the second floor where he introduced him to his home room teacher. Mr. Alexander spent the next couple of hours assisting Anthony with registering for the classes he would be taking. Shortly after Mr. Alexander helped Anthony with registration he said, "Well Anthony, basketball season doesn't start for another month or so, but a lot of players go down to the gym after school for pick up games. I'd love to see you there playing with the rest of the guys when you can."

Anthony suddenly thought he had Mr. Alexander figured out. Mr. Alexander was introducing him to everyone as Billy Beechups' little brother. They probably had the same expectations of Anthony that they had of Bill. As he thought about that, Anthony almost became angry. He didn't want to be compared to Bill in any way, shape, fashion or form. His sport was football, not basketball, and he certainly had no plans to excel in the classroom like Bill had done.

Anthony knew that neither Bill nor anyone else, for that matter, would be able to study and excel in the classroom after living in the conditions he did. Arguments, fighting, whippings and beatings were the norm for Anthony. That is why he seldom stayed at home, and had turned to other things for pleasure, like sex and drugs.

Even though this was what Anthony understood to be Mr. Alexander's intent, he later understood that nothing could be further from the truth. Mr. Alexander was a man who genuinely cared about young people and helped them. There was no exception; Mr. Alexander cared for all of his students, including Anthony. If anything, he gave Anthony a little more attention and showed genuine compassion and concern. Anthony came to believe that Mr. Alexander was one of the only people who saw a sense of hurt in him. However, he also believed Mr. Alexander never knew the extent of the hurt. He was grateful for the help Mr. Alexander gave him.

It only took about an hour for Anthony to figure out University School. Most of the students were wealthy, at least according to Anthony's standards. He could tell by the way they walked in the hall ways, by looking at the clothes they wore, their shoes, and how they were groomed. Many of them drove to school, the majority drove nice, new cars, not old Novas or Impalas, but custom trucks, Mustangs, even an occasional Mercedes or Volvo. Anthony knew right away, he was out of place. He had to make his mark in this new environment, one way or another. He had to earn their respect in such a way that if they didn't respect him, they would pay the consequences, dished out his way.

After about two weeks, Anthony no longer rode the bus to school, he was walking. Anthony was somewhat chubby and this would be the best way to start taking off some weight. This is what he told his teachers and friends at school anyway. The real reason was he was one of the only students who ever took his lunch to school, and this was embarrassing. He knew that in order to impress these students he had to do the best he could to adapt to their world. One of the ways to do that was to eat with them which meant spending the dollar a day he had for bus tokens for lunch in the cafeteria.

Robert and Wanda were not consistent about giving Anthony bus fare, and after a while seldom gave it to him at all. Bus fare was $1 a day which left him a quarter short of the $1.25 lunch even when they did give him bus fare. This being the case, he had to increase his stealing to have extra money. This was rough, especially the times he got caught stealing from his mother or Robert. They didn't take well to it, and used Anthony's stealing as another excuse for punishment. It was worth it to fit in at University School. Having to make adjustments to fit in was something Anthony was used to. He did what he had to do in order to make it at this school. If that meant making a few adjustments or going through additional difficulty at home then that is what he would do.

Anthony had attended University School for three weeks. He was having a tough time adjusting to the new school and environment. One of the difficult areas was the classes he was taking. He had never been a good student, but with walking to and from school, and keeping up with his friends in Keystone, he had even less time to study. This was compounded even more because University School was much harder than any school he had ever attended. He soon realized that studying hard at another school to get a good grade wouldn't have the same impact at University School. This made it even harder on Anthony; he had never studied hard enough to get good grades. He had always been glad to get a C in school. Those efforts would be of little benefit at University School. After three weeks, he knew he could not make good grades at University School and had a great deal of difficulty passing. He had to make his mark in other areas.

While at University School, Anthony felt as if he was looked down on by many of the other students. Many of referred to him as either Billy Beechup's little brother or that new kid from Keystone. Many seemed jealous that he was related to Bill. He wasn't upset about the association with Bill, but he would have preferred to develop his own reputation and persona.

Things were difficult for Anthony and the expectations made school even more difficult. Some separated themselves from Anthony and never spent time with him. Some made things difficult by trying to act tougher than he. Inside, Anthony found those efforts comical. On the outside, he was genuinely trying to make a good impression on others and not let Bill or Mr. Alexander down. On the inside, he knew where he came from and that none of these students would be able to last a week in the environment he went home to nightly.

Anthony put up with the tough attitudes from some of the students for a while, but they quickly learned he would not put up with it for long. One of the students who acted tougher than he and tried to put him down was Anthony Humphrey. He was about the same size, maybe a little taller and a little thinner. He had dark brown hair that was medium length down on his shirt collar; they were similar in many ways. Tony Humphrey was handsome, had numerous girl friends and was one of the most popular boys at University School. Humphrey was someone who put Anthony and others down if he thought he was better than them; at least, this is the way Anthony saw it.

Tony Humphrey hung out with some of the toughest boys at University School including George Likens, James Rogers, Matthew Swenson and a few others, but he was recognized by many, even some of the upper classmen, as one of the toughest kids at University School.

One day during a social studies class Tony Humphrey said something to Anthony as they were leaving class. Anthony didn't really remember just what it was that was said; he just knew he had finally decided he was not going to take it anymore. As the two boys were walking from one building to the next, Anthony ran up and hit Humphrey in the throat and chest before Humphrey knew what had happened. He hit him once squarely in the center of his chest and with the same hand, hooked around and hit him squarely in the throat. Humphrey had a short time to realize what was happening but not before Anthony hit him on the side of his head with his other hand. Anthony yelled at Humphrey right after he hit him, "Come on you son of a bitch. If you've got something to say, say it to me now. I'm not going to take your shit any more. Do you understand, you stupid jerk?"

Humphrey stood there not knowing what to think. At the time, James Rogers and George Likens were walking with Humphrey between classes and just stood there watching Beechup, not believing what they had just seen. Rogers and Likens had never seen Anthony like this and neither had Humphrey. They quickly realized Anthony Beechup had come from a different mold than they had, and they possibly could not handle this new boy.

And they wouldn't be in a hurry to find out. In many ways Anthony was becoming the tutor to these boys that David Jansen had been to him.

"Hey man, I'm sorry. I didn't mean anything, honest," Humphrey replied right after Anthony had jumped down his throat.

Beechup, nervous, anxious, and not knowing what to expect, felt somewhat relieved this would not go any further. Anthony realized from his past experiences that if these boys knew anything about the streets, they would have all three jumped him and there wouldn't have been much he could do. He knew that everyone who saw this take place looked at it as if Humphrey was backing down from him. He would earn some respect for who he was and what he could do. It was clear he would not take anything from anybody at the school, not anyone smaller, older, or bigger.

Anthony responded to Humphrey, "Fine then, you stupid punk. If you ever talk about me or put me down again I'll break your fucking arm in two. Do you understand that you stupid ugly punk?"

"Sure man, I'm sorry. It won't ever happen again," Humphrey replied in a subdued tone, embarrassed because he knew Anthony meant it, and he had to give in to him in front of his friends and the others who had gathered around the fight. From this incident, Anthony began to be accepted by many of the students. Tony Humphrey had a legitimate reputation, and Anthony had dispelled that reputation. Not only had Anthony dispelled much of Humphrey's reputation, but he did it in such a way that other students were talking about it.

There was only one other student who gave Anthony a hard time at University School, James Rogers. Even though James witnessed the episode between Anthony and Tony Humphrey, he saw it as an opportunity for him to take over Humphrey's role of the tough guy at school. James didn't see the fight between Humphrey and Beechup as Beechup saw it. He saw it as an opportunity to take over Humphrey's role. This conflict between James and Anthony continued for a period of time, and Beechup knew it had to be resolved in time.

~ Chapter 13 ~

James Rogers

Anthony finally reached the point where he was fitting in to some extent at University School. He learned who he could run around with at school and he developed his reputation, separate from the identity and association with his uncle Bill. Anthony learned which friends he could trust and those he couldn't. He gave up trying to make good grades and tried instead to gain a leadership role. The only opposition was James Rogers.

James Rogers never relinquished any leadership to Anthony. That was hard to understand since James was present during the encounter with Anthony Humphrey. James was much smaller than Anthony, shorter at only 5' 2" and he weighed less than 130 pounds. He had dark brown hair cut like the early Beatles, kind of a bowl cut with bangs. He had braces which Anthony thought was strange when trying to be a tough guy. Anthony and James seemed to get along. They were good friends despite the rivalry between them. They had played basketball together for some time and spent time together on weekends which contributed to their friendship.

They played on the junior high team where James started at point guard and Anthony started as a forward and wing man. James was small but shot the day lights out of long shots. If the three point shot had been in effect James could have averaged another 6 points a game. Basketball was a favorite past time for both boys.

James and Anthony spent time after school going to the East Tennessee State University gymnasium to play pick up basketball games. The pick up games often involved players from the East Tennessee State University team. Anthony and James also played basketball or football at lunch with other students from University School. It seemed like they always ended up on the same team whenever playing any sport. They played so much together they knew each other's moves and shots, making it hard for almost anyone, even the high school players, to beat them in basketball. They even played respectably against the college students. They seldom won the games against the college players but sometimes were on a team that won. One indication that they weren't too bad, was when playing with the East Tennessee State University basketball players in pick up games or other high school players, they were seldom the last ones picked when choosing teams.

Anthony and James also enjoyed going to University High School and East Tennessee State University basketball games. University School's high school team often played the pre-game before the East Tennessee State University men's and women's college games. They were at almost every game.

Mr. Alexander ran the game clock for the East Tennessee State University games, and Anthony and James always got in free to see the games. They either showed up early, or knew one of the gate attendants or coaches. If that didn't work Mr. Alexander let them in. Basketball was the vehicle which helped develop their friendship. It was also basketball that brought out the confrontation between them.

Anthony decided to spend the weekend with his grandparents. He did this occasionally since they lived a half mile from the school campus. Anthony stayed with them the weekend East Tennessee State University played Austin Peay University. He wanted to see the game because Austin Peay had the nation's leading scorer in James "The Fly" Williams. Anthony and James made plans to see the game together that weekend. It was televised regionally across the Southeast, and they sat directly behind the scorers table, complements of Mr. Alexander. Both Anthony and James enjoyed the game and James "The Fly" Williams was everything he was cracked up to be. Williams scored 28 points in a close loss for Austin Peay while sitting out half the game in foul trouble. "The Fly" was another player like James who would have scored many more points over his college career if the long-range three-pointer was in effect. Anthony realized "The Fly" scored most all of his points from long-range, and was double-teamed most of the game. He was quick and pesky which was where he picked up his nick name, "The Fly."

After the game, Anthony and James went to University School to see if anyone was playing basketball. On the way to the high school gym, Anthony and James talked trash with each other. They started putting each other down, mostly for fun, and most of the time they knew their limits and knew what to say or not to say. Even though they challenged each other and vied for the leadership roles in school, they had enough of a friendship that they didn't want to challenge each other to a fight. They were happy to share the leadership role they did.

This conversation started on the basketball game they saw. "Hey man, 'The Fly' was awesome," James said to Anthony.

"Yeah, he was almost as good as I'm gonna be!" Anthony replied.

"Oh come on man, you suck," James stated emphatically and in a tone Anthony didn't appreciate.

"Like bull man. I'll kick your ass any day!" Anthony teased in a tone not yet serious but with confidence.

"Shoot, man, you can't whip my rear in basketball or for that matter in anything." James responded, now angry at Anthony.

They were now at the front of the University School's gym. Anthony was getting angry at James for the tone of voice and temperament he was expressing. Anthony yelled at James, pointing his finger at his chest. "Listen here you stupid son of a bitch. I can kick your ass any day in basketball or any other way I want to. I'm tired of your bull shit. So go ahead. If you keep it up I'll kick your ass right here, right now."

James had enough with Anthony and started yelling and cursing back, "All right boy, let's settle this right thing now." James drew back his fist as if he were going to go full force at Anthony.

Anthony, angry, and upset yet calm, whispered loudly, "Hold it man. Here comes Mr. Alexander." Anthony said while pointing toward James's back left shoulder. James turned to see Mr. Alexander. At the moment he turned to see Mr. Alexander he realized he was not there. Anthony kicked James in the back with the toe of his shoe. James groaned, and turned toward Anthony. When he turned, Anthony kneed him in the groin with his right knee. As James bent over from the pain, Anthony threw an uppercut with his right hand that caught him in the mouth. The force of James's lips hitting the braces busted his lips immediately. Blood flew everywhere. As James's head bounced back from the force of the uppercut, Anthony grabbed him around the head and threw him to the ground face first with a movement that looked like a cowboy in a rodeo throwing down a steer.

Both boys were on the ground. Anthony was sitting on James's chest hitting him in the face. A college student grabbed Anthony from behind and said. "Hey, man, give it up, you're going to kill the guy. Enough is enough." The college student waited until he thought both boys were going to quit. Just as he thought they were going to quit, he realized Anthony was not going to stop so he stepped in.

After the student stopped the fight, he walked off leaving James and Anthony facing each other. Blood was all over James's face and Anthony's hand. It also covered the ground around where they were fighting.

"Man, you fight like a little girl." James said while wiping blood from his face with the sleeve of his shirt.

"Man, I kicked your ass once. I'll do it again if you keep it up, you stupid little punk." Anthony responded calmly but breathing hard.

"Man, don't give me that shit. You fight dirty. What the hell are you trying to prove anyway?" James was still wiping blood from his mouth and cursing every other breath.

Anthony noticed James also had a few tears in his eyes. "Don't give me that bull, man. You should know there is no way to fight fair. You either win or you lose. I fight to win, and I'll do whatever the hell I have to do to win. You lost, period. And unless you're willing to do what you have to in order to whip my ass, then I would advise you to shut the hell up because I'll do what I have to even if it means biting off a body part that comes near my teeth," responded Anthony, his voice cracking from getting so angry at James.

"O.K. man, you whipped my ass. Let's just call it over, O.K.?" asked James, seeing that Anthony meant what he said. James didn't expect this from Anthony. As far as he knew, he had never encountered this type of attitude in a fight, before.

"Yeah, O.K., it's over," answered Anthony sticking out his hand to shake with James. Anthony valued his friendship with James and was willing to do what he needed to in order to remain friends.

Anthony learned from David Jansen in Keystone that just because you beat somebody up doesn't mean you can't be friends to that person. James was willing to do what he had to, but he also knew how to judge people. James was a good guy.

After the fight Anthony learned he need not be afraid of anyone at the school again. Not anyone his own age or older. He earned the right to be where he was, and he wouldn't let anyone take that from him. He did realize that a lot of the richer kids at University School never had the privilege to learn from David Jansen in Keystone. The University School students wouldn't do what was necessary to win a fight. They didn't realize a fight wasn't won just by whipping someone; it was won by the person walking away with the most fear of the other.

Most of the students at University School came to believe you can buy respect. Anthony had learned the opposite. The people with the money hired people like Anthony to take care of their problems. It wasn't the money that gave respect; it was the street know-how and willingness of people like Anthony to do whatever they had to. Because of this rule Anthony couldn't remember ever losing another fight. He learned from this experience to demand respect even from the older high school students. They could easily whip Anthony because of their size, but they knew he wasn't afraid of them and would fight until someone was either hurt seriously, or dead. For this reason Anthony seldom had trouble with older students. There were challenges but it didn't take long for the older students to walk away.

After a few weeks Anthony and James were back on good terms with each other just as if nothing had happened. They were talking again and spent as much time as possible with each other. They were back to their old ways. They maintained that relationship through the rest of the year and into the next year.

Anthony thought he had done everything he needed to make friends and impress people at University School. He gained respect by putting fear in people. He became more violent towards others at school. He developed a reputation as a trouble maker and someone who willingly hurt people just for the fun of it.

Anthony had to frequently visit Mr. Alexander's' office for getting into trouble. Mr. Alexander always showed concern and compassion towards Anthony. He occasionally made Anthony stay after school but never threatened to paddle him or give him any form of corporal punishment. This surprised him even though he knew he deserved it. Anthony did so many things at school he was surprised he wasn't kicked out or expelled from school. On numerous occasions he even brought bottles of liquid cinnamon to school. It was so hot it would bring tears to your eyes if you put a couple of drops on your tongue. After the tears, one had to worry about the blisters. As bad an effect as the liquid cinnamon had on others, it was not uncommon for Anthony to pour half a bottle into someone's soft drink at lunch. He did these types of things seldom getting caught. Anthony felt he could get by doing these things because people either weren't sure who did it or were afraid to tell on him. There were a number of reasons some of the students were afraid of Anthony. He developed a reputation where if he thought someone was a wimp, nerd, or jerk he walked up to them in the hallway and hit them as hard as he could, in the chest, stomach or occasionally the face. He laughed at the person and walked away while they were either crying or trying to catch their breath. Often times this took place in front of other students, but none of them ever said anything about what he was doing. The hitting took place almost daily. On rare occasions he got caught by a teacher, but most of the time he got away with it. James and some of the other guys started hanging around Anthony because they hadn't seen anyone this mean before, and they liked the attention Anthony was receiving even though it was not all positive. Anthony didn't seem to care about whom he hurt or how bad he hurt them. Yet, deep down inside, without the others knowing it, he did care but was unwilling to change. He cared about being accepted and liked, and this was more important than anything else. What he was doing regarding the abuse and attitudes towards others was the only way he knew how to get any kind of acceptance.

Anthony still missed something in his life, and he knew it. He just didn't know what it was. He started to drink alcohol more during his time at home and took more pills while at University School. He broke into Robert or Wanda's Bacardi Rum or Pabst Blue Ribbon Beer and stole as much as he could on a regular basis.

Anthony spent more time with Gerald Johnson in Keystone, who got alcohol from his family any time he wanted it. He also had some of the kids at University School bring pills to school for him. Anthony was high on some type of drug or alcohol most of the time. He never knew whether the other kids realized he was high, but he suspected many of them did or at least that they suspected it. Anthony brought his lunch to school again, but for different reasons. He did so primarily because he could bring his thermos. He filled it up with either Rum or Vodka and drank it throughout the day. He always carried a bottle of Nip-it breath freshener or cinnamon tooth picks due to the alcohol breath. He seemed easy going and expressed an attitude like he didn't care. He sometimes was high by the next to last period of the day.

Anthony started leaving school early to keep from getting in trouble. He was able to encourage a few friends to participate in drinking or taking pills. He reasoned it was O.K. to participate in taking pills and drinking at school because he never did these things before lunch, well at least not much.

As Anthony drank more, he also got poorer grades. He wouldn't have thought this was possible earlier in the year, but it was happening. His grades dropped from mostly D's to all F's, even in areas like deportment and citizenship. These were designed to tell the parents how the student was behaving at school. Most kids were in trouble if getting B's in this area. Anthony never got into much trouble though because he seldom, if ever, took his report card home. Robert and Wanda eventually found out what kind of grades Anthony was making at the end of the year in a letter they received from the school. It stated that unless Anthony went to summer school and passed the required courses he would have to repeat 7th grade. Wanda told Anthony he would be spending the largest part of his summer in school. She stated, "I'll be damned if I'm going to have you fail at this too."

Anthony didn't mind going to summer school because Anthony Humphrey, James Rogers, and several more friends would be there with him. He brought several of his friends to summer school with him this particular summer. It wasn't the first time he was in trouble with the school, his family, friends, or their parents, nor would it be the last. For a few of Anthony's friends, it was their first time to be in trouble, and if their parents had anything to do with it would be their last.

~ Chapter 14 ~

Summer of Discontent

Anthony didn't look forward to spending 7 weeks of summer going to school all day long. He wouldn't mind if he wasn't walking to and from school each day. He walked almost 8 miles a day in the heat and humidity of Upper East Tennessee.

The temperature got up to the high 80's and low 90's on a regular basis. On rare occasions the temperature got into the high 90's and low 100's. The problem was not the heat, but rather the fact that there was seldom any wind, and the humidity rarely fell below 80%. This made for unbearably hot sticky summers. This was the reason Anthony and his sister Madeline went to the city Rec pool most every day through the summer. Unfortunately, he was walking to and from school and spending time away from the pool. He was also at a school for most of the summer with no air conditioning.

Anthony didn't care if he went to school or not, so it didn't matter if he failed 7th grade or for that matter ever went back to school. Anthony would be content to stay in Keystone with the rest of the guys until he was old enough to get a job. Most of his friends from University School being in summer school made it easier but not enjoyable.

Anthony influenced several good kids into bad behaviors and grades. Anthony Humphrey, James Rogers, George Likens and Keith Testum were all good kids and seldom in trouble before meeting Anthony. Anthony didn't intentionally lead kids down the wrong path; he just went down the only path he knew. To him these kids had their own problems with acceptance before meeting him. If it wasn't a problem with acceptance for them, it was trying to get more attention from their family and others. They saw Anthony get his fair share of attention. He certainly had a sense of pride. If his friends knew what Anthony was really feeling they would not have followed him.

Anthony, if asked and being honest, could've shared a horror story they could not understand. He didn't feel acceptance or friendship from anyone, family, friends, anyone. He certainly didn't like the attention he received from others in his family. Anthony realized that the attention he received at school and with friends was nothing like the little he received at home. Anthony seldom saw his mom or Robert, but he didn't care. Even if he got attention from them, they would likely be drunk and not recall anything. Anthony's uncle Bill was never around now that he was in college, so Anthony didn't care if he was at his grandparents' house. The benefit of being at his grandparents' was that they lived only a few blocks from University School. This was also convenient depending on who was around through the summer to have sex with. Despite the convenience of his grandparents house, most of the time Anthony stayed in Keystone and endured the long daily walk.

Time in the classroom wasn't important to Anthony except he wanted to go on to the 8th grade with his friends. It was obvious the families of his friends had laid down the law with their children: they had better pass summer school. For that reason Anthony went to summer school and made the attempt to pass on to 8th grade. Class didn't start off so bad that summer. There was a new kid named Dwayne who started school. Dwayne was Black and went to one of the other schools in Johnson City during the regular school year. He was tall, slender and had a large afro hair-cut. He was attractive and drew the attention of many girls at University School. Dwayne was also well mannered and polite to his teachers and friends. This was an attitude Anthony was not used to seeing.

The rest of the students at University School looked at Dwayne as a cool token. He was black and different than most of them as they were primarily white and had spent little time around blacks. Dwayne enjoyed the attention but was wise and smart enough to understand how to take advantage of the attention. Anthony liked Dwayne for his wisdom and ability to be deceptive. Dwayne knew how to take advantage of any situation or person around him in order to make things better for himself. Anthony also liked him because of the closeness he had with his black friends in Keystone, and Dwayne reminded him of those friends.

Anthony was friends with Cherry and other blacks. He hung out with them and saw them as any other friends except they had experienced aspects of prejudice. Others, especially whites, hadn't. In Keystone, Anthony learned one thing about prejudice from his black friends. They helped him learn the real color of prejudice is green. They understood the ones who had money, the green, had power. So prejudice was not a color to Anthony. The blacks and whites in Keystone saw themselves as the same; neglected and abused by the rich man.

Anthony was also impressed with Dwayne as an athlete. This wasn't a stereotype; it was a reality. Dwayne was a good athlete. Anthony spent a lot of time with Dwayne playing ball, whether football or basketball it didn't matter. Dwayne was a challenge and a challenge was something Anthony enjoyed. Anthony enjoyed it because he realized it was only from competing against others who were good could one gain a chance to improve. Dwayne helped him get better in sports.

Most of the summer didn't have meaning for Anthony except the relationship he developed with Dwayne. The relationship was good for Anthony, but it also gave his friends something to focus on besides getting into trouble. There were still occasional cut ups in class and Anthony still popped pills and drank when he got the chance, both at home and school. Anthony did spend time on his school work with his friends and Dwayne. He realized learning could be fun and he was not as dumb as he thought. Eventually he passed summer school with all of his friends and had a few weeks left in the summer to enjoy the pool at the Recreation Center. He also had time to enjoy some good times including drugs and other things with his friends in Keystone.

For the first time in his life, Anthony was ready for summer to be over. He was ready to go back to school and be the man. Because of summer school, he was not able to spend much time with his Keystone friends. Even though he got along with them, he had also developed close relationships with some of the students at University School.

Anthony was excited because Dwayne had applied for admission into University School and was accepted. He was excited about this relationship not only because of their friendship, but the contribution made to the basketball team. Anthony was sure the friendship would continue for a long time. Even though Dwayne had a tough reputation, in many ways he was more honest than most of Anthony's friends or for that matter Anthony himself.

Dwayne had a better understanding of himself than most kids Anthony knew, either at Keystone or University School. Dwayne knew what he wanted, and he knew how to get it. He was confident he would be able to get what he wanted. Dwayne did what he had to in order to get what he wanted. This impressed Anthony, and they developed a good relationship built on respect.

Anthony was sure Dwayne had problems, yet he was always open to discussing them with the people he trusted, and he always knew who to trust. Anthony wanted to learn from Dwayne, but had difficulty, especially at first while at University School. The ability to learn from others took years to develop. It was important to Anthony that others accept him. He did not want to take the chance that others would despise and reject him for his imperfections. Love was something he desired and sought whether he recognized it or not.

✱✱✱✱✱✱✱

The rest of the summer was uneventful. Anthony spent limited time with his friends in Keystone. He hung out with the guys in the gang and they went on occasional excursions where they vandalized property around Keystone and the surrounding communities. There were construction and road crews doing work in the community, and Anthony and his friends took pleasure in vandalizing their equipment when it was parked over night. They would put sugar or salt in the fuel line, cut open the seats with a knife, hit the vehicles with hammers and rocks, denting the body or breaking what glass was left and cutting open tires. Most of the time they did whatever hit their mood at the particular moment.

There was an occasional drug excursion where the boys experimented with different drugs coming into the market. The drug usage was not as serious as it used to be for Anthony due to the deaths of some of his friends. He stayed away from the harder drugs but on occasion did a form of heroin, but never by injection. He did smoke marijuana which was the hardest drug to quit. Anthony cut back his drug and alcohol use to weekends unless a special occasion arose. He occasionally had more excursions into the drug world but the death he had seen had taken a toll.

The following year had many changes for Anthony. It resulted in confusion and hurt. This was something he experienced many times before. He would've thought he was getting used to these experiences, but he never did.

✱✱✱✱✱✱

Anthony was in the upstairs counseling room at Manna House in Hendersonville. He and George continued to talk. Anthony was now used to talking with George and felt better after their conversations.

They had been meeting for over a month on a weekly basis. George gave Anthony some materials to take home to read and work on for the next week. "Here, Anthony are some scriptural references I want you to look at this week," he said calmly. "I would also like to give you some of this other material to take and look at," as he reached for another stack of papers to give Anthony. "These are some articles which have been written on the area of Post Traumatic Stress Disorder. This is information which I think will also help you better understand yourself."

"Thanks," Anthony answered. "I'll give it a look over and get back in touch with you in a couple of weeks. I have a meeting I have to go to next week so it will be the week after next before I can get back with you," he said regretfully.

"That's fine. I'll see you then. Just give me a call if anything else comes up," George said as they shook hands.

Anthony read the articles over the next two weeks. It was good he had a meeting in Charlotte, North Carolina. While there he had time to read and reflect on the articles and get additional information on Post Traumatic Stress Disorder (PTSD).

Anthony understood this was an illness which was rare for males but was mostly unique to men who served in war. Some men who had been sexually and physically abused to the point where they thought their lives were in danger or extremely traumatized also had PTSD. It also existed in females who had been abused either physically or sexually.

Anthony never liked labels but he appreciated the association he had with a number of feelings and emotions he had in common with others who had PTSD. Labels are seldom rewarding, but through association with others and the understanding of PTSD for Anthony were beneficial.

The articles helped Anthony develop a better understanding of why he was the way he was and felt the things he did. He was feeling better about himself. He was fine as long as he didn't go to bed and have the dreams and nightmares from his youth reoccur, or he didn't visit the places where the stress and pressures occurred during his youth. The problem was, he had to sleep and he had to visit Johnson City on a regular basis.

~ Chapter 15 ~

Turmoil on the Home Front

The school year started on several positive notes for Anthony. Shortly after school started he found out his art teacher, Mr. Testum, drove by Keystone each day on his way to University School. Mr. Testum had a son named Keith whom Anthony liked and hung out with at school. As a result of this friendship, Anthony and his sister started getting a ride to school with Mr. Testum each morning. He walked home which was not nearly as bad as walking to and from school. Occasionally he was able to ride home with Mr. Testum if he didn't have anything after school.

The most exciting thing for Anthony that year was his mom was pregnant. This was good news for a variety of reasons. Anthony hoped the pregnancy would result in less fighting between Robert and Wanda. Robert was excited that Wanda was pregnant and going to have his child. Robert kidded around with Wanda more and was not as mean to Anthony and Madeline. Madeline was happy due to the pregnancy in place of frequent mood swings.

Once school started Anthony made some new friends including Edward Collins and Charles McGregor. Edward was a little strange to most of the kids but that was O.K. with Anthony. Edward and Anthony Humphrey lived close to each other so they spent several days a week at each other's houses. Anthony and Edward did drugs together and became involved in deep spiritual conversations which seldom looked like any recognizable religion. The conversations were eclectic and very New Age focused.

Anthony spent time with Edward despite him being unacceptable to his friends at school. Edward was a few inches taller than Anthony had long dirty blonde hair. It wasn't just the color. Most of the time the hair really was dirty, but Edward was a guy Anthony enjoyed spending time with. He had an acne problem like many teenagers had. He was perceived to get weirder as he grew older. In the high school year book he had the tag Lucifer under his picture. Despite the weirdness, he was a good friend and a friend Anthony enjoyed.

Sometimes Edward spent time with Anthony at Keystone. While Anthony had friends at school, Edward was one of the few to actually visit Anthony on his turf. Keystone was an environment which was completely foreign to Edward. He lived in the country in a nice large house. Edward had difficulty with the inner city adjustments necessary to make it in Keystone. There were some aspects of Keystone he did enjoy. Anthony occasionally took Edward to see some of his girl friends. Edward was pleased that Anthony took him places either to get free drugs or be involved in sexual activities with others, in this case always female.

Occasionally Anthony took Edward to Sandra's house. She was a girl friend who made efforts to get friends to her place so Edward could have sexual partners. Sandra was a little shorter than Anthony, two years older and sexually active. She and Anthony had sex on numerous occasions and she was one of the more attractive females he was with. She had medium length blond hair and was slim enough to see her bone structure. Sandra never succeeded at getting additional sexual partners but tried anyway. Edward appreciated the effort. She liked Anthony and enjoyed being with him so much that she did almost anything he asked. Sandra was 17, and lived on her own. This was convenient for Anthony and although he knew her through his family, living on her own made it easier to work around the details of spending time together. Anthony was busy with his other friends and didn't spend as much time with her as he would have liked. This likely prevented an unwanted pregnancy and kept him from being pushed into fatherhood before he was ready.

Anthony always remembered Sandra's most distinguishing feature; her little pug nose along with her having a very shapely body. Her nose accented her eyes and lips. She was such a pretty girl, and Anthony wondered why she would have the relationship with him she did.

Another friend of Anthony's at school, Charles McGregor, was another story. Charles was 4" or 5" inches taller than Anthony and had long dark, dirty hair. It was always greasy and it seemed as if his clothes were always wrinkled. The clothes didn't look dirty as much as unkept, hanging off his extremely slender body. Charles had a long face with a sharp pointy nose. He spoke with a nasally tone and came from one of the most educated families at University School.

Charles lived 2 blocks from school and came from one of the strangest family situations Anthony ever encountered. Charles lived in what appeared from the outside a very nice contemporary house in a nice residential neighborhood. Once entering the house one would not believe the filth encountered. The house had bugs everywhere. There was trash all around the house, in all corners. It was as if the family just threw the trash wherever they wanted, occasionally taking it out.

Anthony noticed in Charles's room a stack of Playboy magazines sitting on a table next to his bed. He had seen Playboy numerous times but never so openly displayed in a young person's room. Ms. McGregor, Charles's mother, was a single mom and an English professor at East Tennessee State University. She also appeared to Anthony to be the most understanding parent he had ever encountered. Not only had she purchased the magazine subscription for Charles, she bought light drugs for him and his friends as long as they didn't abuse them. Ms. McGregor seldom bought anything other than marijuana or some pills, and she occasionally joined Charles and his friends in doing the drugs. On a few occasions, Anthony participated with the McGregor's when they did drugs with friends. Though Anthony never experienced it, he was almost certain that Ms. McGregor was also willing to have sex with Charles's friends if they wanted. Despite this, it was hard imagining younger guys having sex with her. She had long dirty black hair, almost identical to her son Charles and she was short and heavy set. Anthony figured someone would have to be drunk or high before having sex with her.

This family had many characteristics Anthony admired, free sex, free drugs and free acceptance. It wasn't long before Anthony and his friends started spending more time at Charles's house. Anthony was not able to get his friends from Keystone to come because they didn't believe such a family existed. Many of his friends from school occasionally spent the night with Charles, but Anthony was unwilling to do this because he couldn't stand the thought of sleeping in the filthy house.

Despite the positive things happening for Anthony, it didn't take long for life to fall apart. One of the earliest problems was the relationship he had with Mr. Testum, the art teacher, who was his ride to school. One day in art class Anthony was supposed to be working on a project. He and Keith worked together in the class but didn't take the work seriously: Keith, because his dad was teaching the class and Anthony because he was never good in art. Anthony wanted to succeed in art because he heard from his family about how good of an artist his father, Charles, was. Anthony never discovered a talent in art and used art class as a social time.

While in class Anthony decided he had no time, patience, or talent, especially with the work he was doing in class. Anthony always enjoyed reading and was reading the book, The Exorcist. He figured art class was a good place to read. Anthony came to the part where the primary character, the possessed child, masturbated with a crucifix. He thought it was funny, in a juvenile sort of way that the author wrote about the crucifix entering the girl's vagina. Anthony passed the book around, joking and snickering with his classmates about the description the sex act in the book. Mr. Testum noticed the disruption taking place in his class.

"Anthony what are you doing?" Mr. Testum asked calmly.

"Nothing," Anthony responded in a matter of fact manner, trying to impress the other students.

"Yes, you are doing something. Now, what are you doing?" Mr. Testum repeated, now raising his voice.

"Nothing, I said," Anthony replied in a tone which was derogatory to Mr. Testum. Mr. Testum spoke in a high pitched, feminine tone, and Anthony was mimicking Mr. Testum's feminine tone of voice. Anthony reacted angrily towards Mr. Testum just as he responded to him.

"Well, I'll just take that nothing," Mr. Testum said as he jerked the book out of one of the student's hands. Mr. Testum opened the book and looked through it. He noticed Anthony's name on the inside cover. "Now, is this your book I have here, Mr. Beechup?" Mr. Testum asked sternly, looking directly in Anthony's eyes as he asked the question.

Anthony knew Mr. Testum saw his name in the front of the book, and answered, "Well, you know it is. You saw my name in it." Anthony carried on with the image he felt the other students expected of him.

"Well, let's just look through it and see what is so funny for you and your friends, Mr. Beechup." Mr. Testum turned to the page Anthony had marked and underlined. He also saw a note Anthony had written for his classmates to read referring to the section of the book dealing with the masturbation.

"Just what is the purpose and meaning of this, Mr. Beechup?" Mr. Testum asked angrily, becoming more upset.

Anthony knew what the note said and it was clear to Mr. Testum what was going on. He knew that most of Mr. Testum's attempts were directed at embarrassing him. Anthony decided he would not be embarrassed by Mr. Testum, or for that matter, anyone else. He made a joke of the situation and turned it around to embarrass Mr. Testum. Anthony responded to Mr. Testum's question with a smirk and yet serious attitude to show the class and Mr. Testum that he wouldn't let anyone take advantage of him and embarrass him.

"Well, Mr. Testum, if you really want to know, I was so bored in your class that I was reading that book and read the word 'vagina'. I didn't know what a vagina was, and I also knew that of all people in the classroom you wouldn't know either. So, knowing how little you knew about vaginas, I decided to ask some of my friends to see if they knew." Anthony said this while trying to hold back his laughter.

Upon the response from Anthony, the classroom erupted in laughter, obviously directed towards Mr. Testum. To Anthony the laughter indicated he had not only maintained his image, he improved it among the students.

As the classroom laughed Mr. Testum took his embarrassment out on Anthony. He angrily grabbed Anthony under the left arm pit and yanked him out of his seat, "Come with me right now, young man."

Anthony didn't have much of a choice as to whether to go or not because Mr. Testum had him by a part of the arm that was painful. After leaving the classroom, Mr. Testum spoke in a stern whisper and pointed his finger in Anthony's face. "You listen to me right here, right now young man. I have gone out of my way to help you in a personal way and I've tried to teach you in my classroom. It is time you learned that neither this earth, nor anyone on this earth, revolves around you and no one owes you a single thing. People don't have to show you that they care for you. For that matter, they don't have to care for you, like you, or give a flip about what happens to you. So if you don't appreciate what people do for you and you are not willing to show your appreciation by, at the very least, treating them with respect, then I'll be dammed if I'll go out of my way to help you now, or any time in the future. As far as I'm concerned I don't care a bit if you have to walk to school in rain, sleet, hail, snow, or excruciating heat. It will be a cold day in hell before I give you a ride to school again. Now get your rear back in the class room, sit down and don't open your trashy little mouth. You may not care about learning, but there are other students in that classroom who do. So keep your mouth and your filthy mind to yourself. If you can't do this, then it's simple. Don't come to my class. Do you understand this Mr. Beechup?"

Through the whole episode Anthony did not display his anger in an inappropriate way. Mr. Testum had not raised his voice. Instead in a calm direct way, he let Anthony know this was the way it was going to be. In the past Anthony would have reacted, but Mr. Testum had clearly gone out of his way to help Anthony, and Anthony in return turned his back on him as a person who was willing to help. As the years went by Anthony realized Mr. Testum was right in what he said and the way he said it, especially when considering what Anthony had just done. Anthony had a respect for Mr. Testum, a respect not shown many adults.

"Yes, Sir," Anthony answered, showing for the first time some respect.

Anthony showed respect to Mr. Alexander for the kindness and concern he had always showed him, but Mr. Alexander was not a teacher. Anthony went back into the classroom with Mr. Testum making the rest of the class wonder what had just taken place. Anthony sat there quietly thinking about how he blew it with Mr. Testum.

This was one of the first times Anthony was truly sorry for his actions and what he had said. He realized his mouth had taken something good and it was no one's fault but his own. He really did appreciate the rides to school from Mr. Testum much more than the long walks. Anthony knew deep down Mr. Testum must have cared for him. Otherwise he would have taken Anthony to the principal's office to see Mr. Alexander. Anthony appreciated this encounter for the learning experience and firmness of Mr. Testum, which was deserved. Mr. Testum continued to give Anthony's sister, Madeline, a ride to school, but Anthony was left to start the long process of walking to and from school again which continued for the next two years.

✱ ✱ ✱ ✱ ✱ ✱ ✱ ✱

"How did you feel about having to walk back and forth to school once Mr. Testum quit giving you rides, Anthony?" George asked sitting in the office at Manna House.

"Well, it really didn't bother me too much." Anthony answered. "It was just a little harder having to get up earlier and all. That extra hour of sleep was nice."

"Did anything else significant happen to you that school year?" George asked.

"Yeah, there were actually several things that happened that I can recall pretty well," Anthony replied. He then told his story regarding his year at University School.

✱ ✱ ✱ ✱ ✱ ✱

Anthony walked back home from school early that spring. The walk took him Northeast from school. It was a 3 1/2 to 4 mile walk. He was walking and going through several business sections of town before coming to the downtown section of Johnson City. Anthony never minded walking through downtown Johnson City because he went by several bars. He might see several homeless people or people who had been drinking too much. He enjoyed walking through Johnson City because of the things in the city to see.

There were businesses including pawn shops where he occasionally went into and looked around. Every now and then he had extra money he had saved or stolen from his mother. On these occasions he stopped by the pawn shops to buy something, usually knives. Downtown was fun, and this was before the building of the mall on the outside of town that almost killed the downtown area.

Anthony heard stories of homosexuals stopping people and offering money for sexual favors. Although he had been involved in sexual acts with both males and females, he had harsh feelings towards the homosexuals who stopped and paid boys for sex. Anthony heard of several people being stopped and was aware that the Johnson City Police Department was on the lookout for whomever it was purchasing sexual favors.

Anthony was a good size for his age, standing at 5' 10" tall and weighing 150 pounds. He was old enough to take care of himself if ever approached by a homosexual. Occasionally he stopped by the pawn shops and purchased throwing knives and boot knives because they were the cheapest knives for sale. He kept the knives for awhile before selling them for a profit to some of his friends in Keystone. He also carried a small weighted stick in his pants leg in case of trouble. These and other things like nails driven into the toes of his shoes always had Anthony feeling safe when on his own.

It was early spring when Anthony left school early. It was quite warm so he took his time going in and looking at several stores. When he was about a mile and a half from home, he noticed a white Impala following him. Anthony was near the large Johnson City Post Office building when he went in and looked around to see if he could lose the car. The Post Office, a large building with a fallout shelter in the basement, was a good place to waste some time. He occasionally went down to the fallout shelter where it was cool, especially during warm weather, to cool off from the walk.

Anthony had been in the basement before, but he was there longer than normal. He was aware of the pick-ups by homosexuals and took out the stick he was carrying and put it in the hollow of his back between the upper pants waist band and his shirt. He wasn't sure but he thought he had been followed for some time. He pulled the shirt tail out just in case he needed to get to the stick in a hurry.

The stick Anthony was carrying was no ordinary stick. It was weighted; he had drilled a hole in the end and weighted it with lead. The stick was 2" inches in diameter and weighed 3 pounds. He carved it in such a way that it fit nicely in the palm of his hand. The stick was a foot and a half long which made it a decent weapon. He had never used it but was confident that if he needed it, it would make a good weapon.

Anthony also had a throwing knife strapped around his ankle and lower calf which was concealed by his socks and pants leg. He had another weapon he carried on a regular basis which Gerald Johnson taught him how to make. The weapon, one of his favorites, was a switch blade knife which was 8" long with the blade opened. A number of kids in Keystone carried similar knives. Anthony took the spring, which normally opened the blade automatically when the button on the knife was pressed, out of the knife. The knife was a little over 4" inches long with the blade closed and had a bone handle with a silver button. With the spring on the knife gone, Anthony oiled the blade so that when he pressed the button, all he would have to do is to flip his wrist and the knife opened just as quick if not quicker than if it had the spring. Many of his friends at school often questioned why he had removed the spring. He knew with the spring removed, the knife opened quicker and remain legal.

Anthony stayed in the fallout shelter for 30 minutes before exiting to see if he had lost the white Impala that was following him. Anthony exited the building, walked down a flight of stairs leading away from the entrance of the Post Office towards Keystone. He did not look around but turned right after getting to the bottom of the stairway in order to get to Keystone. He walked no more than 30 yards when the white Impala pulled to the curb near him and parked.

Driving the Impala was a small man, shorter than Anthony and weighing less than he. The man wore glasses and dressed in a nice suit. He reached across the seat of the car and rolled his window down. "Hey, son, I would be glad to give you a ride home if you want one. Hop on in and I'll give you a ride," The man said to Anthony in a nice way.

Anthony was repulsed by the thought of what his true intentions must be.

What Anthony did next surprised even him. He said, "Thanks, I don't mind if you do give me a ride. It's a long walk home." He opened the passenger side of the car and got into the front seat.

Anthony was surprised the man didn't drive off right away. Instead he started speaking, "Well, where are you going, son?"

"I'm going home from here. I walk home most everyday from school," Anthony answered wondering where the conversation would go.

"Well, where do you call home so I know where I have to take you?" The man asked Anthony in a tone similar to his previous question.

"I live in Keystone, about a mile and half from here," Anthony answered, not looking at the man's face.

The man answered Anthony in such a way that he got his full attention. "Yeah, I've met several boys from Keystone. That is a pretty tough neighborhood. You're not one of those tough boys that live there are you?" The man changed his tone of voice and became almost patronizing.

Anthony knew the tone and question meant more than the man was letting on. "Well, it depends on who you would talk to I guess. I've been around and have experienced my share of tough times," Anthony said, now looking directly at the guy sitting next to him. He had a smirk and smile after saying this.

The man asked point blank, a question Anthony was half-way expecting. "You wouldn't want to make an extra $30 would you?"

Anthony responded, "Yeah, I would like to make some money, but what do I have to do in order to get it?" He knew what the man would say but wanted to hear it directly.

The car was still parked at the curb. "Well, have you ever had sex before?" The man asked point blank.

Anthony responded simply and matter of factly, "Yeah, of course I have. So what do you want to know the answer to that for?"

"Well, have you ever had sex with another man or boy before?" The man asked, now looking at Anthony in such a calm manner that Anthony found it hard to believe the man was being so honest.

Anthony didn't give a direct or honest answer; instead he gave an answer that gave him an advantage. "Well not really, but it might be something I would be interested in if the situation were right."

"Well, what would make the situation right for you?" The man asked. He was up-front with Anthony in his intentions.

"Well, I don't know. What do you mean by having sex with another man?" Anthony asked, becoming more repulsed inside by his actions and questions.

"Well, you wouldn't have to do anything other than let me kiss you on your penis and let me rub it with my hand." The man smiled.

"Is that all you want?" Anthony asked.

"Yeah, that is it. Would you be willing to do that?" The man asked thinking he had Anthony where he wanted him.

Anthony took advantage of the situation to make some extra money. "Well, I would probably be willing to do that, but only if you gave me $40 dollars instead of $30, and I want my money in advance. You still have to take me home when you are done."

Anthony was surprised at the response of the man. "Well, those sound like fair terms to me. I'll be glad to meet your conditions." The man reached into his back pocket and pulled out his wallet, a black leather two-fold wallet. He reached in and pulled out two $20 dollar bills and gave them to Anthony.

Anthony responded, "Let me put the money in my back pocket, and then we can go wherever you want."

Anthony acted like he was reaching into his back pocket to put the money in. He turned his back towards the passenger door where the driver of the car could not see what he was doing. As he reached back behind his back, he grabbed the weighted stick. Then as quickly as he could, he swung the stick around and hit the man as hard as he could in the head knocking his glasses off. Anthony couldn't use a full swing due to the space limitations in the car, but he flipped his wrist to get the full force of the stick. Anthony didn't hear the man respond to being hit. He knew the first blow hit the man in the forehead, and the second hit him in the face. Both blows hit the man so fast and so hard he didn't have time to respond.

Anthony noticed blood on the man's face. He was not sure if the blood was from the blow to the face or the one to the forehead. As soon as he delivered the second blow, Anthony was out of the car and took off running towards Keystone. He ran as fast as he could, for about a half mile, before turning to see if the man was following him. He turned around and the Impala was nowhere to be seen, so he started walking.

Anthony, breathing hard, couldn't believe what he had done. He looked into his left hand and saw the $40, and in the right hand he saw he was still grasping his stick. Anthony took a different route home that day, one a little longer. He went through more of the housing project area. This way, if the man came looking for him, he would out run him, cutting through the yards. Anthony didn't have to worry though because he never saw the man again. He finally got home $40 richer and a little prouder.

******

It was a while since Anthony had spoken with Judith Johnson. She was Gerald's sister and had lived next door to Anthony in Keystone. He thought she was the nicest and prettiest girl in Keystone. She had her rowdy moments, but of all of the Johnson's, she was the one who tried to make something of herself. Anthony admired Judith for her effort to improve her life. She was married the previous summer to a guy Anthony didn't know very well. He was nice and took care of Judith. Anthony saw him on occasion and said "hi," but that was the extent of their relationship.

Judith and her husband moved a few miles outside of Keystone and now lived in the Snob Hill area. Snob Hill was on the eastern border of Keystone. Judith's husband worked at a factory near Keystone but it provided a decent living for the family. Judith became pregnant and had twins. She was living a normal life, in her early twenties, had a husband, two babies, a dog with puppies and a third child on the way. Anthony was amazed at how fast Judith grew up. It wasn't that long ago when every boy in town came by to try and date her. She always impressed Anthony with her friendliness. She saw the hurt and trouble Anthony got into and had with others, yet she took time to be nice and encouraging to him. She used to tell Anthony, "When you get a little older, you're cute enough that I might have to leave my husband for you." Anthony knew she was just kidding. He did wish he was a little older. Anthony hoped that if he ever married, he would marry a girl like Judith.

Anthony came home late one winter afternoon from school. Ordinarily, he got home from school and went to see Gerald. Gerald was not home, which was not unusual; it was unusual that no one was home. Anthony could not recall ever going to Gerald's house and finding no one at home. After waiting there for a little while, Anthony went to his house to see if anyone was there. He didn't like going home and was staying there less. He thought he might find something to eat or drink. He was surprised to see his mother there. It was early, and if he had known she was there he would not have gone home. As Anthony walked into the house his mother, Wanda, told him she wanted to talk. He should have known something was wrong because she was nice had not been drinking. "Hey, Anthony, how did school go today?" She asked.

"OK, I guess. Not much happened. I went to see Gerald, and there wasn't anybody at home. Do you know where any of them are at?" He asked, trying to change the subject.

"Yeah, I do. That is why I am home early. I thought you would want to know what's going on." Wanda began telling Anthony a story that was hard to believe or accept. "Anthony, last night Judith, her husband, and her children were killed in a fire. No one knows exactly what it was that started the fire, but their trailer caught fire and they were all trapped inside and died before the fire department got there. I thought you would want to know, so I came home early today hoping I would see you, and tell you what had happened. The Johnson family is at the funeral home now working out the arrangements for the funeral." Wanda was trying to have a sympathetic attitude.

Anthony was dazed. He didn't recall what happened after he heard the story. He didn't know if he went to his room, up into the woods and huffed glue, or walked around in the projects. He was shocked and hurt more than he let on.

Anthony recalled that spoke to Gerald a few days later about the death of his sister, Judith. It was cold the night of the fire. The fire department narrowed the cause of the fire down to one of two things. The fire had something to do with a water heater explosion or a kerosene heater. Anthony was sure they figured it out later but he didn't talk about it after the conversation with Gerald. The fire occurred when everyone was awake. All the evidence pointed to this. Judith was found in the back bedroom trying to get out of one of the windows, which was too small.

Anthony recalled the horror of these deaths for sometime, especially with the children being in the room with Judith. Due to his imagination, he was uncomfortable in trailers and vowed he would never live in one. He didn't even like spending the night in a trailer, which he did later on, but not by choice.

Later in life Anthony spent some time with friends and coworkers living in a trailer. He hated every night of it and recalled Judith's death on a daily basis. The fire killed everyone in a matter of minutes and Anthony knew that was a possibility when living in the trailer. While the Johnson family was comforted that the fire and pain lasted only for a few minutes, he never understood how this was any comfort.

Anthony missed Judith and put a lot of the blame for her death on God. It was another episode where God allowed bad things to happen to good people. As far as Anthony was concerned, Judith was one of the few in Keystone who deserved to get out and to make it, but she never had the chance for that.

* * * * * *

As the rest of the school year went by there were few other significant events. Anthony could not forget about the fire. He was preoccupied with a few other events that happened during the year, but they didn't seem that important. What was important was that he let his grades stay bad for the duration of the 8th grade. He thought that because his mother allowed him to go to summer school once, she would do it again. If she didn't let him go to summer school, he didn't care if he passed anyway.

Anthony knew his grades were not sufficient to allow him to pass. He had a high grade of a D- once. The D- was in deportment. Deportment was a grade on behavior, and Anthony wondered how he got the D- the one time he did. Every other grade, in every other subject for the year, including deportment, he got an F.

With grades like this, it was obvious what was going to happen. Summer school was as sure as the sun rising the next morning. The year took Anthony and some of his friends down the same road as the year before. It was somewhat different though. Anthony learned that neither he nor his friends, Anthony Humphrey or James Rogers, was going to summer school. Not going meant each of them would fail and have to repeat the 8th grade. While this was of little concern at the time, as summer moved on Anthony regretted not working harder and passing.

That year in 8th grade involved events Anthony never would forget. There was death, events at home and failing the 8th grade. It was a memorable and enjoyable year. Yet it involved heart break.

~ Chapter 16 ~

Failed Summer

Anthony didn't mind not going to summer school. It was a summer where the fun and difficulty caused him to forget about repeating the 8th grade. He was going to spend time with his friends in Keystone and his grandparents. Occasionally he saw friends from University School at various places around Johnson City. Some of them came to Keystone and sometimes he walked to their house or saw them on the campus of East Tennessee State University when he took walks there. He also spent time at The Recreation Center pool.

Anthony enjoyed spending time at the pool. He got to the point where he tried anything on the diving board. He did this on the one meter diving board and the three meter board. He did flips of all sorts, forwards and backwards, gainers and other specialty tricks. He got better at diving as the summer went by and enjoyed his time at the pool.

Anthony spent more time at home with Robert and Wanda. They continued to argue and fight despite the pregnancy. While there was hope that buying the house plus the pregnancy would help with the marital problems, it didn't occur. If anything the relationship was worse. Robert was working a new job in Bristol, Tennessee where he was making good money. Having money was a first for the family and Robert thought improving the material lives of the family would help. He bought several things for the children and Wanda to help them feel better. He also bought himself a new Harley Davidson motorcycle which he enjoyed working on and riding when the weather permitted.

As much as he tried to make things right at home with material gifts, he and Wanda still got on each others nerves. The severity of that relationship was never known until one evening when Anthony saw them get into a serious fight. Robert and Wanda had both been drinking even though Wanda was pregnant. The accusations of her seeking out relationships with other men came to a head. For most of the marriage Robert had been physical with Wanda and the children. He wasn't as violent during the pregnancy but on this night he couldn't take it anymore. It started with a back hand to Wanda's face. She cursed him, calling him a 'worthless son of a bitch,' at which time he hit her with his fist in the face. She collapsed crying. He kicked her in the head and stomach. Wanda tried to cover her body but it did little good. After 15 or 20 kicks he left her on the floor crying, her face bleeding, and she holding onto her stomach. Shortly thereafter Wanda went to the bathroom, crying. She was in there for several minutes. When she came out, still crying, she asked Robert to come to the bathroom. Anthony didn't realize what was going on at first but it wasn't long before he found out that his mother had lost the baby. The hope he and his sister had of a real family and of the violence ceasing was over. They developed an attitude towards Robert that wouldn't change. Robert tried to rekindle the relationships but he started the season off on the wrong foot.

One of the things Robert tried to do to make things right was purchase a black Labrador retriever puppy. They named him "General," after General George Patton. General was one of the first pets Anthony became attached to. He had had a pet mouse, hamster and at times a small cat or dog but the cats and dogs really belonged to his mother and were not pets he became attached to. Anthony worked with General and trained him in no time to sit, lay, and follow other basic and simple commands. He was impressed at how smart this dog was. General could retrieve or do about anything. General also loved the attention and friendship of his master.

The more problems between Robert and Wanda, the more Robert tried to get together with Wanda. One of the ways he did this was to take everyone to a movie. The movie Patton came out that year and the family went to see it. Patton and the movie Billy Jack were the only two movies Anthony remembered attending with his family.

Going to the movies with Robert and Wanda was uncomfortable for Anthony. He was aware of everything that went on between them. He noticed the flirtations Robert carried on while in the theater with Wanda. He was also still aware that Wanda was dating other men—a habit which had picked up again. Anthony saw and felt the hypocrisy between them. Robert and Wanda were spending more time apart from each other for various reasons. Robert was convinced Wanda was seeing other men on a regular basis, and he had a great deal of difficulty dealing with this. He was extremely possessive and jealous of her. Robert knew that before he and Wanda were married she had a habit of cheating. He still thought this should be something he shouldn't have to worry about. Being married meant something to him. Wanda's reasoning for her actions and behaviors was that she was tired of

Robert and the beatings she received from him. She was tired of the arguments she was getting into on a regular, almost daily basis. She was going to find love, someway, somehow, from someone. She didn't care if she had to go out with other men to find that love. In her mind she not only wanted the warm companionship, she needed it.

General and Anthony were together a lot. Anthony took General everywhere he went and he enjoyed his dog's company. While Anthony had friends, he never felt as if they were real friends. Most of the guys he hung out with would be considered friends, but he realized they were only friends when they got something from him that they wanted. Even at an early age, Anthony learned not to trust anyone because of the times he had been taken advantage of and abused. His preconception of others had been formed. He came to realize and believe the only thing others wanted from him were the things that helped them in some way. He never developed close friendships for various reasons and as far as he was concerned, they were good reasons. Anthony didn't have anyone he trusted that he could talk to about the problems he faced in life. General became a friend he loved in a special and unique way and a friend he shared his problems with. Sure he was a dog, but he was also a friend.

Anthony had the puppy for several months and General grew. He was waddling around like most puppies do. Anthony took him up to the woods with some of the guys to walk around and spend the day with him. On occasion, Anthony went to the woods without doing drugs. He enjoyed the scenery and the chance to walk around and spend time outside thinking about things. Anthony was in a unique situation; the woods were near downtown Johnson City, yet were deserted enough to get away from people and spend some time alone in nature.

On this day Anthony, Gerald Johnson and Vincent Patterson decided to go to the woods and walk around. The sky was navy blue and the leaves on the trees were bright green. The wind was blowing which made it seem cooler than usual for a mid-summer day. The temperature was in the low 80's, which for this time of year was cool for the mountains of East Tennessee. Anthony wore shorts, as he almost always did this time of year, and a T-shirt and Converse basketball shoes. Gerald and Vincent were dressed in the same manner as Anthony, wearing the typical things boys wear in the summer. Wherever the boys went, General waddled behind them trying to keep up. His ears and feet were large in regards to his body size and he was as clumsy as any puppy. General tried to gallop more than run. He tripped over his own paws which was funny. As he galloped, and jumped, he fell and kept wagging his tail with his tongue hanging out.

Anthony, Gerald and Vincent were walking around for a couple of hours playing with General when Vincent said, "Hey guys let's go up on the Backbone and look around."

Anthony responded. "It's O.K. with me. How about it, Gerald, do you want to go up?"

"Sounds fine to me, let's go." Gerald answered.

The Backbone was a section of woods with a tall ridge that encircled part of the area. To get up to the top one climbed a barren slate hill 200 feet high. It was steep and difficult to climb. The loose slate made it difficult to climb without falling and while wearing shorts this meant cuts on the legs. There was enough foot traffic up to the Backbone that a small path had formed up the ridge, but it was still difficult to maneuver.

At the top of the ridge on the Backbone was a narrow section of walkway only 5 to 10 feet wide. The ridge was worn down and mixed with dirt and slate. The opposite side of the Backbone dropped off 250 - 300 feet. The drop off was straight down with occasional sections slightly declined or sloped. It was a section some people tried to climb down, but the loose slate made it extremely difficult. Anthony had tried to climb down occasionally, but was only successful a few times at some of the easier sections. He would quit the descent and climb back up, not taking the chance of falling.

The boys walked towards the Backbone with General following close behind. On the way up the Backbone General barked for no apparent reason. The boys stopped and looked around trying to figure out what was causing him to bark. For all they knew, someone was around or another animal was close by. Anthony never heard General bark like this and didn't know what to think or do. The dog barked as if he knew something was going on around him. It barked, and then turned to look at the boys. He stopped barking just long enough to look at them. He turned towards the Backbone and barked again. Anthony noticed General's wagging tail and knew they were not in any kind of danger but something was definitely going on. General barked for a few minutes and turned and ran in the direction he was barking, towards, the Backbone.

The boys ran after General, and as they got closer to the top they realized what it was the dog was barking at. They heard the screams of two people yelling, "Help, Help!" Anthony, Gerald, and Vincent knew where the screams where coming from. General ran to the top of the upper ridge. They were not able to get up the hill as fast as General due to the slate and rock. At the top of the hill they saw General sitting on the ridge looking down the other, steeper side of the Backbone.

The boys looked over the steeper side of the Backbone and saw where the screams were coming from. On one of the narrow ledges below them were two boys. They were stuck on a small ledge and in a position where it looked like they were about to fall if they moved in any direction. The boys on the ledge made it down about 250 feet when they got stuck. Part of their problem was that they had climbed down a section that looked easy until they got down to where they were now at. When climbing down 200 - 300 feet the footing was looser from the slate and rock. The ledges here were also steeper. Anthony never saw anyone climb down this section.

When seeing the situation the boys were in Anthony, Gerald, and Vincent spoke back and forth with the boys on the ledge. Anthony yelled down, "Hey guys calm down. We've got some help up here. We'll get down to you just be patient."

The boys, who were at least 4 years younger than Anthony and his friends, yelled back up. "Thanks, man, but hurry! We feel like we're going to fall any minute now."

Anthony and Gerald started down to where the boys were stuck. The initial descent was easy but became more difficult as they got closer to the boys. Anthony asked Vincent to stay behind and hold on to General because he was afraid that with the dog's clumsiness, if he had tried to go down with he and Gerald, then General would have tripped and fallen down the ravine.

Anthony couldn't believe he was now climbing down the section he was. For some reason he was always afraid of heights and spiders. He looked over some ledges where it was obvious he was up pretty high and could get hurt if he were to fall. When he got more afraid he looked at the two boys stuck on the ledge and realized they needed help. He realized that without his and Gerald's help, the boys might not make it off of the Backbone safely.

"Hold on, guys, we're almost there." Gerald said. He was close enough that he didn't have to yell but could speak now in a calm reassuring tone.

"I think we're O.K. for now. We found a good hard rock to stand on." One answered back to Anthony and Gerald as they climbed down the ledge towards them.

As Anthony and Gerald got closer they saw a problem the boys were facing. Anthony and Gerald were on a ledge 5 feet straight above them. They could not figure out how the boys got into the position they were in but it was obvious they would have difficulty getting them out of it. The boys were on a small ledge just below Anthony and Gerald. It looked like the ledge was no wider than a foot and a half. There was a 20 or 25 foot drop off right below them. The drop off was straight down and then loose slate with a steep descent for another 100 feet. After the drop off it would be easy to walk away to safety if careful on the loose slate. The problem was, would one be willing to drop or jump down the 20 or 25 feet in order to exit that side of the Backbone.

Anthony knew that if they jumped they had to tuck and roll after hitting the ground to keep from getting hurt. This would be difficult with the loose slate at the end of the fall and the steep grade of the hill after they landed.

Anthony helped Gerald down to the ledge where the boys were standing. There was barely enough room for Gerald to stand on the ledge with the two boys. Anthony helped Gerald by taking his hand and holding on to his wrist. As Anthony lowered him down to the ledge he scraped his arm on the slate. Anthony lay on his belly using his left arm to lower Gerald.

"Hold on guys." Gerald said as he got down to where the boys were.

"What are you doing, man? This ledge is barely big enough to hold the two of us!" One of the guys questioned Gerald as he was lowered to the ledge by Anthony, whose arm was bleeding due to the slate.

"We're trying to get your tails out of here. Now shut up and help us out why don't you?" Gerald answered, upset over the question. Gerald finally got his footing and felt safe. Anthony held on to his arm and wrist until he had his balance.

"O.K. guys, what I'm going to do now is help one of you at a time. Anthony is going to get you by the wrist like he had me and pull you up to where he is at. You should be able to climb up to the top and then down from there. Are you ready?" Gerald asked the boys in a stern, yet reassuring way.

"Yeah, I think so," one of them answered. It was obvious to Anthony now, after seeing the two up close; they had been crying and were afraid. Anthony grabbed one of the boys' wrists as Gerald grabbed him by his feet and helped lift him to where Anthony was. As the boy was pulled up Anthony scraped his arm on the slate again. He could not have lifted the boy except for Gerald helping. Anthony's arm bled more. Anthony and Gerald got the first boy up without much trouble. After they got him up they got the second boy off the ledge.

As soon as they got up to Anthony they scurried up the ridge to safety. They thanked Anthony and Gerald as they took off up the ledge. They didn't see the two again. Once they got to the top of the ridge they took off running towards home. Anthony remembered the last one saying, "Thanks! You two saved our lives."

Anthony never knew if they saved their lives but he felt pretty good about what they did that day. Anthony and Gerald were in a strange predicament after helping the two off the ledge. Gerald could not get up the ledge where Anthony was without taking the chance of slipping and falling. He also weighed too much for Anthony to pull up. There was no way to get out of the predicament so he called up to Anthony, "Hey, come on down here. I'll help you down and we can jump down the ledge and say we climbed down this section of the Backbone."

"Shoot man, are you crazy? There ain't no way to get down that section and I sure as hell ain't going to jump from there. That has to be at least 20 to 25 feet until you hit the ground and then it's not an easy climb down from there, especially on this loose rock and all." Anthony said back.

"Oh come on man are you a chicken shit or what? Besides, can you see any other way down from here or up and out for that matter?" Gerald asked trying to convince Anthony to come down to where he was at.

"Oh damn it, man, why the hell not? I reckon if we're careful we don't have to worry about killing ourselves too much." Anthony answered as he turned over onto his belly and slid down to Gerald. Gerald helped Anthony balance himself as he got onto the small ledge. As Anthony turned around he realized the only way out was to jump. Being afraid of heights as he was, this wasn't going to be easy.

Anthony said, "Well, man, are you ready to die or not?"

Gerald said, "Well, I guess you're no chicken shit after all. On three we'll jump together, O.K.?"

Anthony answered hesitantly, "Sure, man. Let's fucking do it."

Gerald began counting, "1.....2.......3."

They both jumped from the ledge on 3. Anthony was surprised at how quick they hit the ground. As Gerald hit he rolled head over heals in a tucked position. As soon as Anthony hit he fell on his rear and slid down the hill. They were surprised at how steep the hill was after landing. They both slid and rolled 40 or 50 feet. They stopped rolling, got up and wiped the dust off. There was a dust cloud from stirring up so much dust.

The slate was unusually soft and padded their fall. Anthony and Gerald figured out why the slate was as loose as it was. The slate gathered where it did as it fell down the Backbone from erosion. It was also in a place where few people ever walked. This allowed the build-up and looseness which eased the jump.

Anthony and Gerald suffered minimal damage. Anthony was still bleeding from his arm. He also tore his pants in the rear and had scrapes on his butt from sliding on the slate. Gerald scraped his legs and arms and was bleeding slightly from them from rolling down the slate once he had hit the ground. Other than that, the boys were fine.

It surprised Anthony how calm they were after the jump. He thought he would be anxious due to his fear of heights and his jumping from where he did. He wasn't anxious though. He was calm and feeling pretty good except for the slight burning sensation he felt on his arm and rear from the slate.

"Great, jump, man!" Gerald yelled at Anthony in an excited, macho tone.

"Oh, yeah, man, we did it. Did you see that, Vincent?" Anthony yelled up to the top of the Backbone to Vincent Patterson who was sitting there with General watching the whole thing transpire.

"I can't believe you idiots did that. Damn, I can't believe you just jumped from where you did." Vincent yelled. "I'll meet you on the back side of the Backbone."

They took out on separate trails that eventually met. After the three boys and General got together on the back side of the Backbone they talked and looked at the injuries Anthony and Gerald received from jumping. Gerald spoke to Anthony about his puppy, General. "Damn Anthony, that's a good dog you have there. If he hadn't heard those kids screaming for help when he did we might not have made it to them in time to help them. They sure as hell didn't know what they were doing up there. They could've slipped, fallen, anything. If they would've done that they could've been hurt real bad or even killed. They sure weren't going to jump like we did; they didn't have the guts for that. You did a damn good job, General. Way to go," Gerald said, bending over to scratch General on the head.

Gerald started to get more excited as he had time to think about all that had just transpired. "Yeah, good job, General!" Anthony said bending over to pet his dog with Gerald. Anthony had a smile and a smirk, proud of what his dog had just done.

~ Chapter 17 ~

The Never Ending Year Part 1

The end of the summer came quickly. The start of the school year and restarting the 8th grade bothered Anthony more than he thought it would. He was not comfortable with meeting new people or going into a grade where everyone knew he had failed the year before. The only benefit of starting the year for Anthony was he had two friends in the same grade, Anthony Humphrey and James Rogers. He had a number of friends who were still at school that he would see on a regular basis.

There were friends Anthony kept in touch with like Matthew Swenson, Charles McGregor, Jeff Thomas and others. There were also a few girls he was close to going back to University School. Some of them were girls he had had a crush on at one time or other. Some looked down on him for failing the 8th grade and wouldn't have anything to do with him. It was clear to them that Anthony had nothing positive in line for his future. It was a waste of time to associate with him unless all they were looking for was a good time. Under the banner of having a good time, Anthony discovered girls who would have fun with him. He spent time with these girls and developed relationships with them.

On the first day of school the students went to their home rooms the first thing that morning and stayed a full day. They elected officers, got schedules, checked out text books, and other housekeeping duties. After the first day of school they reported to their home rooms each morning to check in and get information. Anthony felt better when learning he had the same home room as James Rogers and Anthony Humphrey.

The 8th grade only had one home room. It was nice because it gave Anthony a chance to sit and talk with someone that he already knew. He didn't have to worry about sitting next to someone he didn't know and developing a relationship with them. He was seldom in the mood to meet new people or to make new friends. He decided he wasn't going to allow himself to meet new people or make new friends.

Anthony realized how little control he had in developing friendships with other students. Whether he liked it or not he was involved in enough activities over the previous two years that he had developed a reputation he couldn't change without a lot of effort and time. Ultimately, he thought he didn't want to change.

The 8th grade students had heard of the exploits of Anthony Beechup, Anthony Humphrey, and James Rogers. They were at an age where they admired this type of behavior and they became rebellious and appreciated the rebels who carried on this behavior. As far as they were concerned Anthony Beechup, Anthony Humphrey and James Rogers were the coolest, baddest guys in their class and deserved the respect they gave them.

Each of the boys saw the appreciation the students showed them right away, on the first day of school. Anthony didn't know, nor did he care, that on the first day of school each class elected their class officers along with other class honors. Both Anthony Beechup and Anthony Humphrey were shocked that the class nominated them for a class honor. They were nominated by someone Anthony Beechup didn't know as Class Favorites for the 8th grade class. This was the most prestigious award a student could get.

Anthony Beechup didn't know most of the students in the class with him. He never took the time to be with them if he didn't have to. He was confident that he never gave them any reason to care or like anything about him. As the students voted on their class favorite, it wasn't even close between Anthony Beechup and Anthony Humphrey. He defeated Anthony Humphrey and some other boy he didn't know, hands down. Anthony didn't understand why the students voted for him. Anthony Humphrey was the brownnoser as far as he was concerned. He thought to himself, "Why would these people, most of them people I don't even know, be willing to vote for me for anything? There ain't no damned way I could be their class favorite. What in the world are their intentions?"

Anthony wondered about this over the years. He never accepted that the class intended and felt he was the favorite male student in the 8th grade. He didn't mind getting voted class favorite he just didn't understand it. He had to have his picture taken for the year book but that was no big deal. The photo part of the recognition was kind of fun. Anthony enjoyed the challenge of trying to show many of these students that he wasn't someone they should like too much. He was as mean to some of these students as he could be. It wasn't unusual to pick out a few of the more nerdy students and pick on them. This was a habit he picked up on when younger and that continued for some time. He often saw some of these students walk down the hall and he just hauled off and hit them for no reason. He also grabbed some of these students by the arm, throwing it behind their backs, and then lifting it up to put pressure on their arms and shoulders, hurting the person.

Anthony wanted to get the 8th grade students to get to the place where they never voted for him for anything again. If they voted for him for anything it would be because he influenced them to the point where they were like him. Where they would be running with him, causing trouble, and not being such "goody two shoes".

******

The new school year didn't change for Anthony. He was still doing the same things as the years before. He was also experiencing the same hardships at home. He had many of the same teachers and subjects as the year before which was embarrassing. Anthony had Mr. Jennings for math and algebra. Mr. Jennings was a war veteran who entertained his classes by telling war stories about Korea. He actually made the class fun for Anthony, and he enjoyed math because of him.

For Art, Anthony still had Mr. Testum, who was still angry at Anthony for the situation from the previous school year. He still didn't give Anthony a ride to school. Even though Mr. Testum felt this way towards him, Anthony's sister, Madeline got a ride to school each day. Anthony understood that what he had done the previous year was wrong. Anthony never blamed or got upset at Mr. Testum for not giving him a ride to school.

Mr. Ledbetter taught history and geography. Anthony enjoyed his classes because he cared about the students and enjoyed the subjects he taught. Anthony had fun in this class and he appreciated Mr. Ledbetter more as the year went on. This was due to the attention Mr. Ledbetter gave Anthony. He didn't know it then but he later discovered that Mr. Ledbetter coached his uncle Billy in sports and enjoyed him as a student. Anthony imagined Mr. Ledbetter would get along with any student and would make the effort to help them in their studies.

There were other teachers at University School Anthony felt O.K. about. Mrs. Lewis who taught English seemed to be a nice lady who took an interest in her students. She had a son named Randy at school. He was three years older than him and he was a jerk. Anthony was one of the few students who stood up to him, and Randy respected Anthony. Anthony never held this against Mrs. Lewis because he recognized the difference in attitudes between the two.

There was one teacher Anthony never knew what to think about. His name was Mr. Jackson. He taught science and chemistry on the third floor. He was extremely difficult and most students had a hard time with his classes. This was true for 7th grade up through the 12th grade. Mr. Jackson taught

8th graders college level materials. Anthony recalled a student teacher intern from East Tennessee State saying that his classes were harder than many of the college classes he had.

Mr. Jackson didn't put up with anything from the students. He was by far the hardest teacher on any level that Anthony ever had. As far as Mr. Jackson was concerned, if you were not in his class to learn, that was not his problem and he wouldn't put up with any student not there to learn. His students could pass, fail, or not come to class at their discretion. It was up to the student and he would not decide for the student. Coming to class was the first decision the student made regarding the betterment of their education. "If a student does not want to make that most basic decision in regards to their education, then everything else I could try to accomplish and give them in the area of knowledge would be useless." Mr. Jackson told students who came to class.

Mr. Jackson's attitude was O.K. with Anthony. He felt this way, though, because the class was at the end of the day. This meant he could choose to skip the last period and play basketball or on occasion go on home early. Anthony was making his decision based on his experience and he learned Mr. Jackson was true to his word.

Mr. Jackson had another side that Anthony appreciated. At the end of the day or during physical education class or basketball practice he came to the gym. Mr. Jackson was a tall man, at 6' 5". Anthony was sure he had played basketball. He was in his fifties and balding. What hair he had left was white and he always had a smirking smile.

Mr. Jackson would take a basketball to either half court or three quarters court and shoot either a set shot, jump shot or hook at the basket on the far end of the court. What surprised Anthony and others was that most of the time Mr. Jackson made the shot. He did this no matter which of the shots he took. Mr. Jackson kidded around with the students in the gym after doing this. This talent was surprising to the students having difficulty in his classes. Mr. Jackson was so hard in school and such an academician, yet at the end of the day he was fun to be around and enjoyed himself in a way the students only saw on the basketball court.

There were other things that didn't change during the school year. Occasionally Anthony spent the night with his grandparents who lived a few blocks from school. On most days he walked from Keystone. The walk wasn't enjoyable and he was resentful that he wasn't staying with his grandparents. If he lived in Keystone, he should've gone to school there with his friends. Anthony was not spending as much time with his friends from Keystone and he resented that.

He hoped things would change for him but they were getting worse. He never thought it possible, but Robert and Wanda were fighting more and the fights were more severe. It was obvious to Anthony and Madeline that Robert and Wanda's marriage would not last much longer. The only question was whether the marriage would end in divorce or in one of them killing or severely hurting the other. Anthony was glad he didn't have to stay at home as much and see the fighting. He spent most of the time either on the streets alone or with his friends. He seldom slept at home, although he went there on a regular basis to clean up and change clothes. He was relieved that neither Robert nor Wanda was at home much. They were doing other things, in other places, often with other people.

For Anthony the use of drugs, involvement in the occult and his sexual activities with others had not changed much. If anything his involvement in occult activities increased over the last year. He continued to ask himself questions, challenging God and the concepts of Christianity, especially those he saw practiced by professing Christians. He became more upset at the ways most Christians practiced their faith. There seemed to be a great deal of hypocrisy and that angered him into doing things to get Christians upset. He noticed that while many individuals were quick to point out that they were Christians, very few of them lived out their faith or showed any love towards him or the rest of his friends in Keystone.

Anthony read more about magic and practiced many of the concepts of magic and trickery. He checked out a large number of books from the libraries to get information on these subjects. He was surprised at the number of tricks used in order to do magic. He studied magic trying to find concepts which would work within the realms of Witchcraft and the Occult. He was disappointed because he perceived them as having power but in reality they had no power. All he learned from magic were ways to fool people, by use of psychological techniques and tricks.

Anthony studied people like Houdini, Thurston, Blackstone, Calvert, and other great magicians. He especially enjoyed studying about Houdini because of his belief in Spiritism, the Occult and the afterlife. Anthony found and read every book he could on Houdini. He picked up on many of Houdini's beliefs and found books on various subjects which were related to those beliefs. Over the next few years Anthony came to appreciate magic for its real intent and purpose, to entertain people of all ages as opposed to practicing the occult. He learned new tricks and techniques to entertain people but would not use the trickery for anything other than entertainment. The applause he received brought joy. Anthony enjoyed the attention he got and the smiles he saw on peoples' faces. It wasn't often that he pleased people, and magic was a way he brought pleasure to others while at the same time he received satisfaction from doing something others appreciated and enjoyed. It didn't take long for him to realize that this was the real purpose of magic: entertainment.

Anthony was involved in other techniques related to the supernatural. He studied methods of fortune telling. He learned these methods after stealing a pack of Tarot cards from the bookstore at East Tennessee State University. He started reading as much as possible on ways to tell someone's future while using Tarot cards. He believed in these types of fortune telling techniques and the supernatural intervention that allowed these things to work. For a while, he also believed this regarding magic.

Houdini's belief in Spiritism and his search for evidence of life after death contributed to this interest. Anthony knew that Houdini at one point recognized he had not found adequate evidence of life after death, but he still believed in it. This was proven at his death when he left in his will that he would attempt to return and communicate from the grave. Anthony knew that Houdini never accomplished this; he also knew 'The Great Houdini' must have thought it possible or he would have never promised it.

* * * * * * *

Anthony was at Charles McGregor's house with several of their friends. Anthony, Anthony Humphrey, Charles McGregor, Matthew Swensen, Edward Collins, James Rogers, and Jeff Thomas were all sitting in Charles' bedroom. Anthony Humphrey was looking through the pages of a Playboy magazine, James Rogers was looking at a Hustler magazine and the others started an unusual conversation. As usual Charles's bedroom was disgustingly nasty. There were magazines throughout the room, on the floor, on the bed, all over. The bed had the sheets and covers wadded up all over the bed without any evidence of being slept in. It looked as if it had not been made up in months nor had it had the sheets or covers cleaned or washed. Charles had a decoration in his room which Anthony and the others thought unusual. He had a life sized, standing stuffed elephant in one of the back corners of the room. It had dirty clothes thrown over it.

Anthony Beechup started up the conversation. "I'm tired of all the shit that's going on in my family and at school. I think I'm ready to just leave home and go on down south to live in Florida on one of the beaches or something. "

"Come on man, you don't have the guts to leave home or to run away. After all, you wouldn't know what to do or how to get away with it if you tried." Jeff Thomas said to Anthony.

"Like bull I don't. I could plan it and get away with it with no trouble. I know my mother would never know what is going on and it would take at least two days for her to find out I was missing. Come on Thomas, if it was planned right we could all run away and get away with it." Anthony responded.

James Rogers was becoming more interested in the conversation and decided to get in on it as had the rest of the boys. "Oh yeah, Anthony, I believe you could get away with it as well. I know if you decided to run away I would be right there with you and be ready to go myself. I'm tired of all of this crap at school, and at home as well."

James turned and started addressing the other boys. "I know Anthony and I would do it. It is all of you other guys that are pansies and wouldn't do it!" James said this in a mocking fashion to get them upset.

"This is bull; I would be up for it." Anthony Humphrey replied.

Edward Collins and the rest of the guys jumped into the conversation and challenged James, saying they would be up for running away and going south to Florida. Some of the guys put conditions on it, but everyone voiced that they would be willing to run away if the conditions and planning were right.

Anthony Beechup responded, "Well boys, if you are all dissatisfied why don't we make plans and do it. I could come up with what I think is the way to do it and we could then plan it and work out the kinks together. If you guys are all in agreement or have other ideas, we could either leave in my ideas, or add in the ideas you guys come up with to ensure we get away from all this shit and this town."

Anthony Humphrey jumped in and interrupted Anthony saying in an almost joking way. "Shoot, Beechup, if you want, go ahead and start making plans then we'll do it. Personally though, I don't think you have it in you to come up with a plan that would work, and even if you did you wouldn't have the guts to go through with it."

"You have a deal man, and I'll tell you what. Why don't we meet here again after school tomorrow and I'll tell you what I've worked out? If everybody is in agreement with it and they think my plan will work, well, then we will all make it a go. Is that O.K. with everybody?" Anthony asked. They all responded positively.

Anthony was sure he could work out a decent plan overnight for a successful run away. After some more brief discussion on the subject the boys went their separate ways and headed home. Anthony had a long walk home and had plenty of things to think about on his way home. The walk seemed shorter than usual.

******

The night passed quickly for Anthony. The next day had come and each of the boys was now in Charles's room. Anthony was surprised that all of the boys from the day before were there for the follow up meeting regarding setting up a plan to run away. He was sure some of the boys thought the plan was a joke, or that the plan would not be adequate. This was an area where he would prove them wrong by making sure he came up with a plan that would succeed.

"OK guys, this is the plan, or at least what I think we could do in order to succeed in our running away from here. First of all we need to set a date in the future, about a month down the road when we decide to leave. What I would suggest is we do it on a school day when our parents are at work and away from home. That way they wouldn't start looking for us right away. We would have a good head start of several hours. We would leave early in the morning; about the time we normally get to school or an hour or so earlier, to get as much of a head start as possible."

Edward Collins, who was listening intently, interrupted. "Yeah, but even with a head start they would still catch us, and besides, what would we do about food and stuff like that?"

Anthony answered Edward rather confidently. "I have all of that planned out. Just listen and let me get through with the plan I've come up with. After that if you have questions about what I've said or what we need to do in order to succeed, or anything else I have not covered, ask your questions then, O.K.?"

Anthony continued describing his plan, "First of all, in regards to the food issue, that is one reason we take a month to plan and organize this thing. If we all began bringing in a few containers of food to school each day our folks won't miss any thing. We have to be careful though to only bring in a few items a day when it comes to food or supplies from home. We can bring backpacks to school on the first day we decide to start our long range planning. Then if the run away is planned on, say, like a Friday, we would all have backpacks that are loaded down, and if anyone stops or questions us about what we are doing, well, then we simply say we are out of school on a long weekend, and that we are a scout troop on a weekend hike. That is one of the main benefits of us doing this thing together. It makes the story we tell people that we run into more believable. The key is that before we leave, we have to have our story straight and we have to leave on the particular day which we have decided, no matter what."

Anthony noticed several of the boys listening intently and nodding their heads in agreement as if they agreed with what he was saying. "Now in the area of being found by someone looking for us, even after a full day's head start: I don't know how many of you have ever been up past Elizabethton going towards the North Carolina state line before. I have, and I think there is a way we can do it and not get caught but we would have to be careful. First of all, we would only have to walk about 15 - 20 miles on that first day. This shouldn't take that much time, especially if we leave early in the morning. If we do leave on time we would be to where we're going before school let out and we would normally be home. It would be critical, though, that we stay off the roads as much as possible on the way to this location. We would only have to walk on the roads for minimal periods of time, and there are sections of the road we would have to walk alongside. We could stay over in the woods that run alongside the road and no one would ever see us unless we let them or wanted them to see us. We would only walk alongside the road when we didn't see any traffic in order to make up time we might lose. Just past Elizabethton is an old railroad tunnel which sits off on the right hand side of the road about a quarter of a mile up in the woods. It is an old tunnel and is deserted. There is an old logging road or road that was traveled by cars years ago that is covered with trees, vines, stuff like that. Anyway it is so well hidden that hardly anyone knows about it. This is where we would succeed. We stay in the tunnel for about a week to get the focus of the search for us away from the area and on some place else. This would be easy to do; especially if we left notes or something like that that stated we were heading to California. By that time I think things would start to calm down and people wouldn't be searching as much in this area."

Anthony Humphrey realized that Anthony Beechup came up with a better plan than he thought he would, but he hoped to persuade the boys to not listen to Anthony Beechup. "Yeah, Beechup, but if that tunnel sits off the road like you say it does, then I'm sure there are bums or other people who go there on occasion. What happens if someone comes in on us?"

Anthony answered with confidence; he had thought of that particular issue in his planning stage. "I have thought about that as well, Anthony. You see I am sure there is one of us in this room who has access to a gun, a pistol, or something that is easily hidden. We take it with us and if we have to, we show others that we are not afraid to use it. That means that if we are put in the situation where we have to shoot someone then that is what we do."

"Shoot, yeah, man, I can get my dad's thirty-eight with no trouble. I know I could also get a couple of boxes of shells to take with us," James Rogers responded, excited because he saw the plan Anthony had devised could actually work.

Anthony finished telling his plan, "What we do then is that after about a week in the woods and the tunnel, we take the old logging road up to North Carolina. This will take a couple of days because it is after all an old road. But once we get into North Carolina we can hop trains down to Florida without too much trouble. All we need is a compass, a rail road track map for the trains to make sure we are going in the right direction and a topographical map of the region for the woods. That way we stay away from the roads so we are not seen by anyone and we get to Florida rather quickly. I believe we could be in Florida within three weeks. Once there, we would have to figure out ways to get money to live on. I believe there are enough people in Florida that we could easily get lost. I also believe that if we are smart about it, we can get odd jobs without much trouble. If we have things like fishing poles and stuff like that we can catch food and get by. Once we leave we could be in Florida in three weeks. That is figuring the time we are going to be camping in the tunnel in Elizabethton, hiking up to North Carolina on the old logging trail, catching trains south and everything. So now what do you guys think of the plan?"

Everyone sat there for a few minutes thinking about the plans Anthony had made. Anthony could see that some of them were not going to be in on the run away. This was obvious from some of the questions and statements they were making, like Charles McGregor, who just came out and said so. "Yeah, guys, it sounds like a great plan and all but I don't really want to do it. I get along with my mom and all and am doing O.K. in school. I don't really have a reason to leave. I'll be glad to help out in any way I can, though. You can use my house and basement to store all of the stuff that you need to bring in over the next month. After all, who would ever think to look for stuff like that around here anyway?"

Anthony was disappointed that Charles didn't want to be a part of the group, but he was also glad that Charles was willing to help out. Anthony also understood the situation about him not wanting to leave home. He understood because things were pretty good for Charles. "Shoot man, that's fine Charles, besides I understand. Heck, if you are willing to help like that, then that would be a major help to those of us who decide to leave." Anthony responded in an honest way truly wishing that Charles wanted to go.

Over the next month the boys worked out the details of who did what. Anthony was surprised the other boys were so willing to accept his plan with hardly any revisions. He was also surprised at how willing they were to take part in the plan and be involved over the long month ahead of them. They started making arrangements to run away the next month.

They started the plan the next day. The first thing each boy brought to Charles's house was an empty back pack and canteens to carry food, staples, and water. They started carrying in the foods the next day to start filling the backpacks up. Some of them were responsible for foam for bedding while others brought canned food, matches or other important items needed for the three week journey. James brought the gun and shells on the last day to keep from being found out while Edward and Anthony Beechup brought in a variety of knives, fishing line, and equipment. Anthony Humphrey also brought fishing line and a couple of small break apart fishing poles and other items. Each of the boys started saving their money from work, allowances, lunch or however they could over the next month.

Anthony was surprised how quickly things began to gather and work out for the trip. They packed each back pack with the things needed for each boy. Each boy was expected to carry their own pack in order for the group to succeed. The boys spent from 30 minutes to one hour after school each day at Charles' house making the arrangements needed for the journey. Anthony was surprised how each boy stuck it out. As far as Anthony knew, they didn't discuss what was going on with anyone other than those involved in the planning for the run away.

The month went by quickly. The time was set for them to run away and leave Johnson City for Florida. It didn't seem like it took any time for the month to pass. For most of the boys it was the fastest month they had experienced up to this point of their lives. The day finally came for them to leave and they were ready for the trip they had planned so hard for. All they had to do was go to bed, carry in a few more items the next morning, and they would be on their way to Florida.

~ Chapter 18 ~

Caught

Anthony had a rough night. He had had little sleep and was restless throughout the night. He thought all night about what lay ahead of him the next day. He decided to sleep at home in his bed, which was rare. He was hoping for a good night's sleep in preparation for the long walk he would be taking. The decision to sleep at home didn't help in getting any rest.

Anthony got up the next morning shortly before Wanda went to work. Robert was not at home due to the arguments he and Wanda had been having. It was around 5:30 a.m. when Wanda left for work. Anthony was wide awake. He was up an hour earlier than usual. This allowed him to get to Charles McGregor's house an hour before school started. Getting to Charles's house early would give him and the other boys an hour's head start. Anthony could tell this was going to be a rough morning. One thing that led him to this conclusion was the weather. It was raining pretty hard and he knew the walk to school would be more difficult due to the rain. Nonetheless he got up, determined to follow through with the plans for the journey.

After cleaning up Anthony gathered a few more items to take on his journey. He got a full bottle of rum and another box of bullets for James' 38 caliber hand gun. He also stole an envelope of money Wanda hid for emergencies. Anthony walked to Charles McGregor's house, on time and on schedule. The walk went quickly for Anthony due to him day dreaming about what lay ahead of him on his journey to Florida. He thought about his future in Florida. He was confident his plan would work with no trouble. He was also confident that once there, he would be happy for the first time in his life. Before leaving the house, Anthony left a note for his mother and sister. He said the few things he wanted. The note would throw off the search which would eventually take place for him and the other boys. The note read:

Dear Mama and Sissy,

I have decided to leave home for good. I am tired of living here and am going out west to live in California. I believe I can get a job there without too much trouble and get by O.K. I am not mad at either one of you and don't want you to get upset at me. Mama, Sissy doesn't know anything about me doing this so please don't get upset at her for what I am doing. I will call once I get to California to let you know I am O.K. Take care and I will talk to you later. ~ Anthony

Anthony made sure he let his mother know that Madeline had nothing to do with him running away. He left the message to distract the search that would happen. He felt he was successful with the note he left.

As Anthony left the house he shed a few tears concerning leaving his sister and his dog General. He would miss them and felt bad about leaving his sister in a situation where she would have a tough time at home with Robert and Wanda. He also cursed God for putting him in the situation he was in. He felt it was the situation God put him in which forced him to make the decision to run away.

Anthony was angry at God for putting him with Wanda and Robert. God took two fathers away before Robert and gave Anthony a step-father he couldn't stand, like, or love. Robert beat and abused Wanda, Madeline and him on a regular basis. God put him in a situation where he was sexually abused by his mother and other family members. He knew this led to his perversion and sexual abuse of others at times. His tears were mostly in anger, except for the love he had for his sister.

Anthony didn't have a rain coat to wear, so he was soaking wet in no time due to the rain. He placed a paper sack, used to carry some items in, over his head, but after getting wet the sack was no good. He took the items out of the sack and put them in his pants and jacket pockets to keep them from getting wet. After walking for an hour to Charles's house Anthony had a glimmer of hope regarding the weather. It quit raining and the clouds begin to break up. The sun was ready to come out and the clouds were going away. Anthony arrived at Charles' house thinking the others would already be there. They didn't have as far to travel as Anthony. Most of them were able to get an early ride to school with family who went to school or work early. This should've enabled them to get there before he did. Anthony arrived at Charles's before the others. Charles was up and had the backpacks out. Anthony was grateful that Charles did this but was still upset that Charles was not going on the trip with the guys. Anthony was at the house for 10 minutes when James Rogers arrived. He was in the bathroom changing into dry clothes when he noticed James working on his backpack in Charles's bedroom.

Anthony told James in an anxious tone. "All right, man. You're here, Rogers. Are you ready to take the trip of a lifetime?"

"Shoot, yeah, I'm ready, how about you?" James answered.

"You're darned right I'm ready. I'm ready to get the hell away from here and today is the day I do that. By the way, Charles, are any of the other guys here yet?" Anthony asked.

Charles responded. "No, not yet, I got a call from Edward and Humphrey who was asking if everything was a go for today since it was raining…" Charles didn't have time to finish his statement before Anthony angrily jumped in. "What the hell do you mean since it was raining? We fucking talked about this and said everything was a go no matter what happened or was going on today. Those stinking pussies, I should have known Humphrey would end up being be a shit head, but I never figured Edward Collins would back out. I'll be a son of a bitch, those no good mama's boys."

Anthony was getting more angry, "What about the punks? Where are they at?" he asked.

Charles answered. "I haven't heard from them yet. They might be thinking the same thing about the rain."

"I'll be a son of a bitch. Here we are, supposed to leave in ten minutes and those little bastards aren't here yet. Well, as far as I'm concerned we'll leave without the babies if they're not here when we are supposed to leave. How about it, James, how do you feel about it if we do that?" He asked James, making it clear what he wanted.

"Leave the chicken shits is what I say." James answered confidently, agreeing with Anthony.

Anthony, James, and Charles waited 10 minutes before deciding what to do next. Anthony and James decided to go ahead and leave on time and alone. They couldn't afford to wait or deviate from their plan. This would hinder their chances of success. Anthony spoke to Charles before leaving and said, "Thanks for all the help man. If you hadn't helped us out we would've never been able to pull this thing off. I'll give you a call in about three weeks to let you know where we are at. Just make sure you don't let anybody know where we are."

"You're welcome man. If things start messing up around here for me I'll make sure I come on down. Just make sure you let me know where you are." Charles responded.

Anthony made one last comment about the others who were supposed to take the trip before shaking hands and saying goodbye to Charles. "Man, if any of those other guys come around or decide they want to go with us, tell them that James and I will be following the plans we worked on and set up. They will have to leave out right away though; I would say they have to leave within the next two days if they want to make it. They have a map and plan of the route we're taking and of everything else so they should be able to find us without too much trouble. Thanks again, man, and take care." With this,

Anthony and James shook Charles's hand, gave him a hug and took off on their journey.

******

Anthony and James left on their journey. It was 30 minutes before day light and they felt this would help them make good time. It would help get away from the East Tennessee State University area where someone they knew might see them.

Anthony and James traveled the back roads going northeast from East Tennessee State University towards Elizabethton. This route took them towards Elizabethton, past the Milligan community which was 4 miles away and then through the Happy Valley community which was another 4 miles from there. After getting past Happy Valley it was another 2 or 3 miles until Elizabethton, and then another 5 miles to their destination from there.

After Elizabethton, Anthony felt it would be clear going. They would get on the old logging roads and not be seen by anyone. Even if someone knew where to look, Anthony and James could take off into the mountains and woods and be able to get away. Getting to Elizabethton would be critical to their success. It would be risky up until that point for the two. They had to be careful, staying off the roads when possible to reduce their chances of being seen by people who may have questions for them regarding being out of school.

* * * * * *

Anthony and James stayed on schedule most of the morning. They kept an up tempo pace the first few miles to get as far away from school as quickly as possible. They both wanted to get as far away as they could to reduce their chances of being seen by anyone going to school. This was a critical part of the journey. They walked on the roads leading to the outskirts of Johnson City. They were hot and sticky from the sweat as a result of the high humidity from the morning rain.

When they were on or near roads, their chances of being caught increased, but they were on a section of their trip where they couldn't help being on a main road. There was a section past the Milligan community where they could get back in the woods but they were not there yet. They could stay hidden from the road but this was on the other side of Happy Valley. They could get into the woods for a couple of miles after Happy Valley before coming out again 2 miles before Elizabethton. Once coming out here, Anthony knew the boys would be home free. They would walk a couple of miles in the out skirts of Elizabethton where it would be easy to hide from anyone looking for them. After leaving Elizabethton, Anthony knew that once they were on the old logging road they were good to go.

Anthony talked to James about the journey ahead of them as they started out. They each carried a large backpack loaded down with supplies and a fanny pack. They were heavier than anticipated due to the extra weight of carrying extra supplies that were supposed to be divided among the ones who didn't show up. They also carried a rolled up piece of foam to be used for bedding. They had to take a break almost hourly due to the weight they were carrying after their initial stop.

Anthony and James walked for two and a half hours before taking their first break. They were on the outside of the Milligan community. They went into the woods, away from the road to take the break. They took these breaks like this to keep from being seen by passing traffic. They spoke to each other while in the woods about the trip. They realized school had started and wondered if anyone noticed them not being at school, or if the students and teachers thought it was just a coincidence they were both out. Neither of them was convinced they would think it was just a coincidence. Anthony couldn't recall the times he was out of school and no one from school checked to see why he was absent. The scenario was the same for James. This was one of the reasons they were convinced they would get away with their plan.

Since Anthony and James were ahead of schedule they took a longer break than normal. After spending 30 minutes resting, they decided to start walking towards Elizabethton. After leaving the woods they went back to the road. They had been walking for 30 minutes when a car drove by. After passing them the driver pulled over onto the side of the road and waited for the boys to get to him. He started talking to the boys. He asked them, "Hey guys, I'm going down the road from here for a few miles. If you need a lift I would be glad to give you one. Do you want a ride?"

Anthony looked at James and James looked back. They nodded their heads in agreement. "Yes sir, we would appreciate a ride for a little ways." James replied.

Anthony and James put their things in the man's trunk as he opened it up for them. They were not afraid of this man. He was older, had white hair and looked like someone's grandfather. Anthony and James were sure he probably was someone's grandfather. Anthony was carrying a boot knife and James had a loaded 38 in the front of his pants tucked and hidden between his pants and shirt. Anthony started the conversation, "We sure do thank you for giving us a ride down the road for a little ways, sir. It will help us make up some time. We were not supposed to get a ride with anyone but I don't think there will be any trouble."

"What do you mean you weren't supposed to get a ride?" The man asked.

"Well, we are both in a Boy Scout troop and we have an over night camp out this evening at our camp leader's house. So we were hiking to his house for the camp-out tonight. " Anthony responded confidently.

"That sounds like a lot of fun but why were you not supposed to get a ride in a car?" The man asked.

"Well our mother couldn't take us today because she was working and said we could walk on over to our scout leader's house who's also working today. Well, our scout leader's wife doesn't drive and she stays at home, so we were going to just walk to their house and stay with her so we can ride up to the campout with our leader tonight. Our mom said it was O.K. to walk up there to their house but we had better not get a ride with anyone." Anthony said this as if he had rehearsed it many times.

Anthony's comments sounded very natural. He gave no reason for the man to doubt the story. He was concerned to some extent, as was James as to whether the story would fly or not. It didn't take long to find out the answer.

"Well, I won't tell your mom if you don't." The man said as he laughed. "By the way why aren't you boys in school today?"

James answered, "We go to a private school and were out today because it's a teacher's work day. That's why we couldn't get a ride; all of our relatives are working today."

The man asked, "What about your dad? Couldn't he have given you a ride?"

Anthony and James had the perfect answer. James answered because he looked younger than Anthony and looked sadder when answering the question. "Well not really. We don't see our dad too much anymore. Our mom and dad got a divorce a couple of years ago."

The man responded, "I hate to hear that. There are too many parents nowadays who get divorced when there are children involved. Families just don't stay together like they should." The man pulled over into the parking lot of a lumber company. "Well, this is where I stop, boys. I have to get a few things here and take them back home where I am doing some work in the basement. It sure has been nice talking to you two and I hope you have a good campout with your Boy Scout troop."

Anthony and James got their backpacks out of the trunk and Anthony said. "Thanks a lot, sir, for the ride. We sure do appreciate it."

"You're more than welcome and I hope you have a good day." The man said as he waved good-bye to the boys.

The boys started walking down the road again towards Elizabethton. They talked about how nice the man was but they also talked about how good it was their story worked out. It was obvious to them the man believed every word. This gave them more confidence about the potential of success for their trip.

Anthony and James knew the story was good enough because they experienced this event and they now had more confidence. If the story was this good it was possible for them to do some hitch-hiking in order to make up time on their trip. They were confident that no one from the school would notice they were gone or know anything until after 4 o'clock about their running away. The boys started taking a few more risks by doing some hitch-hiking.

They were one mile past the Happy Valley community and tried to do some hitch-hiking but didn't have any success. They were feeling comfortable because they were making up time by walking on the road as opposed to walking in the woods alongside the road. They only had another mile and a half to go, and they were home free; they would make it to their destination without getting caught.

It was two o'clock and Anthony and James realized that if they had not been caught by now their feelings about no one looking for them was accurate. They stopped at a bridge over a creek to take a break. They were sitting down on the right hand side of the road for five minute when James yelled out. "Oh, crap, man there just went my uncle in his Volkswagen Bug."

Anthony responded. "Come on man, you're kidding!"

"No man I'm serious, he just went by us heading towards Elizabethton." James replied.

Anthony looked up towards the direction James pointed out. Sure enough Anthony saw a bright yellow Volkswagen Beetle turning around a few hundred yards down the road.

"Damn it, James, that car is turning around up there." Anthony looked around to see if James could find a place to hide. Over to his right was an empty field a few hundred yards long. Anthony looked to his left and it was the same scenario. James could not have run and hid without being seen. Neither of them could run away while carrying the backpacks. Anthony realized James could hide under the bridge. "Quick James, run under the bridge and hide down there. If they stop I'll tell them I am here by myself and see if they believe me."

James crawled down the hill to hide under the bridge. It was only a minute or so before the Volkswagen pulled up beside Anthony who was still sitting on the side of the bank. Anthony saw there were two people in the car. As they got out of the car Anthony could tell it was two young men in their early twenties. The person driving the car spoke to Anthony immediately. "All right man, where is James at?"

The man walked towards Anthony and was almost to him. Anthony answered his question, "I don't know what you're talking about, man. I was just taking a hike and am sitting here taking a break."

"Give me a break, like you don't know who or where he is. We just drove by and saw someone else sitting on the bank with you that looked like my nephew." The man spoke in a hateful tone to Anthony.

"Hey, man, I'm telling you the truth. I don't know anybody named James." Anthony responded in a confident tone.

"Come on boy. We know about what's going on. There are people looking all over for you two. We know about your plan." As the man said this he pointed to the other individual with him to go look under the bridge. Shortly thereafter he yelled back from under the bridge. "He's down here Charley. He's hiding under this bridge."

"All right James get your ass up here right now." His friend on the bank yelled.

James walked out from under the bridge with the man who had found him. As James walked out the guy with Anthony yelled. "What in the world did you two think you were doing running away? Your parents have the police and everybody else in the family looking for you. If it wasn't for some kid at school telling Mr. Alexander what was going on with you two you would have had all kinds of people upset and ticked off at you. Shoot, they are already upset and scared to death that no one was going to find you."

James didn't respond as his uncle spoke, "Get the hell in the car, the both of you. We are taking you back to school to see Mr. Alexander and calling your parents to let them know you're safe."

Anthony and James got their backpacks and put them in the front of the Volkswagen Bug's trunk. The guys had Anthony and James get in the back seat. They didn't say a word until James' uncle pulled to the front lot at the school and parked. All Anthony could think was that their plan didn't work. He was upset he had to go home and face his mother. Would this entail another beating for him? Anthony knew if he was lucky, he would be placed in a foster home or turned over to his grandparents. He was angry that one of his friends talked to someone to turn them in.

Anthony wanted to know the details of who it was but he never did find out. It was probably best he didn't know. If he had he may have killed them for breaking his confidence and ruining his future. He also thought about James. It was obvious that James' family cared about him. After all, they sent out people to look for him.

******

Mr. Alexander was the first one to the Volkswagen as it pulled up to the school. Anthony and James saw him running out the front door. Anthony thought it kind of funny to see Mr. Alexander run. He was short and the little tuft of hair on the top of his head bobbed up and down with each step. He waddled more than ran. Yet, there he was running to the car. It was obvious to Anthony and James that he cared about them. The boys Anthony and James were riding with didn't stop to call anyone so there was no way Mr. Alexander could have known that Anthony and James were in the car. It was obvious to Anthony though, Mr. Alexander knew what the car was there for. Mr. Alexander was heavily involved in the coordination of the search. As soon as Anthony and James got out of the car, the first words out of his mouth was, "Thank God you're both safe. I've been worried to death about the two of you." He said this in a caring non-judgmental tone which was reassuring to Anthony.

Anthony knew Mr. Alexander was a good man and he liked him very much. In many ways he was a hero because of the things he did and the way he treated Anthony with respect. Mr. Alexander showed a caring attitude to Anthony, not judging him, or letting himself compare him to his uncle Billy, like so many others had done. To Anthony, he was the first person he could look up to and respect. He was an example on how one should care for and treat others.

Anthony didn't realize this now but as he got older, he understood the role Mr. Alexander played. He was a positive male role model. Mr. Alexander put his arms around the boys' necks and shoulders and walked them to his office with one arm around each. He had his arm around the boys in a friendly, loving way to let them know they were cared for. Mr. Alexander led the boys into his office. He had them sit down in two chairs at the front of his desk as he also took a seat behind the desk. He sat there for what seemed like a couple of minutes of silence before anything was said.

Mr. Alexander put his chin in the palms of his hands with his elbows on the desk; he rested looked at the boys, and shook his head no. He was the first one to break the silence. "Boys, do you know how many people have been looking for you because they care for and love you?"

Anthony and James didn't answer other than to shake their heads no.

"Well, James, almost everyone in your family is out looking, and Anthony you have your mother and grandparents scared to death. Boys there are people out there who love and care for the two of you very much."

As Mr. Alexander spoke Anthony listened to what he said. What Mr. Alexander had said could be put another way. "Boys your folks care for you and love you. James, everyone is out looking for you because they love you. Anthony your family loves you and is worried about you but they don't have the time to really be out looking for you." This momentarily helped Anthony forget about finding out who turned them in. It was an unfortunate reminder of why he wanted to run away in the first place. This was another example on how his family really didn't care for him. He was sure his grandparents Velma and Oscar cared, but he was sure his mother either didn't care or didn't know how to care. Either one of these reasons was unacceptable. He tried to do something about his situation but that effort was spoiled by getting caught.

This was another area where Anthony put the blame on God and Christians. He was convinced God knew what he was like, not what people thought of him. Anthony believed it was this reason God allowed things to happen to him. He was convinced and he wouldn't let God win the battle between them.

As Mr. Alexander was talking to Anthony and James, he had the two who drove the Volkswagen go and call Anthony and James' parents, the police department and the others involved in looking for them. It took them 30 minutes to make the calls and while they were doing this Anthony and James sat in Mr. Alexander's office listening to him more than talking with him. The longer Mr. Alexander sat in the office with the boys, the more he let his anger show for what they had done. Anthony wasn't sure if it was anger or hurt. He chose to believe it was more hurt. Mr. Alexander seldom raised his voice, nor did he give any inclination that he was going to discipline them.

In his concern, Mr. Alexander wanted to help the boys understand they could have been hurt or gotten into serious trouble. Mr. Alexander brought up various issues and asked questions. "Boys, what you did today was dangerous. I don't know how you would have ever gotten to where you were going. Did you ever stop to think about that?"

They sat there for a few seconds not saying a word when the question was answered for them. In came one of James' relatives from the Volkswagen carrying the maps Anthony and James had with them. They included railroad track maps, and topographical land maps of the region and terrain. There was also a compass and a few survival tools. Upon entering the office, James' relative stated, "We are cleaning this stuff out of the car. James, are these things yours or the other guy's?"

Mr. Alexander asked him to bring the rest of the items in and to set them in the corner of the office. He told him the boys could sort it out later. To Anthony and James it was funny Mr. Alexander's question was answered so appropriately. They didn't say a word and it was obvious that Mr. Alexander had the question answered by what he had seen. That was evident from the next question he asked in a caring way, "O.K., boys, I can see that you made plans in that regard as far as the maps and all. But how would you have slept? What would you have slept on? Don't you think you would have gotten tired from sleeping on the ground?"

As soon as he finished asking the question, James relatives walked in carrying the padding which James and Anthony had carried with them for bedding. Mr. Alexander's reply was again filled with surprise. "Well it is clear to see that you had that one taken care of, too. But boys, you would have gotten hungry after a while. There is hardly any way you would have been able to get where you were going without food. Did you stop to think about how you would eat?"

Just like clock work, as soon as Mr. Alexander asked the question, in walked the two guys carrying the backpacks loaded with food. They walked in not knowing what Mr. Alexander had just asked. The one who Anthony thought was James' uncle said, "Darn boys, how much food did you two have? It feels like you have enough food here to feed yourselves for a month or more."

Mr. Alexander's response was short and made in such a way that he knew he had not been able to make any points to either of the boys because they had covered their bases. "Thanks boys for bringing their things in. Now is there anything else of theirs in the car?"

The boys responded. "No sir, there isn't anything else."

"Well thanks for bringing their things in. Now if you don't mind I would like to spend a few minutes with them alone please. I would appreciate our being left alone so I can talk to them about a few more things. Is that O.K.?" His question was direct, and in a straight forward tone which plainly insinuated to James' relatives that he wanted them to leave his office.

They responded back to Mr. Alexander showing they were not upset with the question. "Yes sir. We wanted to get something to eat anyway, by the way Mr. Alexander; James' parents are coming to pick him up. We called Anthony's mother and she said he should walk on home like he normally does."

"Thanks again," Mr. Alexander said as they walked out of the room.

"Sure Mr. Alexander, no problem." This would be the last Anthony ever saw of these two.

Anthony, James and Mr. Alexander sat in the office for a few more minutes without saying anything. Mr. Alexander thought that he had a point which would nail the boys and make them think about their attempt to run away. He asked the question, while at the same time reaffirming that they had made good plans for their run away. "O.K. boys, it is obvious that you made plans for everything. I'll bet there is one area though you didn't think of. Did you ever stop to think about what would have happened if someone came up to you to either try and assault you or to beat you up?"

Anthony and James had been sitting in the office for close to an hour, not saying a word other than an occasional "Yes, sir." or "No, sir." Mr. Alexander did most of the talking and the boys sat there letting their supplies do the talking for the questions he asked. When Mr. Alexander asked the last question, James responded. He simply stood up, reached for the front of his shirt, lifting it, to expose the 38 caliber hand gun he was carrying. He then told Mr. Alexander as he pulled out the gun, "We would've shot his ass."

Mr. Alexander looked at the gun and the two boys in astonishment. "Is that thing loaded?" He asked.

"Yes Sir." James replied. "We also have another couple of boxes of shells for it and another gun and knives we have with us."

Anthony sat there trying to keep from laughing when Mr. Alexander responded. "Well, I guess you boys had this thing planned out pretty well after all. But it still doesn't change the fact that there are people who care for you and miss you."

They all sat there for a few more minutes talking about various things but none of them regarding the boys' attempt to run away. Mr. Alexander talked about basketball and a number of other things with them. It was his ways of letting by- gones being by-gones and letting the boys know he wouldn't think any less of them. He cared for them and had a unique way of communicating that concern and care.

James' father came and picked him up from school. His father discussed a few things with Mr. Alexander regarding James' attempt to run away. It was obvious to Anthony; James was due for some type of punishment when he got home. It was also obvious that James' father loved James. He left with James telling Mr. Alexander. "Well, I'll assure you of one thing Mr. Alexander. There are going to be some changes in our household for James."

As they left Anthony realized that James' dad didn't speak to him or recognize him while he was in the office. Anthony wondered why this was and believed James father put much of the blame of his son's behavior and actions on Anthony. Anthony wasn't all together sure this wasn't true.

Mr. Alexander decided to take Anthony home after James left. He was concerned that Anthony's mother was not willing to pick him up from school. While Anthony didn't show it, Mr. Alexander felt he shouldn't be alone due to everything that was going on. He didn't understand why Wanda had requested he go on ahead and walk home. Mr. Alexander wanted to give Anthony a ride home.

Anthony was amazed and pleased that Mr. Alexander didn't bring up the issue of running away on the ride home. They talked about a number of things. Mr. Alexander was not aware how far Anthony walked to school. He was surprised Anthony lived as far away as he did and walked to and from school each day.

Anthony was concerned about what Mr. Alexander would say or think once he saw where he lived. He had been to Mr. Alexander's house a number of times and he knew that he lived in a nice home and neighborhood. Anthony was sure that he was one of the poorest students at University School and he knew he lived in the worst neighborhood in a small house. There likely wasn't a student at University School who came close to living in a neighborhood and environment like the one Anthony did.

The drive to Anthony's house took less than thirty minutes. Anthony was afraid his mother would either cuss him out or hit him in front of Mr. Alexander. When Mr. Alexander pulled up to the side of the house, Wanda was at the car to see Mr. Alexander and Anthony almost immediately. Anthony was surprised at her reaction when he got out of the car. "Thank God you're safe. I was worried to death about you. Why would you go and do something like what you did?" Wanda asked while giving Anthony a hug.

Anthony didn't answer the question other than to shrug his shoulders. He couldn't figure out his mother's polite response. Was she genuinely concerned, or was she putting on a front for Mr. Alexander? He had not seen his mother act like this before. He felt his mother knew deep down why Anthony ran away. He wondered about her response, but was she willing to accept the truth as to her part in why he wanted to leave. He didn't think his mother was willing to do this and certainly wasn't willing to admit the truth.

Wanda and Mr. Alexander exchanged a few words before Mr. Alexander left. Wanda asked Anthony to enter the house after Mr. Alexander left. Anthony was sure this was the place, time and setting where his mother was going to take it out on him. He was surprised though; his mother didn't do or say anything. Anthony knew she would revert back to her old self and start cussing him or hitting him but it did not happen. She said nothing. Anthony was confused; he didn't know how to react or what to feel regarding his mother in this incident.

The next weeks at school involved a lot of discussion about Anthony and James' one day adventure and attempt to run away. Most of it started from the other students. Their planning was well known. Many students wanted to hear more about the details. Many of them wanted to know about Mr. Alexander's reaction when James pulled out the gun out in front of him. Anthony and James told the stories but eventually got tired of the questions. Anthony also saw that James was not responding well to talking about the episode.

Anthony started to notice that James' behavior changed and he never was quite the same. James mellowed out and started taking his studies more seriously and didn't get into as much trouble. Anthony was sure this was due to the reaction and action of his father after they were caught. Anthony never knew for sure what James' father had said or done but it certainly changed James. Anthony however, did not change, for him the year was only just beginning.

******

In the office at Manna House, George asked Anthony a question. "Anthony, how did you feel about James changing after this happened with the two of you?"

"I guess I felt pretty bad because while James was someone I always considered a friend, after this happened I didn't really see him or talk to him that much anymore. I am sure it was because of his dad's feelings towards me and the guidelines he must've given James. I believe he spoke to James in regards to him not spending time with me, you know running around together, that type of thing. I don't believe he wanted James even talking to me."

Anthony responded in somewhat of a disheartened tone. He was obviously upset when thinking back on this episode in regards to James.

"Why did it bother you so much?" George asked, trying to get Anthony to talk more about losing one of his friends and the feelings he still felt in regards to losing this friendship.

"I don't know. I guess it was because I always felt close to James and he was one of the few friends I had. As I think back about it, it is like he was the only guy out of five or six who was willing to take a chance and run away with me. I really felt closer to James than any of the guys in Keystone I had been around for years. It seemed as if we understood and cared for each other. I guess I was responsible for blowing the relationship with James. I still think it was because I got him involved in the attempt to run away. That certainly made things worse between him and his dad. I guess I still accept and take blame for that. I still miss James. I often times wonder what happened to him, did he finish school, go into the service, or what? I don't even know if he is still alive. It has been years since I have seen him and I don't know if I'll ever see him again. I really would like to see him again at some point and see what ever happened to him." Anthony was sad and upset. He said these things believing he would never see James again and he regretted that.

George asked Anthony a question which made it obvious that he was trying to get Anthony to see and accept things differently than he did. "Anthony, don't you think James was responsible for his actions and that he made the decisions to be involved with you in those situations?"

Anthony answered George, not really wanting to accept the truth but mentioning it none the less. "Yeah, I know he was ultimately responsible for his actions and his decisions. I guess I just want to put additional blame on myself for those things, though, because if I had not been around he probably would not have done the things he did."

"It seems as if this is a pattern that follows you quite a bit, Anthony. That is, that bad things happen to you and you want to put the blame on yourself. That is not necessary and most of the time has not been true. You need to understand that people are responsible for their own actions and that you have very little if any control over that. A lot of this goes back to when you were much smaller. Even then you were conditioned to put blame on yourself for the actions of others. I want you to understand that you don't have to punish yourself like this anymore. I want you to think about this over the next week, O.K.?" George asked in a caring and concerned voice.

Anthony responded favorably but was almost unemotional in his response, he simply said, "O.K."

Anthony went home thinking about the things George said in regards to him oftentimes blaming himself when he shouldn't. He knew deep down this was true, even in his present life. Anthony tried to change, but had difficulty doing so. While he knew that others had contributed to the formation of his personality, he also knew he was ultimately responsible for the bad decisions. Understanding the mistakes and why he made them did not change the fact that he made the decisions he did. This helped reassure him of not only his own imperfections but the imperfections of all humans.

Through the week Anthony thought more about James Rogers and Mr. Alexander. They were people Anthony had learned to appreciate and enjoyed being around when younger. Mr. Alexander was like a hero and friend to Anthony who he learned to respect and appreciate as he got older. Many of the things Mr. Alexander did for Anthony went unnoticed until he got older. Anthony realized more the influence and help Mr. Alexander had given him. He was a leader and mentor for Anthony in many ways. This was important for Anthony because he never had a male mentor who gave him any type of positive examples.

The attempt to run away was the last time Anthony really spent any time with James. It was the event that changed their relationship. It was obvious to Anthony that it was not their choice, but the choice of James' father. Things would never be the same again and it was something Anthony regretted for years.

~ Chapter 19 ~

The Never Ending Summer

Anthony was amazed at how well he was doing in his studies. He was coming up to the mid-term testing and realized he was doing better than he had done before. Anthony had received mostly C's in his classes with an occasional D. For Anthony these were passing grades and this was the first time he had actually made those kinds of grades on his own. He realized that if he passed this year he would have no trouble passing to the next grade at University School.

Anthony believed if he could get these grades while goofing off and having a good amount of fun, it may be possible to catch up with his original classmates from the previous year. If he caught up with them then he would get some respect back from his family and friends. If he did this then the benefit would be that he could actually graduate from high school with his original class. He knew this was possible if he took a few courses in summer school. He would even pay for the classes if he had to. He had studying to do, but he was motivated. School had a purpose, and while self serving, it was still a purpose.

Anthony spoke to Anthony Humphrey about the possibility of graduating with their original class. He was in agreement; getting their grades up should be something they worked towards and tried to accomplish. Anthony Beechup realized that if he made an effort he could obtain positive results for his studies.

While this was his second year in the same grade, it was the first year where he started a serious studying effort. He blew off the previous year; if he made an effort at anything it was to do as poorly as possible. It was also true that if he tried to study he had other things going on which prevented him from taking his studies seriously. Anthony knew there were a number of factors which prevented him from excelling in school. He also knew that many of those factors were not entirely his fault. He was still hanging out as much as possible with his friends in Keystone, especially on weekends. He was still involved with drugs, gang activity, and numerous aspects of the Occult. The only activity which increased in any significant way was the Occult.

The abuse Anthony received when he was younger was a contributing factor in him still being involved in various sexual activities. He continued to include both male and female partners. He also continued his involvement with the Occult, which created problems for him. The problems were not so much the activities he was involved in as much as the spiritual aspects of it. Anthony was involved in the Occult to the point he was continually looking for some kind of power. Along with some friends from Keystone, on a few occasions he caught stray pets and sacrificed them in hopes of obtaining power. In truth, he realized he never gained any power. The stories Anthony had heard about the Occult were not entirely true. There was as much, if not far more, deception regarding the Occult as with other religions. While Anthony became more disheartened with the Occult, he accepted Demonic and Satanic powers as real.

Anthony realized there were spiritual forces which were clearly evident within the Occult. He believed the type of power he was looking for was not possible through the Occult. He looked for a form of power to enable him to love and be loved. Anthony realized the greatest fault of the Occult was in the ability to love or be loved. It was based on anger and destruction. Anthony realized this was the opposite of what he was looking for. He had experienced these things from his surroundings including his family and environment. He was not looking forward to more of those things in his life.

During the winter months Anthony started to spend more time on campus in the evenings. One of the things he did when he stayed over was to spend time at the East Tennessee State University Student Center. He often met up with various college students who went to different functions and meetings around campus. Many of the students saw him and invited him to these events. Many of the discussions ranged from philosophy and religious beliefs to different cultures. The meetings Anthony took the most interest in were the Baha'i meetings. They made him feel welcome.

The Baha'i topics and beliefs were of interest to Anthony. They taught about the universal love of God and how humanity had distorted the message of love that God provided to humanity. It was an interesting message because it seemed the people attending these meetings practiced what they preached. It was also interesting because the Baha'i faith encompassed all major religious beliefs. This interested Anthony, because he knew that if a belief structure learned to encompass and accept those who where in disagreement, they had to be a loving and caring people.

Anthony went to a number of meetings of the Baha'i and spent almost every Tuesday and Thursday evening at East Tennessee State University attending these meetings. Most of the time he walked home to Keystone from the meetings but on occasion stayed with his grandparents. Anthony was impressed that many of those attending the Baha'i meetings went out of their way to show him they cared for him and was glad he was there. It was as if they knew he was troubled and had a number of problems in his life. No one ever addressed this with him at the meeting but he knew they felt this by the way they spoke to him.

Anthony's involvement with the Baha'i was confusing at times for various reasons. One of the reasons was they observed and recognized all beliefs. They referred to Jesus as the son of God, gave full honor to Mohammed and other religious leaders. They believed that through the ancestry of Bahaullah there were currently sons of God which are present with us in order to lead us. The Baha'i recognized all of humanity as being children of God and that we have potential to become God.

Anthony felt he was a rational person. The longer he associated with the Baha'i he realized he had problems that led to the eventual rejection of the faith. He saw rather easily that different leaders such as Buddha and Jesus spoke two very different messages. To try and encompass an eclectic view of all religions was not possible. Anthony felt that if there was a God, and he believed there was, God had to have one universal truth, not many. For many truths to exist there had to be many Gods and Anthony did not accept this as a rational assumption. "After all," he would think, "if there were many Gods which one would be in charge? All civilized structures generally have one person in charge and I don't see how many Gods could get along with each other. If God does exist; there must be one God. He may have forces he fights against but they are not Gods."

Anthony wanted to know what the truth was, but did he want to be a part of it? Anthony disassociated more with the Occult and looked at various beliefs, like the Baha'i and other Eastern and New Age concepts. He knew things were getting deeper within the Occult and he didn't like what he saw. It was like he was seeing the lies of Satan through his involvement. Anthony believed in a literal Satan and that he was the master of lies and deception. He was disassociating and moving away from the Occult, but he had strong feelings about the reality of Satanic and Demonic powers. He felt the Satanic and Demonic powers were limited. He could not fully explain what was going on in his thought process but he knew he wanted to get his focus back on love, especially in trying to find love for himself.

Anthony started to disassociate with the spiritualistic things he was involved in. While he still had a vested interest in magic and was learning new tricks, he was also limiting his involvement with things like séances, spells and fortune telling. Magic was nothing more than a form of entertainment. When used appropriately it brought pleasure and joy to those observing it. This was the main reason he continued to study magic. He was always open to the idea that what he was doing was nothing more than trickery.

Regarding séances, spells and fortune telling, it was another story for Anthony. One weekend night he was with his grandparents, Velma and Oscar. He was alone waiting for his mother to either come to get him or for his grandparents to take him home.

It was a Sunday night and everyone was at church except Anthony who didn't enjoy going to church. He took out his tarot cards to do some readings. As he held the cards, dealing them to do a reading, he heard a voice inside him say, "Those cards are evil, get rid of them right now." He didn't hear the voice audibly but he was certain he felt a voice telling him to get rid of the cards. Anthony had mixed feelings and wasn't sure if it was real or even if it was his consciousness. He was certain about what he thought the voice said. He was sure something was wrong with him having and using the cards. The more he contemplated the feelings, the more he sensed evil coming. Anthony felt evil come over him telling him to ignore the voice. He was trembling, and didn't know what to do with the tarot cards he was holding. He realized something going on with the cards that he didn't want to experience.

Anthony did what he had to do in order to eliminate the feelings he had. He searched his grandparent's house and found a cigarette lighter of his grandmother's. He went outside on to Virginia Street to burn the cards. He was going to destroy the cards just as he had felt the voice inside him telling him to do. Anthony spent the next 30 minutes trying to burn the cards. He didn't know if there was a coating on the cards which prevented them from burning, but they wouldn't burn. He believed that even if there was a protective coating they should still catch fire. The tarot cards never did catch fire though, no matter what he did. Anthony grabbed the cards and went to a nearby sewage drain near a turn around for cars on Virginia Street; a dead end street. He threw the cards down the access opening. He felt a sense of relief after he threw the cards down the drain. He knew, deep down inside, that for what ever reason, he had done the right thing.

Over the next few months Anthony spent as much time as possible with his grandparents. He attended different activities at East Tennessee State University during that time. He was impressed with the Baha'i meetings but didn't limit himself to those meetings. He attended other meetings of various beliefs, including the Unification Church (Moonie) and some Christian meetings which took place around campus. He was looking more at spiritual matters and there was no better place to look than a college campus. At one of the Christian meetings Anthony met one of the high school seniors. He didn't remember the student's name but on occasion during the evening the student spoke to Anthony about various aspects of the Christian faith. Anthony still disliked Christianity but was impressed with this one student's friendliness and openness. He accepted Anthony and went out of his way to talk to him, letting him know that he genuinely cared for him. Anthony was impressed and outside of his grandmother, this student was one of the first Christians who actually seemed to practice what he preached. Anthony was impressed with the message but due to so many poor examples, he was disheartened towards the faith and resented what others had done to him.

Anthony recognized that he was searching for spiritual truth. He was easily persuaded by some people regarding spiritual issues. He was still involved with activities including sex, drugs and gang activity. He wasn't willing to give up the friends or things which brought pleasure. They were the things that brought him pleasure in a life full of hurt. He still had overall bad feelings towards Christianity, its approaches, methods and attitudes.

* * * * * *

Life got progressively worse at home for Anthony. Robert was convinced Wanda was seeing other men. Anthony knew this to be fact because he met the man his mother was seeing on a regular basis. His name was Walter Hudgins and Wanda was seeing him almost nightly. Anthony knew his mother was sleeping with this man and occasionally spent the night with him at his home.

Wanda took all she could take from Robert before she filed for divorce and was legally separated. This was an easy time for Anthony because neither Wanda nor Robert spent much time at home. The two of them not being together enabled Anthony to sleep in a bed instead of on a bench or at a friend's house. Robert did not spend time at home because he had found another place to live. He was still infatuated with Wanda and tried to get her back.

There were two specific events that impacted Anthony regarding Robert's efforts to get even with Wanda. They were devastating for Anthony, Madeline and Wanda, and caused Anthony to have difficulty forgiving Robert. Anthony wished he were an adult. If he were, and he saw Robert, he might not control his actions. Robert willingly hurt him, his sister, and his mother, and showed little remorse for his actions.

Anthony was young and had a great deal of difficulty in knowing how to respond to Robert. He didn't have an option how he responded towards Robert. He complied whether he wanted to or not. While Robert was not a big man and had been beaten up by his uncle Billy, he was capable of taking care of himself and had the experience from numerous bar room fights.

* * * * * *

With the exception of a night every now and then, or on the weekends to occasionally go out, Robert and Wanda rarely saw each other. They were together no more than ten to twelve times a month and even then for only brief periods of time. Robert continued to make efforts and showed up for brief visits but Wanda had nothing to do with him. She had had it and was satisfied not being together at all.

It was early March and the weather was getting nice. The trees were in full bloom and the temperature was getting into the low 70's on a regular basis. There was an occasional cold spell but the winters in Johnson City were relatively mild and usually ended by mid-February. Anthony was at the point where he did not mind walking back and forth from school, especially in nice weather. He was starting to spend more time in Keystone during this phase. His dog General had grown up quickly and was a smart and fun dog to be around. Anthony trained and worked with General to the point where he did many things with a simple verbal or hand command. Anthony loved playing with General and taking walks with him up in the wooded areas near Keystone. He also enjoyed riding his bike and having General chase him through the woods. One day Anthony was walking home, having a good time during the walk enjoying the scenery and listening to the sounds of spring. Anthony often sang to himself along the walk and wrote songs to go with the rhythms of the sounds. Sounds like jack hammers, car horns, or hammering in the background made nice rhythms to sing to. He enjoyed making up songs as he walked and sometimes he even impressed himself with how easy this came to him. The songs ranged from love songs to simple songs about relationships, religion or whatever topic happened to be on his mind. The songs varied because Anthony made up songs about anything and everything. He was easily influenced by the things he heard, saw, or was thinking about. Anthony loved rock and roll and the music of the period, the mid-1970's. He listened to the hard core music of the time that most of the kids listened to and enjoyed. His favorite bands were Aerosmith, Fog Hat, AC / DC, Nazareth, Bachman Turner Overdrive, and The Electric Light Orchestra, among others. He listened to the radio or stereo all of the time, and whenever he could go hear music he went. Anthony patterned the songs he made up after the tunes and styles he listened to on the radio.

Anthony loved one of the local stations, WQUT. They played what was known as album oriented rock, and this was one of his favorite stations. He especially enjoyed listening late at night on the weekends when disc jockey The Tennessee Midnight Rambler came onto the air. The Tennessee Midnight Rambler was a one of a kind DJ who seemed to always be in trouble with the FCC for his inappropriate behaviors, actions and attitudes while on the air. Anthony was convinced that the Rambler was one of the earliest 'shock jocks', as they came to be known. The Rambler had an edge and was unique. He had a following that covered five states and people of all ages. It was his attitude that influenced Anthony's made up songs. The Rambler obtained a following that stayed with him long after he gave up his radio gig.

As Anthony sang his songs while walking home, General recognized him even when out of General's sight of vision. When General heard Anthony singing he started barking, anxiously awaiting Anthony's return and their play time together. When getting home either Anthony or Madeline fed General and then played with him. Anthony knew General awaited his return home. It wasn't for his singing but the fact that he was getting ready to eat and play. Another reason General awaited Anthony's return was that Robert and Wanda kept General tied up in the back yard for most of the day. The family lived on a busy intersection off of Main Street, and without a fence the only way to assure General's safety was to keep him tied up. General was tied up near a neighbor's fence in the back yard with a thick chain tied to a fence post and connected to the choker collar.

The chain was 20 feet long, but hooked up to the fencing in such a way that it allowed General to run up and down the fence. He had more room to run this way. There was a large oak tree General lay under when he was tired or hot. He was, as far as Anthony could tell, a happy dog. He got a lot of attention and enjoyed being around people.

Anthony knew something was unusual as he walked home, and couldn't hear General barking. Anthony figured he was just asleep under the big oak tree and having such a good dream that he didn't want to wake up, even to his singing.

Anthony went into the house through the front door to get his dog some water and food. He walked back into the kitchen, which was on the back side of the house facing the back yard. Anthony reached under the sink and got two empty one gallon milk containers to fill them up with water. As he filled up the second container he looked into the back yard. He went into shock as he saw his dog dangling lifeless.

There hanging from a low tree limb, not moving, was his dog, General. Anthony ran out the back door towards his dog. Anthony had used General's choker collar whenever he walked him. The collar made it easy to control and train the dog. It also made it easy to choke him to death when he was hung from the tree.

General was hanging from the tree limb, about 3 feet from the ground. It was not obvious at first to Anthony because of his tears, but General was beaten and then hung. Anthony didn't know if he had been killed from the beating and then hung from the tree or hung first and then beaten. What was obvious to Anthony was that he was there struggling to get his dead dog down from the tree.

Anthony was crying because of the love he had for his dog. General was one of his best friends and someone took him away from him in such a cruel way. This was another friend Anthony had lost. A faithful friend who was now gone. Anthony had been critical of people who were close to their pets, but he now understood.

Anthony had a rush of adrenaline and was able to get General down from the tree. He pulled down on the chain with all of his strength until it broke. After it broke he was able to get the collar off of his dog. Anthony didn't know why he wanted to get the collar off. Maybe it was because the collar is what choked the life out of his dog, and he wanted to relieve his dog of the thing that helped cause his death.

General lay on the ground in front of Anthony as Anthony was on his knees petting his dog from head to tail. The petting was more for Anthony's feelings of grief. It seemed to help and was something he had to do. He was crying and asking out loud, "Why? Why? Dear God, why would anyone do this?" Anthony didn't know the answer to that question. Even if he knew, he would not have accepted the answer.

Anthony realized that at times in his life he was no different than the person who had killed his dog. He was just as vile and despicable. There was a component about him that he knew was evil and if honest, others would recognize there was an evil component in every human. After all Anthony had killed animals. He had sacrificed them to Satan and on occasion killed them or abused them for the fun of it. He would never kill or abuse an animal for the fun of it again. He realized the life of an animal had value. It was a life he would respect and value for the purpose it was created.

Anthony was willing to hunt and kill animals for food; this was in tune with why some animals existed. He enjoyed being out in nature, the surroundings, the benefits of the food, but even then he hurt for the animal when it died.

Anthony stayed on his knees, petting his friend and companion, crying out loud for 20 minutes before his mother arrived home. When she arrived she heard and saw Anthony upset. After she saw what had happened she was upset but in a different way than Anthony. For all of the bad things she had done she was still his mother and at times showed Anthony she cared for him. This was one of those times.

Wanda's response was, "Who the hell killed your dog?" She was shocked, confused, surprised and caring.

"I don't know, but he's dead. I had to pull him off the tree from where they hung him." Anthony said while choking back sobs.

Wanda looked and saw the chain with its broken link still hanging from the tree. The chain was swinging back and forth from the slight breeze. She didn't say much, but what she said was enough to get Anthony thinking about who must have killed his dog. "That no good son of a bitch. Surely he didn't so this?" She asked herself as if she knew the answer.

Wanda knew who killed General and she was going to do something about it. She quickly went into the house, up the back steps and into the kitchen to get the telephone. Anthony followed her because he wanted to know who killed his dog, and he wanted to see what his mother was going to do. She picked up the phone as soon as she got to it. "You rotten, no good, piece of shit. You killed Anthony's dog didn't you?" She paused for a moment and responded in an angry, violent manner cursing the whole time. "I don't care if you did fucking buy him, you stupid piece of shit. You didn't have no fucking right to kill it. You stupid mother fucker! If you want to get back at me then get back at me, but don't you ever think about taking it out on my children."

Anthony heard that it was Robert who killed General. He would have figured it out but he was upset over his dog's death and wasn't thinking about anything other than that. Anthony heard his mother yelling again, cursing throughout the conversation. "You listen here, you stupid, son of a bitch, if I ever see you around my house or my children again, I'll be damned if I don't kill you. And you better watch your ass because if I see you out I'll kill you. I don't want to ever see your fucking face again, you bastard." Wanda slammed the phone receiver down screaming at it, "You stupid murdering mother fucker. God damn you!" It was clear to Anthony that her anger was not directed at him but at Robert, who had been on the other end of the line.

* * * * * *

At Manna House, George spoke to Anthony who was crying. "Anthony, how did you feel toward your mother, knowing that she was supportive of you in what had just happened with your dog?"

"I don't really know. I guess I was appreciative but all I could really think about at the time was General." Anthony wiped the tears from his eyes as he spoke, still upset all these years later.

"How about your feelings towards your stepfather, Robert?" George asked. "How did you feel about him?"

"I never referred to Robert as my stepfather. I still to this day have never referred to any of my mother's husbands as my stepfather. I never had good memories of them so there was no reason to refer to them that way. As far as Robert goes, I still feel about the same way towards him now as I did then. I didn't care for him then and I don't care for him now. I'll never forget what he did to my dog, to me, my sister, or my mom. As far as I'm concerned he was, and still is a jerk. It is kind of strange though; he is still alive and was a part of my life for a large period of time." Anthony answered still showing anger for what Robert had done.

"Have you seen him any since this happened?" George asked.

"Well, it wasn't much longer after this happened that I saw him again." Anthony started telling George another story involving Robert.

* * * * * *

Anthony was at home with Madeline just prior to the start of summer. It was late in the evening and it was a month since Robert had killed General. Robert and Wanda were legally separated and she was staying with another man named Walter Hudgins. Walter lived in a small town called Erwin, 10 miles to the south east of Johnson City near the North Carolina state line.

It was 9:30 in the evening on this warm night. Anthony was listening to music in one of the front bedrooms with his sister. Anthony was acting like the musicians and singers performing the music. Madeline was laughing and having a good time. Anthony enjoyed seeing his sister laugh because he seldom saw her having a good time. He liked the attention he got when he made people laugh. He had learned to come back at teachers and other students with one-liners. He was a class clown and a practical joker. The students found him funny when he did this and they supported his behavior. Sometimes it got him into trouble with his teachers because they didn't always see the humor, or even when they did, they couldn't allow certain activities in the class room. To Anthony they didn't have the sense of humor the students did, or at least they didn't show it.

Anthony and Madeline had just finished listening to several songs and he was now imitating Richard Nixon singing a Bachman Turner Overdrive song, "Taking Care of Business." Madeline was laughing hysterically at Anthony's interpretation of the song and his mimic of Richard Nixon's mannerisms and voice. Anthony had learned to imitate several prominent people and Richard Nixon was a fairly easy impression for him. He did this impression because he couldn't think of anything much stranger or out of place than Richard Nixon singing "Taking Care of Business." While he was doing this impression they heard a car come to a screeching halt outside of their house. They looked outside and saw Robert, who had just driven up in his blue Chevrolet Malibu. Robert slammed the door as he got out of the car and stood there for a few seconds looking back towards the garage at the rear of the house. The lights in the house were down low and Robert couldn't see in the house but Anthony and Madeline could see out. Anthony saw that

Robert was carrying a gun, in his right hand, with his silhouette in front of a street light.

Anthony told his sister in a loud whisper. "Quick, Sissy, go lock the back door and I'll get the front door." No sooner had Anthony said this than his sister Madeline ran towards the back door to lock it. Anthony ran to the front door to lock it. The lights in the living room were off and it was dark outside so they knew if they got behind the couch Robert could not see them if he looked through the front window or door. Anthony and Madeline also knew Robert was not supposed to have a key to the house.

As soon they locked the doors they went immediately and got behind the couch in the living room. They were crouched and quiet, listening for any sound Robert made. It didn't take long before they heard Robert knocking on the back door. They could hear him yelling, pounding on the door and cursing. "Come on you two timing whore, let me in."

Anthony was sure that he must not have a key; if he had he would've let himself into the house. After what seemed like 10 minutes Robert quit pounding on the back door and Anthony hoped he would leave. It took no longer than 2 minutes when Robert was pounding on the front door, just as he had the back door. This door led into the living room where Anthony and Madeline were hiding behind the couch. "Let me in, you slut."

After a few minutes Robert quit pounding on the door. Anthony and Madeline stayed behind the couch not saying a word. Their hearts were beating quickly and they felt drops of sweat on their foreheads. They were scared, not knowing what would happen next. After a few minutes of silence Robert yelled out again scaring and shocking the children. "Anthony and Madeline let me in. I know you're in there! I hear the music playing." Anthony realized that in their fear and confusion they forgot to turn the radio off.

They both sat behind the couch not saying a word. Robert yelled out, "Get to it, Anthony and Madeline, let me in before I kick the damned door in. I know you're both in there."

Anthony and Madeline didn't know what to do. They were extremely scared. "Damn it, let me in. I promise I'm not going to hurt you two, but if I have to kick the fucking door down and you are in there I'm going to beat the shit out of you. Now let me in."

Anthony knew Robert would kick the door in and keep his word if they didn't let him in. Without saying anything to Madeline, Anthony got up from behind the couch and unlocked the door. He left Madeline behind the couch crouched down where Robert could not see her. He unlatched and unlocked the door and was surprised when Robert did not come into the house after he opened the door. "Where is your sister?" Robert asked as soon as he saw Anthony.

"She is out with Mama someplace. I don't know where they went," he said with a quivering, scared voice, trying to protect his sister still hiding behind the couch. Robert asked Anthony, this time putting the gun in Anthony's face, while cocking it. "Where the hell did they go to? Tell me or I'll kill you."

Anthony answered, afraid of what was going to happen next. "I promise I don't know where they are. I got in from school late and there was a note on the table that said they were both out and wouldn't be in till late."

Anthony didn't know why, but it appeared as if Robert believed him. "Come out here with me." Robert said as he reset the trigger on the gun to its normal position.

Anthony hesitated before leaving the house. "Come on, damn it, I'm not going to hurt you." He didn't know why but he believed him, even after the harm he had done in the past, and in particular killing General.

Anthony walked outside with Robert shutting the door and leaving his sister in the house. Robert placed his hand on the back of Anthony's neck and led him to the car where he was parked. "Anthony, if you see your mom tonight tell her I love her. I don't want this marriage to end, but damn it, if I can't have her no one will. I don't want to see her with another man or there will be hell to pay for the both of them. Tell her that, do you understand? Tell her that if I see her with another man that I'm going to kill her."

Anthony simply said, "Yes sir."

"I mean it, damn it, if I see her with another man I'll kill the both of them. I wouldn't hurt you or Madeline for the world but I'm not going to put up with this shit from your mother. I'll fucking kill her and her boyfriend. Do you understand?" Robert was raising his voice.

"Yes sir. I understand." Anthony was scared and afraid.

"Good. Now give your ol' man a hug before I leave." Robert told Anthony as he reached to give him a hug. Anthony still saw the gun in his hand and was afraid to do anything other than hug him. Anthony felt this was the last thing Robert was going to do before he left, so he decided to hug him back. Anthony didn't feel he had any other choice, Robert still had the gun.

"I love you and your sister Anthony, and I don't want this divorce. I hope you know that." Robert said as he gave Anthony the hug. Anthony smelled alcohol on his breath. It was obvious to him that Robert had been drinking, which was one of the reasons for his behavior. Anthony gave Robert the answer he felt that he wanted to hear. "I know you don't want it, Sissy and I don't want it, either."

"I love you and your sister, Anthony. Make sure you tell your mother that as well as the other shit I told you to tell her, O.K.?"

More relaxed now, Anthony answered, "O.K." Robert kissed Anthony on the cheek. This was strange to Anthony because it was the first and only time he recalled this type of contact with Robert. It felt strange for Anthony to feel his beard stubble after days of growth. After Robert gave Anthony his hug and kiss he walked towards his car. Robert got into the car without saying another word and left. Anthony didn't know where he went or what would happen. He couldn't get in touch with his mother because he didn't know where she was. He assumed she was with Walter, but he didn't know where he lived, nor did he have his phone number. It was obvious that Robert didn't know or he would have gone there first.

He thought about calling the police, but he knew if Robert found out he had called them, he would be back for him. This scared Anthony to the point he did not call. He decided to go back into the house with his sister.

Anthony walked into the house and Madeline was not behind the couch any more but was hiding in her bedroom closet. After calling out and reassuring her that everything was O.K. she came out of the closet. One of the first things the two did was to make sure the lights were turned off, the windows shut and locked and the doors all locked. They also turned off the radio. They decided to go into the bedroom to sleep in the same bed in case Robert came back. They didn't know why, but being together kept them from being so afraid.

Anthony knew fear, but he knew Robert would really hurt them and even kill their mother. He was sure Robert would come back that night. He was confident he would come back until he found Wanda. Anthony and Madeline lay in the bed not speaking for what seemed like hours. They finally went to sleep, not knowing what would happen with Robert and Wanda. They woke up the next morning and got themselves ready for school as they normally did. They were pleased that neither Robert nor their mother came back from the previous night.

As they got ready for school they worried about their mother throughout the day wondering what would happen if Robert found her before they saw her and told her about the events of the night before. Anthony went straight home as soon as school was out. He left school early to beat his sister home from her ride with Mr. Testum. When Anthony got home, he saw his mother. When Madeline arrived home they told Wanda about the night before. Wanda took appropriate actions to get a restraining order. The restraining order worked because there were no additional problems with Robert. It would be years before Anthony would see him again.

* * * * * *

"How did this affect you Anthony?" George asked as they sat in the office at Manna House.

"Well, I was scared, but I am still surprised at how it all went down. I think I've actually handled this pretty well over the years. I just wish it hadn't been the last time I had contact with Robert, though." Anthony responded.

"How long ago was it that you saw Robert?" George asked.

"It was actually about a year ago. I was visiting my mom and I was going to the store with her and he drove up next to us in his car. My mom spoke to him but I didn't know who he was until after he drove off. She asked me if I knew who it was she was speaking with, and I said no. She told me it was Robert. I had no idea. I guess that was the first and last time I've seen him since I was a kid." Anthony answered. He didn't mind talking about Robert or the things he went through during their time together.

"How do you feel you handled the break up of Robert and your mother?" George asked.

"Pretty well, I guess, but by then I was pretty much becoming my own person and I didn't let him or my mom affect me too much in how I felt or acted. I still think he was a jerk and I would have been better off without him in my life, but there is nothing I can do about that now. I think I learned to deal with the whole thing regarding him pretty well. I don't hate him or anything like that. I just don't think about him too much anymore. He was the only guy my mom was ever married to who is still alive. So I guess I'm like most kids, I would have liked for things to have been different." Anthony said this without being upset. He was having a good day and wasn't going to let this part of his life bother him. It was obvious to George that he had learned to deal with this aspect of his life. George decided not to pursue this any further. They agreed to end early. Anthony had a good day with the exception of the memory of General but he got over it as well as could be expected. George didn't know why Anthony responded as well as he did. Anthony knew he would share one of the few pleasant memories of youth the next time they got together.

~ Chapter 20 ~

The Cross & the Switchblade

Anthony had been walking around the campus at East Tennessee State University now for 30 minutes. It was early morning on a Saturday and he had left Keystone earlier that day. He came to the campus to meet up with some guys from school to play football and watch the ETSU. football team during their spring practice.

It was early in May so the weather was a little chilly in the morning hours and there was usually frost on the morning ground. Anthony wore a wind breaker along with comfortable broken-in blue jeans. During this time of year he still wore a couple of shirts, one to keep warm, and the other to pull off when it warmed up later in the day.

Anthony arrived early. He liked getting there early especially on Saturdays when he came to the campus for whatever reason. On Saturday mornings, the campus was littered with trash from the partying the night before in the dormitories, fraternities, and sororities. He was often surprised at the things laying around on those mornings.

There was another reason Anthony got to the campus early on Saturdays. He found out several years ago that the campus organizations which were planning activities displayed their events on campus bulletin boards Friday nights and Saturday mornings. This was also the day the ETSU. campus newspaper came out. He could get the newspaper and find out what was happening on campus. He used the newspaper to schedule activities with his friends from Keystone and school. He found a number of activities he and his friends had gone to from the listings in the paper. Not everything was fun but most of them were worth looking at and using for free or cheap entertainment.

Anthony also walked around campus to scout out dormitory row for the left over trash and some sign of the activities the night before. This didn't take long because it was obvious that nothing of significance had happened the night before.

He was bored and headed over to the student center to see what was going on. He knew that while there he could watch T.V., get something to eat, and sit down and read the college paper before checking out the activity boards. After finishing a glazed donut and a Sprite for his drink, he went to check out the activity boards. While walking down the hallway, a large poster of movie recently in theaters caught his eye. It was about the movie, "The Cross and the Switchblade." Anthony didn't know much about the movie other than it being about one of the gangs they had patterned their gang after in Keystone, the Mau Maus out of New York City. He knew this was a movie which was doing well at the box office. He was surprised they were going to be showing it on campus. He wanted to see it with some of his friends from Keystone and University School. He expected after seeing the poster from a distance down the hallway that someone on campus was going to be showing this movie. He hurried down the hallway to see what the poster was announcing.

Anthony was surprised at what he saw on the poster. The movie was not going to be shown on campus, but something better was taking place. The poster looked like the movie's poster, but there was a smaller picture in one of the corners of a man who looked to be in his mid-thirties to early-forties. The poster stated, "Coming to the ETSU. Memorial Center, May 27, 28, 29 - David Wilkerson, The inspiration of the movie and book, 'The Cross and the Switchblade' Starts at 7:00 p.m., with special musical guest Dallas Holmes." Anthony couldn't believe it! This guy who knew something about gangs was coming to Johnson City to speak. Not only that, but the gang he knew most about, the Mau Maus, was the gang Anthony and his Keystone buddies had patterned their gang after. Anthony knew this was something he and his friends would want to go see.

Anthony was excited enough that he couldn't wait to finish playing football with his friends and get back to Keystone and tell his friends there. Anthony had some football to play first and even though it wasn't football season, the spring practice that the ETSU. Buccaneers team was going through seemed enough like football season to where he was glad he had played football with his friends. Football was still one of his first loves and he enjoyed the chance to play no matter the time of year. This was especially true since he didn't get to play for an organized team at school.

Later that morning, Anthony spoke about David Wilkerson coming to the ETSU. campus in a few weeks. He was surprised that some of his friends had already seen the movie, 'The Cross and the Switchblade.' The movie had been out for a few months, but that didn't mean much to Anthony because he had to work to get the money to go to the movies. He found odd jobs to get money, or he went with his uncles when they or his grandparents took him and paid for it. He was surprised by what some of his friends from school had said about the movie. Anthony Humphrey was one of the boys who had seen the movie. "Yeah, man, I saw the movie and it was pretty good. Lots of cool stuff in it and all."

"What was it about?" Anthony Beechup asked.

"Well, it's about this preacher guy. That David Wilkerson guy you say is coming here; anyway he moves to New York City and starts working with this gang. The gang he works with has just had some people arrested for killing someone or something like that. He is one of the few people who start helping them and showing any kind of interest. He starts a church for gangs and works with one of the gang leaders, Nicki Cruz. It has some religious stuff and all like that in it, but it is a pretty good movie and all otherwise." Anthony Humphrey told more about the story and this interested him even more. He knew now that he had to see David Wilkerson. "Tell me, man, do they show much about the Mau Maus and all?" He asked with interest and curiosity.

"Shoot, yeah, man. That is about all the movie is about. Those guys are mean as hell." Humphrey answered.

Anthony already knew the Mau Maus were tough. He also knew that he and the rest of the guys in Keystone had probably done their image and reputation justice. Anthony was a little confused about the David Wilkerson guy being a preacher, but his response was, "Shoot man, if this guy's a preacher who is willing to set up a church for gang members and all, he must not be that bad of a guy. Sounds like the kind of church I would be willing to go to on a regular basis or at least give a try. One where, if any of these uptight religious people were to come in we would just kick the shit out of them, take their money and humiliate them right there in front of everyone." The rest of his friends laughed but Anthony believed every word. He couldn't imagine any church with gang members as a part of it doing anything other than what he had just described.

The boys finished playing football then watched the ETSU. Buccaneers Spring practice. It wasn't much longer before Anthony left on the long walk to Keystone. He didn't waste much time. He ran most of the 4 or 5 miles back to Keystone. The running wasn't so hard, after the years of walking between Keystone and University School Anthony had lost quite a bit of weight and was not as chunky as he used to be. He wore blue jeans and they were the only discomfort. He ran home numerous times before and was starting to make good time when he ran home. Today was one of those days he made exceptionally good time.

* * * * * *

Anthony had had very few reasons to get excited about something, yet he found himself more excited than ever about David Wilkerson coming to the campus of ETSU. He planned on going to see the author of the book, The Cross and the Switchblade. He was excited and there nothing that could stop him from hearing this man. Wilkerson was a friend of people like Anthony and he was looking forward to hearing what he had to say.

Anthony saved up enough money and saw the movie "The Cross and the Switchblade". He worked hard to save the money so he would have some idea as to what the story was about. The movie did focus on the preacher David Wilkerson and how he went into New York City and worked with the Mau Mau gang. Anthony was impressed with the sincerity and concern this preacher had towards the gang members he worked with and especially their leader, Nicki Cruz. Anthony was a little put off by some of the preachy attitude the movie had, but he still felt it was a good movie and it didn't detract from his desire to hear David Wilkerson speak. Anthony wanted to see this guy, who had worked closely with the gang he and the rest of the boys in Keystone had patterned their gang after. To him, going to see David Wilkerson was a way of showing respect to a person who was willing to help the Mau Maus, and a way of showing support for the gang in Keystone. David Wilkerson had as good an understanding of the Mau Maus as anyone in Keystone could ever have. Few if any of the guys from Keystone would ever come into contact with the Mau Maus like Wilkerson had. For this reason Anthony and some of the guys from Keystone and University School decided to go hear the preacher.

Anthony walked home after school on the Thursday evening of the opening night of the David Wilkerson Crusade. He did this to get some of the guys from Keystone to go with him. They agreed to go and were as excited about going to the event as Anthony was. Anthony left right after school and walked home. He didn't have to wait long on the rest of the guys from Keystone who were going with him. Gerald Johnson, Vincent Patterson, and Jerry and Joseph Smith were going with him. When they got to the campus, Anthony introduced them to several of his friends from school who had decided to go as well. This included Keith Testum, James Rogers, Anthony Humphrey, and a few others.

The initial meeting and introduction of Anthony's friends from Keystone and those from University School was awkward. Anthony realized how different his friends were from each other. The guys from Keystone were rough, tough, and just flat out mean. His friends from school thought they were all of those things but in reality were just kids from fairly good, and, in Anthony's view, wealthy families. They lived much different lives and had little in common with the boys from Keystone.

The relationship Anthony had with his friends had him feeling different with both groups. In some ways he lived in two different worlds at the same time. One of those, the world of Keystone, was unfortunately all too real for him. It was a constant reminder of the difficulties he had endured. It was a reminder of who he really was and that he didn't have much to be proud of. His family had problems and to others, he was from the projects. It wasn't the nice world his friends at school were accustomed to.

The other world Anthony lived in, the world at University School, was an escape and reminder of what he would like to become or at least have a taste of at some point in his life. It was a world where few people, if any, knew the reality of what he had experienced in life. They didn't know because they came from families that were mainly intact and where there was more money than Anthony would ever see.

While at school, Anthony was in a world where the expectations on him were based on what others had seen from his uncle Bill. To Anthony, it was a world which was sometimes fun, while at other times difficult. The difficulty caused a lot of confusion and hurt. It was difficult because Anthony knew the truth of who he was, not what others saw or thought.

All of this was a reminder of the games he carried on to make the friendships he made at school. Anthony's Keystone friends later on told him how wimpy his friends from school were after spending the evening with them. Anthony didn't say anything to his friends at school about the impressions the boys from Keystone had towards them. He knew it would hurt his relationship with them and put him in an uncomfortable position at school. Having to defend one group of friends to another was not something he wanted to do so he accepted the fact that he would not talk about one group to the other.

Anthony was concerned to some extent about the image some had of him. He wanted to impress others due to his own feelings of being unworthy. He knew of his own desire to have friends. His life at home had him in a situation where he had not experienced love and compassion. Anthony had few real friends, and the friends he had either had died or were not trustworthy. Many of them sought attention for themselves because of their own environment. Anthony knew they sought the same things he did and they had to take advantage of others to survive. This wasn't something Anthony and his friends looked down on each other for. It was just a way of survival.

Anthony's friends from school knew he was a tough kid, but they had no idea what type of environment he grew up in or what he was really like. Only a few of his friends from Keystone knew anything about what he was going through, regarding the abuse. It was something he kept a secret. It was years later before he shared with anyone about the physical and sexual abuse. Only a few people knew of his sexual perversions, and they were involved with those actions in one form or another.

******

Anthony and his friends from Keystone arrived at Memorial Gymnasium early in the evening. It was 45 minutes before the David Wilkerson presentation started. The first thing Anthony and his friends noticed was the number of people who were already on campus for the event. The gymnasium held several thousand people and there must've been over two thousand people already there.

Anthony and his friends sat farther away from the stage than they wanted but still saw the stage pretty well. They sat two-thirds of the way back from the stage, 20 rows up on the right, with a side view of the stage. This was disappointing because they could see the stage set up with instruments where a band was going to play.

The boys didn't know much about the musical artist, Dallas Holms, other than he was a recording artist who had played with a number of rock and roll bands. They were expecting a rock and roll concert with the presentation from David Wilkerson. This being the case they would have preferred to sit on the floor where they could see the band better and party during the concert. The boys didn't know what it was that David Wilkerson was going to be presenting on, but they hoped it was going to involve detail regarding the gangs in New York City and gangs in general. His work with gangs and their respect of Wilkerson was the focus of the movie and the book he had written. Anthony and the rest of the boys noticed in the lobby of the auditorium a number of other books and audio tapes David Wilkerson had written and recorded. They didn't take the time to stop and look at them due to the number of people who were around the tables looking at them. The boys wanted to get the best seats as possible.

There was little that surprised the boys other than the number of people already there and the types of people who where there. While there were a number of other kids who came from the streets and rough backgrounds, they were surprised at the number of people who appeared to come from church backgrounds. This was also somewhat disturbing. They would not have guessed that David Wilkerson would have many church people there to see him. Anthony and the rest of the boys, especially those from Keystone, were already making fun of and harassing people who looked like they came from church backgrounds. It was obvious to Anthony's friends from school that Anthony and his Keystone friends did not have much respect for the people around them. They were cussing during their conversations; it was how they always spoke. This was disturbing to those around them and to Anthony's friends from school. The friends from school were not as accustomed to this type of behavior. For Anthony and his friends from Keystone, it was just a way of life and no big deal. An elderly lady sitting near them asked them to watch their language. Gerald Johnson turned to her and said, "Shut your stupid mouth you ugly old hag." The lady was shocked. The rest of the boys laughed. The lady and her husband got up and moved to another seat. This didn't bother the boys though, especially those from Keystone. This was the attitude the boys from Keystone had most of the time, no matter where they were, including an event with a lot of Christians.

The boys finally took their seats and talked about a number of things for 35 minutes. They talked about drugs, girls, and the number of people coming into the gymnasium. They talked about the number and types of people coming in and where they were coming from. Occasionally they saw someone they knew across the gym and yelled at them. With all of the activity, the time passed quickly.

✱ ✱ ✱ ✱ ✱ ✱

The gym was filled to capacity. The floor was filled and they set up extra chairs. The sides of the gym were also filled. There were people standing around the perimeters of the gym who could not find seats. The fire department refused to let any more people into the gym because they were over capacity. They turned away a couple thousand people. The East Tennessee State University Memorial Gymnasium was at standing room only.

It wasn't long until everyone started clapping, almost spontaneously. A heavy set man in his 40's with short graying hair, wearing a dark blue pin striped suit, stepped up to the microphone. "Ladies and gentlemen, it is my pleasure to present to you, Dallas Holms and Praise." Anthony and the boys started yelling and screaming, anticipating the concert. They yelled assuming they were going to be experiencing a rock and roll concert. Everyone else in the gym was yelling and clapping their hands, but not as loudly and rowdy as Anthony and his friends from school, and especially those from Keystone.

Anthony and his friends were disappointed in the concert. They were used to listening to The Doors, Led Zeppelin, Bachmun Turner Overdrive, Foghat, and other hard rock and heavy metal groups. Dallas Holms and Praise was a good band who played a variety of rock styles but the style was more pop and middle of the road than the hard rock style they were used to. They were also turned off to the overt religious message. That might have been tolerable if Dallas Holms didn't stop so often to talk about God and religion. Their style was more like the style of America or Cat Steven's, good music but not for a bunch of rowdy friends. Dallas Holms would stop between songs and talk about Jesus. That was O.K., but to Anthony, it was something you just didn't do at a concert. You went to a concert to hear music, not preaching.

Anthony and his friends laughed and mimicked the events at the concert. They yelled "amen," and "Preach it brother" at the top of their voices making fun of Dallas Holmes and the people sitting around them enjoying the concert. For some of the people the concert may have been a big deal, but to Anthony and his friends the concert was lame. The boys distracted the people close to them. It didn't bother Anthony and his friends though. If anyone said anything, the boys became rowdier. The people around them didn't know how to respond. One of them finally told one of the security guards and he came to confront them. "Boys you are going to have to calm down or you're going to have to leave. We can't have you disturbing the people around you like this." The security guard was hesitant due to so many of them sitting there. "We're just enjoying the concert like everybody else. Are you going to make them leave too?" Anthony asked with a smart aleck attitude while pointing to large groups of young people sitting around the auditorium who looked like they had come with their church group.

"Boys I'm not going to tell you again. You need to calm down or..." The security guard stopped in midsentence. He noticed some of Anthony's friends from University School. They sat somewhat quietly not knowing what to expect from what was happening, and feeling embarrassed. The security guard noticed them because some of their parents worked on campus. "I guess you boys are O.K. If you would, though, just hold it down a little. These old people around you just don't know how to have any fun and we don't want to get them too upset." He said this with a wink and loud whisper.

Anthony knew everything would be O.K.. "Yes sir we'll be a little calmer."

"Thanks boys. Enjoy the show now." The security guard said in a calm manner as he walked away.

While the boys from Keystone mellowed down, they became in some ways more obnoxious to the people sitting around who had complained. They were extra loud and rowdy during the times everyone else was clapping or yelling. They stood up jumping up and down like many of those on the floor did. This disturbed those around them because they couldn't see what was happening on stage. One of the men sitting close to them started to say something but when he did, Anthony and the others turned and stared at him. The look they gave him was one which let him know he was messing with something he didn't want to mess with. He stopped short of saying something, especially when his wife grabbed him by the shirt sleeve and pulled him down into his seat and whispered something into his ear. He sat down without incident. The people around them knew the security guard was not going to do anything. They sat down, and left Anthony and his friends alone, letting them have their fun. This was the best thing they could do. The boys did not become as obnoxious when they thought they were not bothering the people around them.

The concert with Dallas Holms lasted between 30 and 45 minutes. The boys enjoyed parts of the concert, especially the more up tempo rock-oriented songs. The music was good even though it was Pop and Middle of the Road Rock. The musicians were good and most of the people in the gym seemed to have fun so that made the concert more fun for Anthony and his friends, although it wasn't what they were used to.

After the band was finished, the man who had come out earlier to introduce the band came onto the stage again. Everyone was giving a standing ovation to Dallas Holms and Praise. The man spoke after the applause. "Ladies and gentlemen, let's hear it one more time for Dallas Holms and Praise." Everyone clapped again but this time not as long or as enthusiastically.

"Ladies and gentlemen, we are going to take a 20 minute break before introducing David Wilkerson." As soon as he finished people got up to go take a break. Anthony and some of his friends took turns going out and using the bathroom, getting a drink of water and looking around. Anthony went and looked at some of the books and tapes which were for sale. He didn't have money to buy anything but he figured that with so many people looking around, if he saw anything he liked he could steal it before he left. He figured there would be more people looking at the end of the presentation, and with everyone leaving no one could catch him if he took something.

* * * * * *

Anthony was surprised at the physical appearance of David Wilkerson as he went to the microphone to speak. He was expecting someone much tougher. David Wilkerson stood 6 feet tall and was thinner than Anthony expected. He didn't look that old but was older than Anthony thought he would be. Anthony couldn't see him very well but guessed he was in his early 40's. He may have been older or even younger, but Anthony couldn't tell. David Wilkerson was wearing a nice suit but not dressed in a high dollar suit like the preachers Anthony had seen before.

Anthony and his friends were pleased that David Wilkerson started off talking about his experiences with the Mau Maus in New York City. He shared much of the information that Anthony and the others from Keystone had hoped he would. The Mau Maus were as tough as they thought they were. David Wilkerson worked with them and gained a great deal of respect from them and other gangs in New York City. He was not judgmental of them and accepted them.

It was obvious to Anthony that David Wilkerson had seen more in them than their violent actions toward others. Wilkerson understood why they did the things they did. To David Wilkerson it was more than kids being mean. They had been abused by the systems, families, and others around them.

Anthony was impressed; here was this man, telling these church people how they had failed to love those who they should be loving. He couldn't tell how the people received this message, but it was a message he appreciated. It was a message he was glad was being taught to those in attendance, especially the church groups. Deep down he knew that if they practiced what it was David Wilkerson was teaching then he would look at Christianity in a different way. Anthony was impressed that David Wilkerson was willing to say these things to the people in attendance. He said this without preaching or talking about God so much. Anthony was impressed that the church people were the ones getting preached to. After 30 minutes, the direction and manner of his message changed. David Wilkerson addressed those in the gym who were in gangs, or not Christians. Anthony knew he was now speaking to him and many of his friends from Keystone, school and others in attendance who had only come because of the reputation David Wilkerson had in regards to working with gangs and street people.

The way his message was received changed. Anthony listened intently and tried to understand what David Wilkerson was saying and trying to get across in his message. As David Wilkerson changed his message, many of those in gangs or from the streets didn't appreciate how he presented the message. They didn't handle confrontation well. It was O.K. for the confrontation with the church people but they had difficulty when it came to being confronted themselves. It probably had more to do with the fact that David Wilkerson knew what he was talking about and was honest with them. Anthony and a number of the guys from Keystone started talking loudly, disturbing those around them, and not caring if they disturbed David Wilkerson's presentation. They mocked David Wilkerson, Christianity, and those sitting around them. Anthony laughed at some of the mockery taking place among his friends but in other ways he was embarrassed by their actions. This went on for no more than 5 minutes when the boys in the group and the rest of the people in the gym were surprised at what David Wilkerson did next. The noise the boys made was heard over most of the gym, including by David Wilkerson. David Wilkerson had had enough; he stopped in midsentence and addressed the boys directly. "I am tired of you boys disturbing me as I speak. What I am sharing is the message of God Almighty and of his Son Jesus Christ. I will not allow a mockery of God in any way as I am speaking. If you don't like what I am saying, then leave. Otherwise keep your mouths shut or I will have each and every one of you thrown out of here. I will not tolerate God being mocked when I am speaking." David Wilkerson said this while pointing right at the boys.

David Wilkerson added one more point, "I want security to go over to where those boys are, and if they or anyone else creates a disturbance while I am speaking I want them thrown out of here. If they don't want to hear God's

Word then get them out of here. I expect respect." Anthony saw people from security come over and stand behind them. They observed them for the rest of the presentation.

Anthony and his friends for some reason were too embarrassed to get up and leave. They sat and listened intently to the rest of the presentation. Anthony was afraid; he and his friends were in an environment where they were out numbered by the majority of church people around them.

David Wilkerson impressed Anthony and his friends. The confrontation and demand for respect was something they respected and understood. They knew enough about David Wilkerson to know he meant exactly what he said. If he demanded this type of respect and had received it from the gangs in New York City, they needed to give him that same level of respect while he was in Johnson City.

David Wilkerson shared concepts of Christianity that Anthony had never heard. It was a presentation he wouldn't forget. David Wilkerson didn't take long to get over the confrontation with the boys. He spoke to those who were either from gangs, the streets, or not a part of the church. He was calm, caring, and spoke in a meaningful way which showed he understood what he was speaking about.

* * * * * *

Anthony listened intently to what he said. "I know that many of you have been hurt by the church and people who are in the church. What I am about to share with you though is something I want you to separate away from the church. I want you to understand that what I am about to share with you is the truth, a truth that has been distorted and taken advantage of by the Church and people in the Church."

"Here is the reality of what I want to share. We are all liars and deceivers. I don't mean we do that intentionally, what I mean is that we are all human. You need to understand something the Bible says in the book of Romans. The writer of that book tells us that we are all born into sin and are all sinners. The writer also tells us that without the shedding of blood there is no remission or forgiveness of our sins. Do you understand that? We are all sinners, even those of us who are involved in the church and profess to be Christians. We are all, and I mean all, including each of you in this gymnasium, sinners. That means we have all made mistakes and are all poor examples to others around us. You need to think of that when you look at people in the Church and other Christians as your examples."

David Wilkerson spoke some about the person who wrote Romans. "Understand who it was that wrote those words. The person's name was Saul and he later came to be known as Paul. Now Paul was someone who at one time hated Christians with a passion. He hated them to the point that he even assisted in the murder of many Christians in the early Church. Despite all of the hatred that Paul had towards Christianity, God still loved him enough to confront him about his life. Paul later became a Christian and wrote most of the New Testament. He eventually died because of his faith in Jesus. In reality, Paul was not much different than many of you here tonight. He had a hatred and rejection of Christianity yet he was willing to listen to God when Jesus Christ called him to follow Him."

David Wilkerson then addressed some of the issues relevant to Anthony. "I know this is why many of you have rejected Christianity, because of the examples you have seen from people from in the Church. You have looked at poor examples of Christianity and a faith many of us profess and claim." Anthony listened intently. He understood what David Wilkerson was talking about. Anthony had looked at Christians for most of his life as examples of why to not accept Christianity. He knew he had seen poor examples all around him throughout his life. The imperfections and abuses of those Christians was the primary reason he followed Satan at one point.

After pondering what David Wilkerson had said, Anthony listened, hanging on to every word. "Many of you have felt that you could work your way into heaven and into the presence of God, but let me tell you something else the Bible says. Jesus said who He was very plainly a number of times. I would like to quote a simple passage that is really easy to understand. It is a passage where Jesus Himself was speaking. Jesus said that no man comes to the Father except through me. Do you understand that? Jesus says that no man comes to the Father except through Him. How much simpler could this be to understand? You can't get into or experience the presence of God through Buddha, Mohammed, Confucius, yourself, or any other way except through Jesus Christ."

"There is another passage which many people learn but few accept. That verse is John 3:16. 'For God so loved the world that He gave His only Son. If anyone believes in Him he shall have everlasting life.' This is another passage which makes it clear who Jesus is. Jesus was and is, simply, God's only Son."

"Now there is something else we need to understand in this message. How and why did God give His only Son, and what does the shedding of blood mean to each of us? The answer is quite simple. There are several passages of Scripture which refer to Jesus as the perfect sacrifice. Early in history the only way to find favor with God was through the shedding of blood and sacrificing the best animal you had possession of, the first born. That is why so many would offer sacrifices to God. Despite the fact that many sacrifices were made, the reality of it is that none of them were good enough. That is one of the reasons you don't see sacrifices like this anymore. There is no way they can offer the quality required."

"That was why God was willing to offer Jesus as a sacrifice and Jesus was willing to be sacrificed. God offered and Jesus was willing to give the perfect sacrifice in order that each of us could receive salvation. That perfect sacrifice was Jesus Christ. He lived a perfect life, as a man, yet, still divine as God's Son, holy and perfect."

"Jesus was taken into custody by the Roman government and beaten, kicked, spit on, humiliated, and then crucified and killed on the cross. He was nailed with spikes to a cross through his wrists and feet, had a crown of thorns placed on his head in mockery of His kingship, and then had a spear thrust through his side at which point water and blood, or a blood and plasma mix came out of his side indicating that he was in fact dead."

"Jesus died on that cross as a sacrifice for all of our sins. Many would question this but there are several things I would like to bring out. First of all the largest selling book of all time is the Bible. The most researched book of all time is the Bible. The book which has changed the lives of more people than any other book in the history of mankind is the Bible. Now let me ask you a question in regard to this. Why? That is it. Simply, why do you think these things are? Is it because the Bible is a fairy tale? If so why does it continue selling, and changing lives like it does? I will tell you why. I have seen the most awful of men and women come into the presence of God, accept Jesus Christ as their Lord and Savior and their lives have been changed like nothing I have ever seen. Why do their lives change? Is it for a fairy tale? I will assure you that men don't change their lives around and dedicate themselves to fairy tales. I will assure you that miracles do not happen because of fairy tales. I will tell you instead that these things happen because someone has seen a truth that is larger and more real than them. That truth, ladies and gentlemen, is Jesus Christ."

Anthony found himself drawn into what David Wilkerson was saying. He was thinking about things he had not thought about before. David Wilkerson was saying things about God and Jesus in such a way that Anthony thought about and made comparisons in his own life. He could not get over the fact that so much of what he had seen was poor examples from Christians. He knew Jesus was a figure in history who had actually existed. He knew Jesus was real. Anthony knew that every time a check was written by someone to pay a bill or every time someone wrote down the date, whether they realized it or not they were putting down the number of years ago Jesus was born. He questioned why this magnitude of change took place if Jesus was not instrumental to mankind's success or hope? This was a truth Anthony knew, but he also knew he could not accept the lifestyles and examples of those around him he had seen profess Christianity.

Almost like clock work David Wilkerson addressed Anthony's questions. He spoke in a calm and persuasive style that had Anthony thinking. "I know many of you are skeptical of Christianity and Christians. For that reason I would like to address several things with you. As I mentioned earlier, people, people like you, people in churches, and yes even I, are not perfect. As long as you look to them for examples you will see imperfection. I want to tell each of you that if we are looking at others or we are looking at organizations like churches, then we are looking at the wrong things. Jesus said, 'I am the way the truth and the life. No one comes to the Father but by me.' People, Jesus is the one we need to look to for our example. Do you understand that? Jesus is the one we look at. It is His example, His leading, His teachings, His life."

"I know many of you have looked at other religious figures. Let me ask you this. Was Jesus Christ a liar or did He speak the truth? There can be no other alternative. Either we believe what He said and what He said was true, or we don't believe what He said and everything he said was a lie. Let me tell you this, Jesus' tomb is empty. We know historically that He lived, walked and talked on this earth, yet His tomb is empty. How do you suppose that came to be? After all, the Roman government was afraid of Him and His teachings, enough so that they had Him crucified on Calvary. On a hill called Golgotha Jesus was crucified and died. We know that, yet his tomb was empty after three days. Why was it empty? Especially after we know the government was so afraid of Jesus that they actually placed guards around the tomb? They knew the teachings and prophesies regarding the resurrection! The answer is simple folks. Jesus rose from the dead just like the Bible tells us he did. If you look historically at Christianity the largest growth of the faith per capita took place after his crucifixion. The reason for that is there were so many people who saw him alive after He was crucified. The Bible records many of those sightings and that is the perfect explanation of the growth of Christianity and why we know Jesus rose from the dead."

"I want each of you to think as to why Jesus was willing, yes willing, to give his life up. If you truly think about it and ask yourself, seeking to find the honest answer, you will know that Jesus was willing to do this because He loved you. Jesus loved each and every one of you enough that He was willing to give up His life for you. The Bible says, 'Behold I stand at the door and knock. If any man hears my voice and opens up the door I will come in and dine with him and he with me so that he may have everlasting life.' Jesus is knocking at your door, at your heart because He loves you, and wants you to have everlasting life."

"Jesus would choose that each of you find that true and perfect love in order that you may live with Him in Heaven forever. The only question is, will you accept that offer? Will you accept a perfect love that Jesus wants to give to you?" David Wilkerson spoke these words with a ring of truth and honesty.

Anthony knew in his heart of the sincerity and honesty with which David Wilkerson was speaking. He had been around enough people who were dishonest that he had learned ways to manipulate and take advantage of people. He saw honesty in David Wilkerson. It was evident to him that the message was an honest one. It was a message David Wilkerson believed in and one which deep down Anthony knew was true. Anthony was impressed by the perspective and methods of David Wilkerson. Here was a man, standing before thousands of people admitting his own faults, the faults of Christianity, and those calling themselves Christians. He didn't put them down, but helped those like Anthony know they were really no different.

Anthony didn't know exactly what it was, but he found himself feeling, in some strange sort of way, the presence of God. It was as if he could hear something say, "Anthony I know my people have let you down, but I want you to know I love you very much. I want to give you that love you want and need. Please, Anthony, make me your Savior." This was a strange, almost supernatural experience. He knew he was not having a drug flashback, but the voice was as real as anything he could explain.

Anthony focused on what David Wilkerson was saying. He was speaking in a much calmer tone now, reassuring those in the audience, "Many of you need to come to know Jesus Christ as your Lord and Savior. I want to make that experience and opportunity possible for you. Many of you are asking how do I come to know Jesus. Will God accept me after I've done so many evil or horrible things? Some of you will say, "I've been involved in drugs. I've prostituted my body. I've worshipped the devil. I've killed someone. You will say many things but let me tell you this. God's love and Jesus Christ's love is bigger, better, and stronger than any of the things you have done, it is bigger than you."

"The Bible gives us all kinds of examples where prostitutes, murderers, adulterers, abusers and so forth have come to know and love Jesus and, better yet, turn their lives around from their sin to the love Jesus offers them. Not one time, in the whole Bible, did one person come to Jesus, willing to give Him their lives in its entirety, did Jesus refuse them salvation. That is also the key for you. You have to be willing to give Jesus Christ your life in its entirety. You have to be willing to make the effort to live your life in its fullest in order to allow Jesus to live as an example in you. Many of you know what I am talking about now because you hear God's Spirit speaking to your hearts right now. That is the start. It does not stop there, though. You have to be willing to ask Jesus to come into your heart, into your life and tell Him that you are willing to live for Him, that you will love Him, and that you will do your best to serve Him. You have to make Jesus your Lord and Savior."

"Many of you are asking and saying that I want that for myself, but how do I go about getting it? It is simple. I won't go into all of the details but I will tell you that essentially the Bible says you have to do several things. First you have to ask. You have to say, 'Lord Jesus, I know I need you to come into my life to live. I have not had much of a life and I want my life to be the best it can be. Dear God I want you to be my Lord and Savior. I know that I have done wrong and there is no way I will ever see you or Your Kingdom of Heaven unless you come into my life to live. Dear God I ask that you will do that. I know that I have done wrong. I have sinned. It is because of that sin that I will not be able to enter into your perfect Kingdom. I ask you to come into my life now and I ask you to forgive me of the things I have done wrong. I thank you for forgiving me and I love you God. In Jesus' name I pray, Amen."

Anthony thought more about his need to make Jesus Christ his Lord and Savior. He heard that voice of persuasion more in his heart. He didn't know what to do, though. He noticed his friends and they were listening to the message, but a couple of them started joking about the things David Wilkerson was saying.

Anthony didn't want to embarrass himself or let his friends down. He didn't want to get caught up in the emotion of what was going on either. He didn't think that was what was going on in his thoughts. He felt that the message he was feeling in his spirit and the message David Wilkerson gave was convincing, real, and honest. He didn't know what to do. So he listened a little more to David Wilkerson,

"Many of you are saying, 'How is this possible and why do I need to make Jesus my Savior in order to be saved?' The answer is simple. You see God is a perfect God, full of perfect love. The Bible even tells us that God is love. With love like that, it is impossible for that love to be in the presence of wrong, hate or sin. God created man to have companions who would worship and respect Him, yet man sinned and chose to follow his own ways. Each of you has done things wrong which were either against God or against your fellow man. God is so perfect that He can not be in the presence of those of us who have done wrong and do not have forgiveness for that wrong."

"It was for this reason that God created hell. Not for man, but for a former angel named Lucifer. Lucifer wanted to be like God and was one of God's favorite angels yet he wanted to overthrow God in Heaven. It was for Lucifer or the Devil that God created hell. If we don't follow God then we follow Satan and will live with him in the place which was created for him. But God doesn't want that for us. That is the very reason why God was willing to send us His only Son to die for us, to be sacrificed for us. That is why Jesus allowed God to do that. So you see, Jesus freely gave his life up for us, so we could live with Him in Heaven forever. He did this because He wants to give us His love and salvation."

"When God looks at us he sees the things we have done wrong. He sees the sin. Yet, when we accept Jesus as our Savior, when God looks at us, instead of the sin, He sees nothing but the blood that Jesus shed on that cross for us. Jesus was the ultimate and perfect sacrifice. He never did any wrong and was perfect love. He was such a perfect gift of love that if we accept Him into our lives, then that is what God sees when he sees us. That is what will allow us to enter Heaven as opposed to hell. The problem is that each of you individually choose who you follow. God loves you so much that He wants you to decide who you will follow. Either follow Him, a perfect love, or Satan, a perfect deception. He gives you a free choice and the opportunity to make your own decision."

"That is the decision God is speaking to many of you about at this very moment. Who will you follow, and what will you do with your life? For those of you who feel God speaking to you, we are going to give you an opportunity to come down front so we can pray that prayer with you and then go back in the back into a private room in order to explain a few things to you. Dallas Holms will come back and sing a couple of songs while we go to the back with those of you who come down front deciding to give your life to Jesus."

"I would ask that if you need, to come up front if you want to experience the love Jesus has for you. Don't be afraid to get your life in order with God. He loves you to the point that He gave the ultimate gift, His Son to die on a cross. Many of you may have known God and have either fallen away from Him and need to get your lives back in order or haven't been living for Him in the way you know you should. This invitation is for you as well. Please come and accept God's love for you."

"Many have asked me who the toughest person I ever met is. The answer is simple, Jesus Christ. What tougher person could there be than the person who loved you so much that He was willing to give up His innocent life in such a way that it would be tortured, beaten, kicked, spat on, and abused in the way Jesus' was. He went through and experienced the ultimate rigors of pain. Yet Jesus could have stopped all of this at any time and left us all to our own destruction if He had wanted to. Yet He didn't. If Jesus was willing to do that for us, shouldn't you be at least willing to take a few steps and come down to the front of this stage and pray for Jesus to come into your heart and life. Jesus said in the Bible that if you are not willing to confess Me before men on earth then I will not be willing to confess you before my Father in heaven."

"So, that question about the toughest person I ever knew is easy. Jesus was, and is, by and far the toughest yet most loving person to ever live. Yet He was not just a person, He was the Son of God. You can have a relationship with Jesus if you are willing to invite Him into your life. Will you come down and start that relationship with Him tonight?"

Dallas Holms came to the stage and started playing and singing as David Wilkerson walked to the front of the stage to meet the people coming to get saved. There were hundreds of people who went up during the invitation. Anthony noticed people pouring out of the seats they were sitting in and walking down to the stage. He felt in his heart the need to go down and get saved. He didn't know what it was but he knew he needed to go. He felt the need to make Jesus his Savior. He had done exactly what David Wilkerson had spoken about. He had looked at the wrong examples. He realized that he should have been looking at Jesus and not those in the Church, his family or friends. Jesus was the example he should have examined.

Anthony started to walk down front. He started to get out of his seat when he heard one of his friends, Keith Testum laughing with Anthony Humphrey. Anthony looked over as they pointed to one of the students from school walking down front from one of the other sections of the gym. Anthony's friends from Keystone were also getting restless and were already talking about leaving the gym and going on home. Anthony didn't know what to do. He knew he didn't want to embarrass himself. He didn't want them laughing at him. He realized it was a decision he didn't need to make right then anyway. Anthony made his decision about what to do, at least for this night. He reached over and poked one of his friends from Keystone. "Hey guys, are you ready to leave, after all we have a long walk home?"

Gerald Johnson responded, "Yeah man, let's split this joint."

Anthony whispered over to his friends from school that they were leaving and told them good-bye. Anthony and his friends from Keystone started their long walk home. They talked some about the David Wilkerson Crusade, but not as much as Anthony thought they would. He was glad for that because he still heard that small voice telling him that he was loved and he needed to accept that love. He didn't know where it was coming from but he was sure it had to be from God. Anthony was not involved in many of the discussions on the way home. It was a good walk home though, the night was clear and they enjoyed each others company. The Keystone boys broke into a pay phone to get them some money to buy something to drink. They usually got into more trouble than that but this night would be different. They had just come from a church function and that was new to all of them.

~ Chapter 21 ~

Saved

Anthony stayed at his mother's house for a change instead of with one of his friends or the streets. After walking home from the Crusade he lay in bed thinking for what seemed like hours regarding the things he heard at the crusade. The voice inside him was a constant, telling him he needed to give his life over to Christ. He didn't know how to explain what was going on but he couldn't deny his experience.

Anthony felt the voice telling him God loved him. Better things awaited him if he only gave in to and accepted God's love. This meant recognizing that he had done wrong and yielding his life over to Jesus Christ. It was as if the voice reminded him of the things he went through while growing up and how much he wanted to be loved.

Anthony was reminded of the words of David Wilkerson. People needed to look at the example of Christ when deciding to follow Him or not. It was clear to Anthony; the message of Christ's love was true, he couldn't argue with the facts of the Gospel, facts he knew were historically and spiritually true. He knew he had to do something with his life. He could either follow God or reject him and go his own way. What he thought were Christian practices were not. He saw imperfect people pretending to be perfect. He was confident that many of the people he had observed never had a relationship with Christ. He knew from experience that following Satan had no promise. He also knew he had made mistakes and that if God was perfect and loving he couldn't be in the presence of God without being represented by Jesus. He felt that if he gave his life to Christ he would be no different than the Christians he had observed while growing up.

It was getting late and Anthony finally responded to the voice heard in his heart. He said out loud, "Let me sleep on these thoughts and see how I feel tomorrow. If I'm still having questions about who you are and what I should do with my life and this is not just an emotional thing then I'll go to the crusade tomorrow night and see what happens from there." After saying this he went to sleep.

Anthony got up early the next morning and got ready for school. He slept well and was feeling good. It was Friday and it was supposed to be a nice, warm, clear day. It was a day he looked forward to because if his walk to school was in nice weather; odds were the rest of the day was going to be good. Anthony was getting dressed when he started having the same thoughts from the night before regarding Jesus. The feelings from the previous night had not gone away. He was convinced that what he was experiencing was real. He couldn't explain what was causing the feelings but he knew they were there. Anthony didn't know what he needed to do regarding accepting Jesus into his life. He was convinced he wasn't going through an emotional episode but something supernatural like he had never experienced before.

Anthony's walk to school seemed to take an unusually long time. He was still trying to decipher and understand the feelings he was experiencing. He didn't know what to do with his life. The decision to follow God required sacrifice and change. He didn't know what would be involved but he knew there would be critique from his friends at school and from Keystone. He struggled through the day weighing both the positives and negatives of the decision that he knew deep down he was going to have to make. While at school Anthony continued to struggle with his decision. He stayed out of trouble but was not focused on the work taking place in the classroom. This was unusual because he had been enjoying school and maintained his C- average. For him this was a good average and an indication that he was spending time in the classroom thinking about what he was doing and occasionally getting his homework. The fact that he was passing was an accomplishment, considering his past experiences at school.

All day Anthony went back and forth on the inevitable decision he had to make. His friends knew something was going on, but they knew better than to confront him. He had a bad temper and it was not unusual for his temper to show by hitting someone or finding some cruel way to get back at them. He wasn't in a bad mood, but this only confused his friends which caused them to stay away from him. He was confused by what was going on in his heart and mind but in a strange sort of way he was calmer than he had been in some time.

If anything, Anthony was nervous. His nerves were on end throughout the day, on occasion he even found himself breaking out in cold sweats. It was this way through most of the day until he decided at the end of the day to go on back to the David Wilkerson Crusade that night. He knew he needed to go to the Crusade again, but on this night, it would be best to go alone.

* * * * * *

Anthony arrived at the East Tennessee State University Memorial Gymnasium even earlier than the night before. He believed that getting there early would assure him of getting a good seat. He was alone but that was O.K., he knew he had a lot of things to process in his own mind and he didn't need the distractions from the previous night. Anthony was surprised when he arrived and saw there were just about as many people there as the night before, despite him arriving earlier. He was able to get a better seat but it was not much better. He was 12 rows down from where he sat the night before. He was sitting in the bleachers instead of the seats with backs on them.

Anthony sat back listening to the voice inside him telling him that Jesus loved him and that Jesus wanted to give him a new life and perfect love. He was struggling like never before. He knew his experiences with Christianity. He didn't want to be the hypocrite he had seen from observing Christians in the past. Despite these feelings he was more confident than ever before, that God was real and that Jesus was God's Son. Anthony wanted to give God a chance. He wanted to do this because he needed the love God was offering. He was tired of the heartache and hurt that was such a dominant part of his life. He sat in his seat for what seemed like hours. He knew he needed to give God a chance. He was oblivious to what was going on around him and the things that were being said and done from the stage. Anthony was deep in prayer asking God questions and trying to come to some type of decision for his life. Dallas Holms was already playing his pre-crusade concert, and Anthony was not sure how long he had been playing. He missed the introduction and much of the concert. Anthony didn't notice the concert or the actions of people sitting around him who enjoyed the concert. He continued to pray with his face in his hands as his arms rested on his knees.

The more Anthony prayed and sought to understand himself the more he was convinced he needed to give his life to Jesus. As he thought about making this decision he felt a sense of peace and comfort like he had never experienced before. He also felt a sense of love like he had never known. He didn't know how to explain the feelings but it brought a warm sense of emotions over him. This peace Anthony felt provided peace for a number of reasons. He didn't feel the voice telling him he needed to do anything other than ask Jesus to come into his life and trust him as his Savior. Anthony needed forgiveness and knew deep down, that others would fail but that was O.K. It was his obligation to look at Jesus as his example. When that happened he would make every effort to follow Jesus as his leader and guide. Anthony knew that the bad things in life that had happened were not Jesus' fault. There were many people who had done wrong to him. Anthony was also responsible for his own actions to others. Anthony knew he was doing the right thing if he gave Jesus a chance.

David Wilkerson was speaking for some time, but Anthony had no idea what he was speaking about. It wasn't that he wasn't listening; it was that he was preoccupied with listening to what he came to know as Gods Holy Spirit who helps give consciousness. Anthony knew the decision he had to make when the time came. In many ways Anthony was carrying on a conversation with God. He heard many of the things he needed to hear in regards to love and forgiveness. He was sure about what he had to do and it was then that he became conscious as to what was going on around him. David Wilkerson finished speaking and introduced Dallas Holms to come up and sing for the invitation.

Dallas Holms sang the traditional praise song, Alleluia. He hadn't finished the first line and Anthony found himself getting up out of his seat and walking down front to ask Jesus to accept him, faults and all. He was going to ask Jesus to be his Savior and try and live his life for God. Anthony took a few steps and realized he was crying. He had cried before in front of relatives and others but this was different. He was sensitive but as he got older he got over his sensitivity. He became callused to the need for sensitivity that went on in his life. He even cried on occasion to get his way but the tears he shed here were different. As he walked down the aisle toward the front of the gym, he felt an overpowering sense of love come over him. The closer he got to the stage the more he felt the love. His tears were a mixture of sorrow and joy because he knew how much wrong he had done but he also experienced a powerful sense of love that could not be explained as coming from any place other than God. Only God could love as much as he felt at this moment. Anthony made the decision to make Jesus his Savior, and as he did this he felt peace and love. The more he walked, the more he felt that sense of love; with each step the love grew. He had a sense of peace and joy like he had never felt. He could feel the power and love he was looking for. He now understood why so many Christians he had seen became emotional. If God was capable of doing this for him, then he knew he was making the right decision for his life. The love he experienced at this moment was strong enough that he knew he never wanted to turn away from the God who loved him despite the heartache and hurt Anthony had perpetuated on others.

Anthony was on the front row of what seemed like hundreds of people. People stood there to turn their lives over to Jesus. The closer Anthony got to the front of the stage the more he cried tears of joy. He wasn't the only one experiencing this love. He saw others just like him, some who were a part of a church and others that had never set foot in a church. Anthony was crying almost uncontrollably. The tears were in many ways due to the things he had done wrong. He was embarrassed for the way he had treated others, yet he knew that God was taking away all of his past wrongs. It was as if each tear symbolized the wrong things he had done. Anthony knew this and was excited and as happy as he had ever been. He wanted to shout at the top of his lungs, "Thank You God!"

After getting up front, David Wilkerson had those responding to the invitation pray a simple prayer. Anthony prayed the prayer with the all of those standing alongside him, "Dear God, please forgive me of the things I have done wrong in my life. I know that you love me and that is why you sent your Son Jesus to die on the cross for me. I accept that love and ask Jesus to come into my heart to live as my Savior. I thank you for the forgiveness of my sin and I will try to live my life for Him. I will allow Jesus to live through me. I know that Jesus is your only Son, born of the Virgin Mary. I know Jesus gave up his life up for me on the cross because He loved me. Dear God, I also know and accept the fact that Jesus rose again from the grave on the third day so that I might have eternal life. Jesus is now with you in Heaven, and I will see both of you some day. I thank you for that love and I thank you God for saving me and allowing me to experience your love, the most perfect of all love. Thank you God, it is in Jesus' name I pray this prayer. Amen."

As Anthony finished praying the prayer he realized his hands were extended towards heaven. He did not know why this was. He only knew it felt right. Maybe in some way he was trying to reach up to God. Shortly after praying with the others on the floor there beside him, and some still sitting in their seats, he walked back to a private room with some volunteers from the crusade who were on the floor helping those who made decisions to follow Christ. They walked to a large room behind the staging area. It was crowded due to so many people making decisions. The room was hot from all of the bodies, yet no one complained. The counselors spoke to those in the room. "Many of you are making the decision to follow Jesus for the first time in your lives. To those of you I congratulate you, and want you to know that you have made the most powerful and important decision of your lives. I also want you to know that the Devil is not happy with the decision you have made. He will make every effort to pull you away from Jesus. When that happens, try to get in touch with a friend who is a Christian or start calling on Jesus to fight those battles for you. Do not allow Satan to get a hold of you and do not allow yourselves to go back to doing the things or following the ways of Satan."

"We also want you to take a little book with you, a book David Wilkerson wrote a while back called The Jesus People Handbook. This little book is a wonderful book that will help you in your walk with God. Take it and read it. The book is free and will help you a great deal. We also want to get your names, addresses and a record of what decision you have made tonight in regards to following Jesus. We will gather this information and give it to local pastors so they can follow up on you and help you out with your walk with God."

Anthony did as he was asked to do by the counselors. He filled out the information sheet and got a copy of the small booklet. He got ready to leave the room when he saw someone he knew but had not seen in years. Anthony saw the Black kid who used to take up for him when he lived in Northside. He was now a Junior or Senior in High School and was one of the better football players in the city. He eventually played college football and in the NFL. Anthony went to speak to him. He also remembered Anthony and they gave each other a hug. Neither of them could believe that they made the decision to follow Jesus on the same night after not seeing each other for so many years. This was a blessing to Anthony because he realized he wasn't there alone. It was a reminder to Anthony of where he came from and what God was taking him out of. Anthony was pleased and felt the happiness and love from God. He was glad God gave him someone to experience this moment with.

✶ ✶ ✶ ✶ ✶ ✶

At Manna House George asked. "Anthony, how did you feel about becoming a Christian, or do you feel that you became a Christian?"

"Oh I know this was the moment I became a Christian. I know even though I had prayed the sinner's prayer before, and even though I had been baptized. It was and still is one of the most meaningful if not the most meaningful events in my life. I know now that what I had been hearing was God's Holy Spirit. He was ministering to me, trying to get me to make that decision which I ultimately made. I know now after all these years that this is the one experience, the one event which allowed me to experience love and obtain eternal life. From this point in my life I never worried about death because I knew that if anything happened to me I would live and be with Jesus in Heaven."

Anthony changed his attitude; he wasn't as joyous about what he was now sharing. "I only wish the David Wilkerson Crusade people would have done a little more to help me and some of the others who went down front that night. It was years later before I experienced the joys of being a Christian."

George looked at Anthony somewhat confused and asked, "What do you mean, Anthony?"

"Well, they really didn't tell us what we needed to do to grow as a Christian. I guess that was supposed to be the stuff the preachers and all were supposed to go over with us in the follow up, but no one ever followed up on me. I mean, well I know, that I truly made Jesus my Savior that night, but I really didn't know what it meant to be a Christian. How was I to grow as a Christian? What was I supposed to do? Stuff like that." Anthony was confident, and had thought a great deal about this over his life.

"What types of things are you talking about?" George asked.

"It was some years later before I stopped being involved in sexual activities or drugs. I sort of had some sense that what I was doing was wrong, but I really didn't understand. I know this sounds weird, but I really wanted to follow Christ but I didn't have anyone helping me. I didn't even really know or understand the importance of reading the Bible, going to church or anything like that. Imagine someone growing up in the streets, being involved in the things I was. How are they supposed to know what to do if no one tells them?"

"But that eventually came and you learned what to do didn't you?" George asked.

"Yeah, but it took some time. I guess it was a few years later but I did eventually learn how to grow in my faith." Anthony said confidently.

"Can you give me an example of something that happened after your salvation to help me understand?" George asked.

"Heck I could give you all kinds of examples." Anthony said, "Do you want me to give you one from right away or later on?" He asked.

"Tell me about something that happened shortly after your salvation experience" George said.

"Well if I had to pick one, it would be an episode that happened just a few weeks later."

* * * * *

Anthony tried to understand what his new faith was all about, but he was confused. The confusion lasted for some time. While his faith and belief was a critical part of his life, he had many of the same associations, some good, and some bad.

Andre Gilliam was a member of a rival gang from Tyler apartments who had a beef with Anthony. He was several years older than Anthony and had a reputation. Anthony had a reputation too, but he was never in a place where he faced life and death decisions. Andre forced him to face this one afternoon when Anthony was home alone.

Anthony was listening to music. While sitting in the living room he heard Andre yell at him from the back yard. "Beechup, get your ass out here, now."

Anthony didn't know what was going on but he realized it wasn't good. He went to the kitchen, looked out the back window and saw Andre standing there. Andre wasn't at the door; he was in the yard yelling toward the door. "Come on man; get your ass out here." Anthony immediately ran to his mothers' bedroom and grabbed a 38 caliber hand gun out of the bedroom night stand. He went to the back door, opened it, and stepped out onto the back step. "What do you want, man?" He asked.

"I've come here to resolve a problem, we need to settle some things, and I'm going to take it out of your ass." Andre said as he walked towards Anthony.

Anthony took the 38, pointed it at Andre, one hand on the trigger, the other hand bracing and supporting his wrist. "Stay put man; we ain't going to settle anything. You take another step I'll shoot your ass."

Andre looked straight into the eyes of Anthony as he took another step.

With a quick motion to the ground, Anthony shot, hitting the ground close to Andres' feet, Anthony immediately pulled the gun up pointing it to Andre's chest. "Take another step man and I'll blow your ass away!"

Andre stood there, he wasn't shaking, wasn't afraid, he maintained eye contact. "I'll leave this time mother fucker, but if I ever see you alone on the street, your ass is mine and they'll be reading about finding your body in the newspaper."

Anthony was emphatic, "I said leave mother fucker." Andre turned and walked away. Anthony realized he was the one shaking.

*****

"Would you have shot him?" George asked.

"I have to say, yeah, if he had taken another step I would have shot him." Anthony responded.

"You would have had no reservations about shooting him?" George asked.

"I honestly don't think I would have." Anthony responded. "There was that components of the streets that hadn't left me, I guess I sometimes wonder if it ever left me. Don't take it wrong, it isn't that I would want to or would resort to shooting someone, but I don't think the streets where I came from will ever leave me."

"That is interesting." George stated. "I can sort of understand where you are coming from a little more."

Anthony and George carried on their conversation for a little while longer. They spoke more of some of the issues they had just talked about so George would have a better understanding of where Anthony was coming from. Anthony was confident in what he was talking about. It was a difficult concept for Christians to understand but he was sure of its truth in his own life. It was a concept which to him made perfect sense. He knew he made the decision to follow Jesus with sincerity and honesty. He also knew he didn't know what to do. He didn't have the help to grow in his faith like he needed.

Anthony knew the love and peace he experienced after making his decision to follow Christ. That was a love and peace he never turned away from or denied. He still had trouble in a number of areas including his home life. That trouble and others even got worse. He was sure though; he wouldn't have to go through those things alone; he had the Creator of the universe with him.

~ Chapter 22 ~

Goodbye (For Now)

Anthony was up early for a Saturday morning. He was looking forward to a good weekend but didn't know if telling his friends about getting saved would have an impact or not. He thought about what to say to them for most of the morning. He had until noon before he saw Gerald and the other guys in Keystone. He was excited and up early, he knew they would sleep until later in the day.

Anthony was sure he was saved the night before. He still felt peace in his heart and the love of Christ. This was new and unusual and something he had never experienced. As the day went by he thought about the decision he made the night before. He decided to tell his friends. He was excited and felt he could share the good news. At mid day he went to Gerald Johnson's house to make plans for the day. They got several of the guys from the neighborhood together.

Anthony, Gerald, Vincent, and some of the other guys played basketball, and went up into the woods. While playing basketball at the elementary school Anthony told them of his decision the night before. He was sure he needed to share about what he had done, but he didn't know what to say or how to say it. This was the first time for him talking about God. "Hey guys what did you all do last night anyway?" He asked.

"Ah, shit man, we didn't do much of anything, tried to go out and get some girls but we didn't have any luck. Where the hell were you anyway? I thought you were going to go out with us but you never showed up." Jerry Smith answered.

"Well, I went back to the David Wilkerson Crusade last night." Anthony answered.

Before being able to go on into more detail Gerald Johnson interrupted with laughter. "Shit, man, you went back to see that preacher? Why the hell did you go and do that? You got religion on us or what?" Gerald asked, laughing.

Anthony tried to explain in such a way that it would open up the door to tell the guys about getting saved, "Well, you guys remember the night before when we all went. Well, I just couldn't stop thinking about what David Wilkerson said in his message. He seemed like a cool guy and all, and I don't think he was lying to us so I decided to go back and hear him again. I wanted to see what I felt after hearing him a second time. Would I still be thinking about what he said or what? I didn't know. I had to answer that question for myself."

"Goodness gracious, if Anthony Beechup hasn't gone out and found religion on us." Vincent said as everyone else stopped playing basketball to listen in. They laughed because they didn't expect Anthony to be one of the people from Keystone who would ever find religion and they knew he would take what Vincent had said as a joke. Everyone was surprised though when they didn't see Anthony laughing.

"Well, guys, to me it really isn't that funny, because I did. I went up last night during the altar call to get saved." He said waiting to hear his friends' response.

"Jesus Christ," Gerald Johnson responded. "What does this mean; you can't party with us or what? I guess this means you can't do any more drugs or hang out either, right?" Gerald was angry because he thought one of his friends was going to leave him or start pushing religion.

Anthony thought about the question because he didn't know the answer. He knew something didn't feel right about the conversation but he really didn't know the answer to the question Gerald asked. He knew Jesus would give him the love he needed but he didn't know the answer to what it was he was supposed to do with his new found faith. He was not hearing or experiencing a voice or feeling from God like he the previous nights. He didn't know the answer to the question he was just asked. Anthony wanted to do what God wanted him to do but had no idea what it was he was supposed to do. Did being a Christian mean he had to go about things differently? He didn't know so he came to the best conclusions he could. He finally came to the conclusion that God said He would take him like he was and all he needed to do was give his life over and believe in Jesus and allow God to love him and for him to love God. After some thought and struggle Anthony answered Gerald, "Come on man, just because I decided to get saved doesn't mean I can't do the things I did before, and you guys of all people should know why I got saved. I mean if God is as powerful as David Wilkerson made Him out to be then I want a part of that. There are other reasons I got saved, too, but I don't think you guys would understand. I just did and I'm glad I did. I don't see it changing me that much, though."

"Well, if it doesn't change you that much I guess that's O.K., but if you start to get that religion shit and start preaching to us, well we'll just have to beat the shit out of you like we have some of those preachers coming into Keystone before." Gerald said while laughing, yet accepting of what Anthony had said. After all, Anthony had not laid any religion talk on them, because he was back in his environment.

It was the day after and this was all new to Anthony. He didn't know much about what he was supposed to do with his new found faith, so, why make things worse until he had an idea of what being a Christian was all about. He wanted to learn but he expected to be taught by someone. He knew he needed to be taught in order to learn. He anxiously awaited the follow up phone call or visit he was told about from the counselors in the room at the crusade. He would learn to do the things he was supposed to do with his new faith. Anthony felt the love he experienced from his salvation. He didn't know the details of his new faith or how to allow the love to grow within him or how to show it to others.

The boys played basketball for another hour and then went up into the woods outside of Keystone. Some of the boys talked about going to the Jiffy Mart and buying a few tubes of glue, after all, it was the weekend and the weekend was for getting high. Anthony had some reservations about sniffing glue but didn't know exactly why he felt this way. He didn't know if his new found salvation had anything to do with him being hesitant or not. He decided that if God didn't want him doing glue then He would make it clear to him like He did his need for salvation. Anthony sniffed the glue but didn't know what God thought about it. It wasn't as if the glue was okay, he just didn't feel anything. As the glue started to have an effect Anthony heard one of the boys say, "Beechup man, if getting saved means that you can still keep doing drugs, girls, and all that shit, I might want to get saved, too." The others laughed. Anthony wasn't sure who said this; his head was spinning from the effects of the glue. He just heard it and knew something about the comment made him sick in his spirit, something was wrong.

* * * * * *

George Wilson looked at Anthony, squarely in the eye when he asked the question, "Anthony, do you really think you were saved the night before? I mean why were you still using drugs, still cursing and hanging around these guys?"

Anthony was surprised by the question. He was offended because he had mentioned that he had only been saved for one day and no one had bothered to tell him what he needed to do as a Christian. It was obvious to George from his tone of voice that Anthony was upset by the question. "Yeah, I know

I was then, and am now. The thing is, George, that it was like I said earlier, no one had bothered to tell me what I needed to do or what being a Christian was all about. There was no support then and really any for quite some time thereafter. That is one reason why I have so many problems with these preachers who do their altar calls and never work at helping someone grow in their faith. I think it is about them getting trophies instead of really caring about the people who responded to their message about Jesus. Even in the Bible, Jesus and His disciples made the effort to train and help the people who had made their decisions. I mean, after all, I didn't really know any Christians that I trusted; they had hurt me while I was growing up and they would have been some of the last ones I would have depended on to give me any kind of help and understanding of my new faith. All I had was the same friends I had while I was growing up. They were the ones who had grown up on the streets and seen the same poor examples of Christianity I had seen. I don't know why it was that way but that was all the friends I had." Anthony was emphatic and sure of the things he said.

Anthony changed the direction the conversation. "In many ways, I still hold the church responsible for what happened with me over the next few years. They should have been there to help in the follow up, and they were nowhere to be seen."

George was somewhat understanding; seeing the sincerity in Anthony's explanation, but he was still confused. He asked, "You mean you never got any type of follow up or help after you got saved but still felt that you were saved and accepted that salvation and Jesus for who He was?"

Without hesitation Anthony answered, "Most definitely, I was, and still am, saved. I knew who Jesus was, I accepted it, and I sought His help and desired His love. I wanted so much to have a relationship with someone who would love me unconditionally and Jesus was that person. The reality of it though, was that I didn't have any Christians or church to help me grow spiritually or explain spiritual things to me. All I knew of spirituality was what I had experienced with Lucifer and my friends from the streets. That certainly wasn't the same type of relationship Jesus desired for me. I mean, I still felt then and even to some extent now, the same about many of the churches and the lackluster role they take in helping new believers. I didn't and don't trust very many of them, but yeah, I loved Jesus then and I love Him now. I accept and know that Jesus is my Savior and I made that decision that night. The confidence of that decision has never wavered and I know that I will be, well, literally forever grateful for the relationship I have with Jesus."

Anthony was assured in what he was talking about. He began to grow more confident as the shared. "For me, the difference is that I now accept Him as my Lord and Savior, my Forgiver, my Leader. I also understand the role of the Holy Spirit in my life which I didn't understand or know about then. The truth of it though, as far as getting help, is that I never did go to anyone until it was almost too late. I expected to have someone from the crusade or some church start to help me. I had given them my address and everything. I thought there was a reason for that. To this day, I have never received any follow up or help from David Wilkerson's group. I don't know whose fault that was. I tend to believe it was the churches in the communities who helped put on the crusade, who was supposed to do the follow up. I believe that David Wilkerson's people gave the information to the churches that those of us making decisions filled out, but it was the churches that didn't do what they were supposed to do with it. I just don't know. I do know it was some years later and after a lot more stuff happened in my life before I grew as a Christian."

George accepted what Anthony had said because he saw and heard the earnestness and sincerity in his face and voice. He asked Anthony, "O.K., Anthony, if you don't mind, go on ahead. What happened next in your life and journey?"

* * * * * *

Anthony was surprised to see Wanda walk into the house as early as she did. He had been home for some time and was watching television. He had not seen his mother much lately so he usually went home and watched television or rested after school before going out with his friends from Keystone. It had been at least a week since he had seen her.

Wanda was going out more with her new boyfriend, Walter Hudgins. She and Robert went through a bitter divorce but they had only been separated for weeks before she started seeing Walter on a more open basis. He was 6' 2" tall and had a medium to heavy build. He weighed 200 pounds, had dark hair and long sideburns like Elvis. Anthony thought Walter was in a time warp. He loved professional wrestling and had a combed back duck-tail hair-cut. He even had the little loop in his dark hair that fell down over his forehead. Walter lived in a small town 10 miles south of Johnson City called Erwin. Erwin, Tennessee, was a small town with a population of 15,000 – 20,000 people. Erwin was not thought well of by most people in Johnson City. Many thought Erwin was racist and backwards. It was unique because in the entire county there were no minorities who lived there. Everyone who lived in Unicoi County was Caucasian.

The school and town had a reputation for racism, especially towards Blacks, whether the town fit the stereotype or not was another matter. Anthony didn't know about the reputation the school had. He assumed that since no Blacks or minorities lived or went to school there the rumors were true. Erwin had such a bad reputation that it was the only small town surrounding the Tri-city area which many residents in the Tri-cities did not recognize as being a part of the Tri-cities. Much of Erwin's reputation was a shame for various reasons. Many people who lived in Erwin worked in and spent a lot of time in Johnson City. There were a number of the city and county residents who had numerous friends who where Black or from other racial persuasions. While it was true that many were racists, most were not. In reality Erwin was not much different than other towns in the South during the period. The problem for Erwin was a few residents gave the town and county a bad name.

It was unfortunate that Erwin and Unicoi County had the reputation it had. It had to be one of the most beautiful areas in the United States. Even the name of the county, Unicoi, was an indication of the beauty of the area. Unicoi is a Cherokee word which means "The valley beautiful." Unicoi County and Erwin are just that, a big, beautiful valley. The town of Erwin is surrounded by the Blue Ridge and Smoky Mountains. Running through the center of the large valley is the Nolichucky River. The Nolichucky is a river with history behind it, history that involved some of Anthony's earlier relatives. Areas that had some of his ancestors knowing others who lived on the river as neighbors, residents and neighbors like Davy Crockett and Daniel Boone. There was more to Unicoi County and Erwin that Anthony knew about, and for him that was too bad because that knowledge had a lot to do with the development of his ideas about the community. Because of that reputation and the attitude he had developed about Erwin and Unicoi County, he was hurt terribly by what his mother was about to tell him.

"Hey Anthony, what have you been doing lately?" Wanda asked in a nice way, which confused Anthony. She was nicer lately but he figured it was due to her spending so much time with her new boyfriend Walter Hudgins.

"Oh, not much I guess. I just got in from school a little while ago and wanted to sit down and watch the Braves play on T.V. You know, Hank Aaron is still playing pretty good." He was hoping his mother would express some interest in him and baseball. He was disappointed because baseball was not what she wanted to talk about.

"That's good, honey, but there is something I need to talk to you about." Wanda said, not paying attention to what Anthony had said. Anthony recognized this unconcern on her part and was why he answered her in a defeated, non-caring tone. "Yeah, what is it?" He was shocked at what he heard his mother say,

"Well, honey, you know that me and Walter have been seeing each other lately. Well, we've actually been doing more than seeing each other. I've been spending a lot of time with him and staying with him some at his house over in Erwin. Well, honey, we love each other and we want to get married. We've talked a lot about it and he is willing to accept you and Madeline as his children. I think it will be good for all of us if Walter and I get married. It will give you and Madeline a father, and I know you won't have to worry about him. He is so much nicer and kinder than Robert ever was. Anyway, we have decided to get married and we are going to be moving over to Erwin where Walter has a house we can all live in. Besides we are going to have to look for a place to move into anyway. Robert and I are going to sell this house and split up the money from the sale for the divorce settlement."

Anthony was in a state of shock. It was a few minutes before he said anything. "Could I stay with Mamaw and Granddaddy Beechup?"

"No I don't think that would be good for us. You need to live with me, Walter and Madeline." What Wanda said next did excite Anthony a little, "Besides, Erwin has a football team and you can get back to playing football. I know how much you love to play and this will give you a chance to play on a high school team. Wouldn't you like that?" Wanda asked, knowing what the answer would be.

"Yeah, I'd like to play football again for a school and all, I just don't know if I want to leave my friends at University High or Keystone." Anthony answered the question, confused. He didn't want to move, yet he appreciated the chance to play football again.

"Well, Anthony, this is what we are going to do. So you can either go along with it and see the positive side of things or go on and be miserable. It's up to you how you deal with it, but we are moving." She didn't raise her voice and yell but she stood firm. Anthony knew better than to argue with his mother. She had calmed down since the divorce with Robert, and was not as violent. She was drinking more but was usually with Walter when this took place. Anthony knew she still had a bad temper and he would not argue about the decision to move. He tried to keep his mother from getting angry and agreed to the move. It was not as if he had any choice. He knew this and was willing to accept it. Madeline felt the same as Anthony about the proposition once it was presented. Both would leave another school where they had developed friendships, and would have to start all over again.

******

Anthony told his friends in Keystone and at University School what was coming down regarding the move. It hurt to tell his friends at school and Keystone about the move. He had mixed feelings about the loss of friends and the gain of playing football. No one understood why he had to go and they had a hard time understanding why he would consider going to Erwin. The only thing most of his friends understood was that he loved football and this would be an opportunity for him to get to play.

It was amazing to Anthony how fast the time went. It was no time before school was out and he was telling his friends at University School bye for what he thought would be the last time he would see them. It wouldn't be long until he went through the same procedure with his friends in Keystone. Anthony would miss the neighborhood where he had developed most of his persona and friendships.

The day of the move came quickly, all too quickly. It was a day Anthony regretted for the rest of his life. He was saying good-bye to Keystone and to University High. He didn't let anyone see him after he had told Mr. Alexander at University School bye. He walked home with tears in his eyes, often wiping them from his cheeks. He thought of the friendships he was leaving behind and many of the teachers at University School, especially, Mr. Alexander. Anthony never thought of a teacher or principal in the same way again as he did Vernon Alexander.

~ Chapter 23 ~

Erwin

What was left of the summer went by quickly for Anthony. He had lived in Erwin for a couple of months and he was quickly learning about his mother's new husband, Walter Hudgins. Many of the things he had learned about him, and where he was living, were things he didn't like very much. One of the things he didn't like was the house he lived in or where it was located. The house was located just out of town on Rock Creek Road. Anthony had never lived out of town. Running parallel with the road was a good sized creek, appropriately named Rock Creek.

The house was a small wood framed home with an unfinished basement. The basement was on ground level but since the house sat on a hill, the house gave the appearance of being a two story home, especially from the back yard area.

Anthony didn't like the house from the start for one primary reason; neither he nor Madeline had a bedroom to stay in. The house only had two bedrooms, one occupied by Walter and Wanda, the other by Walter's father who lived at home. Walter's father was in his eighties and almost deaf. He exemplified the typical old man who had grown up in the country. He drank whiskey from the time he got up in the morning until the time he went to bed. His old, wrinkled frame was small and topped off with solid white, but thick hair. The old man spent most of his day watching professional wrestling or fighting shows on television. He believed that what he saw on the tube was real. He believed this whether watching soap operas, westerns, monster movies, or whatever. His whiskey of choice was 'Rock And Rye,' the kind with the fruit in the bottle. His sport of choice was professional wrestling because it had so much action and theater. The old man couldn't hear very well if at all, but he would sit back in his easy chair, watching the television, drinking his whiskey and cussing out the television show he was watching.

Since Walter's father occupied a bedroom, Anthony and Madeline slept on the two couches in the living room. Anthony stored his clothes in one of the dressers in the hallway and the rest of his things in the basement. He lost all of his privacy and since he had no friends he became miserable with his new living situation. He tried praying to God to find out what he needed to do with his life. He wanted to grow as a Christian but he didn't get any answers from his prayers, at least none he recognized.

Anthony was still reluctant to accept the things he had heard at church or the Christians he was around. Most of the Christians he was around had hurt him in one way or another and he didn't want any part of their religion. Their faith could not be based on the loving relationship with Christ he wanted for his life. He knew what these Christians had done and he wouldn't forget the hurt they had put him through. He knew the attitudes and actions these Christians took towards people like him, like his friends from Keystone and the children of the streets.

Anthony knew deep down that if these Christians had a real relationship with Jesus they would attempt to love others the way Jesus had loved them. If they did have a real relationship with Jesus they didn't bother to show the lost and hurting world around them that love. They either chose to be disobedient or simply thought they had a relationship with Jesus and didn't know what to do, either way was not acceptable.

Walter Hudgins was a big man. He stood over 6' tall and weighed over 200 pounds. The large bulk of his weight was in his belly. His large belly was from the drinking. Anthony never saw anyone drink as much as Walter and his drinking had a direct impact on Anthony's mother and the amount she was drinking. Not only was she drinking more but it impacted her behavior in a negative way. Walter followed a specific pattern in his drinking. It could be counted on like a cheap Timex watch. He awoke every morning at 4:30 to go to work at Mor-Flo Industries. Mor-Flo was the factory where he worked with Wanda. The factory made water heaters. After getting up he started smoking cigarettes. He smoked at least 2 cigarettes and then took a shower. This took him 30 minutes. After taking his shower and dressing he had a beer, a Colt 45. He continued to drink beer while packing his lunch. He got his Thermos and filled it up with whiskey and coke. He got Wanda up and she got ready for work. They went to work where he worked in quality control and Wanda worked on the assembly line, stapling boxes shut. Walter drank his whiskey out of his thermos throughout the day. After work they went by a local package store to buy a case of beer and sometimes a bottle of whiskey which they consumed that night before going to bed.

Anthony and Madeline watched Walter and Wanda drink through the night and over a short period of time they observed them getting into verbal arguments with each other. Arguments were different than they were between Robert and Wanda. They were not as violent, and on occasion Anthony and Madeline watched a reversal of roles for Wanda. It was not uncommon for Wanda to be physically abusive to Walter. He responded to her hitting him by walking away or getting into his truck and driving off. Even though he was drunk he drove intoxicated on a frequent basis. Anthony couldn't figure out Walter's behavior. His lack of actions was new for Anthony. He couldn't figure out if it was because he was too drunk or he just didn't want to hit her back.

Anthony hated the small house he lived in. It smelled of stale cigarettes, but more than this he didn't have anything to do. Occasionally he walked in the woods near the house looking for animals, or fished in the creek bed. Anthony enjoyed walking up the road to Rock Creek State Park. The park was 3 miles from the house and wound up a 2 lane road lined with trees on both sides of the road. The park was part of the Cherokee National Forest and was a beautiful area. It was much different than the woods near Keystone. Here, one could walk for miles and see all kinds of wild life and beautiful scenery. The Park had everything the mountains of Appalachia were famous for. It wasn't unusual to come upon deer, snakes, rabbits, and on occasion see signs of bears.

There were numerous paths one could walk on at the park, but the one Anthony liked best led up to a waterfall. The path included a 3 to 4 mile walk. It went across various manmade bridges such as single log bridges, cable bridges and swinging bridges. Anthony enjoyed the beauty and peaceful yet loud roar of the water as it came down the ledges of a nearly 150' foot fall. He devoured the time he spent there alone because it was one of the few places he didn't have to worry about what was going on around him. It was a place where he felt and experienced God's presence. Because of the peaceful atmosphere, he spent a great deal of time at Rock Creek Park. He spent it on the trails, and at the waterfalls, questioning and seeking God. Anthony felt the presence of Jesus in the serenity of the mountains and park like no place he had before. He was beginning a new life, in a new town, and a new environment. He was convinced; if not for this park, he would have gone crazy and not been able to adapt to Erwin and his new surroundings. Then again it was debatable if he did in fact adapt.

* * * * * *

The summer passed quickly and the main thing Anthony looked forward to was the start of football. He was going out for the high school team, playing in full pads, with full contact once again. No more sand lot football, he was going to play real football. He didn't mind when he found out he had to walk to practice. He was used to that. He was used to it from his time at

Rock Creek Park and from walking to school while living in Keystone. The walk was the same distance as his walk to school when he lived in Keystone. There were a few more hills but after a few miles of this he knew he would only get in better shape.

Anthony arrived at the first day of practice 3 weeks before school started. It was hot and humid in Erwin in late August. Once practice started, he was impressed with himself and how well he was doing. He would start on the junior varsity team. His head coach was Philip Davidson. It also looked like he would play some on the varsity team. He was pleased; he would play some on the varsity and start on the junior varsity team.

The name of the school and team was the Unicoi County High School Blue Devils. Despite their poor performance over the past few years Unicoi County was a strong football community. The town's people insisted the school play in the Big 9 Conference. The conference schools were much larger than Unicoi County. The Blue Devils should have played in a conference for smaller schools, but the townspeople liked the idea of trying to compete against Johnson City, Bristol, Kingsport and the other larger towns in the region. The residents didn't understand how the athletes felt, almost always coming up short on the score board. Football was king in Tennessee though and if competing, one needed to compete against the best competition possible.

Coach Davidson was a tall, blond, slim man who made no gripes that his favorite sport to coach was not football, but rather baseball. He was a good coach though and got along well with Anthony and the other players. Coach Davidson seemed to like three players in particular. Jeff Thomas, the starting quarterback, also played defensive back. Jeff was short, blond, only 5' 11", cocky, and everything else one needed in a good quarterback. He could scramble, run, read defenses, was durable and took a good hit. He had a decent throwing arm and was a take control kind of guy. He came from good stock. He had a big brother Mike, who as a sophomore was a sensational running back for the high school and one of the top backs in the conference.

Reggie Taylor was another player who was a favorite of Coach Davidson. He was 6' feet tall and weighed 200 pounds. Reggie was a lineman on offense but specialized as a middle linebacker on defense. He was a linebacker with great vision and reaction time for the pass and run. He was a hard, devastating hitter. It was obvious he was going to be a high school star and play in college if he wanted. He had the brains to go with the position. While many referred to football players as "dumb jocks," Reggie was a contradiction to the stereotype. He was intelligent and one of the smartest young men at Unicoi County High.

Anthony was also doing well and receiving the favor of Coach Davidson. He was playing linebacker on the defense and tight end on the offensive side of the ball. He did well in both positions but especially at tight end. He had good hands, was a good blocker and was a positive yardage receiver after catching the ball. He made gains after his catches from running the ball and he seldom fumbled. He had a knack of protecting the football and knowing where to run once he had it. He had good size, making it hard for the defense to tackle him. Anthony also watched professional games, studying running patterns of receivers. He watched their cuts and patterns to make up for his lack of speed. He felt he could develop quickness and he studied and practiced his moves as much as possible to do this.

As bad as living in Erwin was for Anthony, he enjoyed playing football. He made friends on the team and had something to do with his afternoons and evenings. Practice was twice a day during the preseason so this took up a chunk of time. He practiced through the end of summer and went with the varsity team to camp a week before school started. For the first time in a long time things were going well for Anthony. He liked football and he was not thinking as much of his friends from University School or Keystone.

✱ ✱ ✱ ✱ ✱ ✱

School had been going on for a week and Anthony was surprised at how well he was doing on the football field and in the classroom. As hard as school was at University School, it was as if there had been a complete turn around for Anthony. The hard work and struggles at University School actually made Unicoi County High School easy. It was strange to excel in the classroom for Anthony. He was playing football and in a strange sort of way, worrying that his new friends would think he was smart. He was having fun, but with all he had been through, he knew a good thing could not last.

Problems at home soon started with Walter and Wanda. Anthony had been in school for less than 2 weeks when everything fell apart. He was shocked by the occurrences. He was fitting in and making progress in getting his life in order.

Anthony was sitting at the table for supper. If there was supper it was always late and this night was no different. It wasn't dark yet but it was after 8:00 PM. Late enough so that by the time supper was served Walter and Wanda had time to be drunk. They had been drinking quite a bit and got into an argument, which was not unusual.

Anthony wasn't sure what the argument was about. He tried to block them out once they started. This was a reflex mode he developed from the time Wanda was married to Robert. Anthony had heard the arguments numerous times before. He heard them from the years with Wanda and Robert. Maybe it was those memories that got to him. He never knew what it was but something happened that changed him, something which pushed him to the point where he would not deal with the conflict, as he did in the past.

******

"Shut up, you big fucking idiot, before I knock the shit out of you." Wanda yelled at Walter at the top of her voice.

"I didn't do anything, Wanda." Walter responded slurring his speech.

For no reason Wanda jumped up from the table and slapped Walter across the face, yelling, "You ugly piece of shit, I'll be damned if I don't knock your brains out."

It was obvious to Anthony this was going to be another incident he would rather not witness. What happened next though surprised him. As soon as Wanda slapped him, Walter hit her in the face with an open hand, knocking her back into the kitchen cabinet. As soon as Walter hit her, Anthony was up, out of his chair between them.

Anthony shoved Walter in the chest towards the table, yelling at him, "If you ever lay a hand on my mother again I'll fucking kill you."

As soon as Anthony yelled at Walter, Wanda jumped on Anthony's back, pulling him by the hair. She was yelling at Anthony, "Leave him alone, you smart assed little bastard."

Anthony couldn't believe what was happening. For the first time, he took up for his mother and she had the nerve to grab him, curse him and yell at him. Anthony could not accept what had just happened. In his own mind he concluded this life was over. He would not put up with this type of treatment anymore. Anthony looked at his mother, with tears in his eyes and told his mother and Walter, "That's it, you don't want me here and you treat me like shit. I'm out of here!"

Wanda, still angry and taking it out on Anthony, yelled back, "That's O.K. run off. Go to Velma and Oscar. You always wanted to run off to them anyway. Go ahead, I don't care. I'm sick of all your shit anyway."

Anthony yelled back, "Fine then. I'm gone but I won't go to Mamaw's and Grandaddy's. I'll go as far from here as I can. I'm gone; I don't care if I ever see you again." He stormed out the back door.

Anthony went into the woods back behind the house and followed the creek bed to the main highway between Erwin and Johnson City. Once at the highway he hitchhiked to Johnson City. It had been getting dark when he got a ride to Johnson City. He arrived in Johnson City after dark and went to his grandparents, but not right away. He walked around town and visited a few of his friends in Keystone first.

In some ways visiting Keystone first disturbed Anthony more than it helped him. Many of his friends were not at home and the ones who were reacted differently than he expected. He had not seen them in almost 4 months but it seemed as if it had been years. It was almost as if the friendship they once had never existed. It was a strange feeling and he didn't know how to deal with it.

Anthony eventually went to his grandparent's house. Before going there he walked to the north side of town where he went to the mall and walked around. He put in at least 20 miles of walking that evening.

Once entering the house, Velma spoke right away to him. "We were expecting you. Your mother called a few minutes ago and told us that you left home and would probably come here."

Anthony responded, "I didn't just leave. She told me to leave."

"Now Anthony, your mother wouldn't do that. Wanda loves you and Madeline. You can stay here as long as you want, but you need to think about going back home to your mother." Velma believed what she told Anthony. She didn't accept the things Anthony and Madeline had told her about what they had been through. This type of problem in a clean and decent Christian family was not acceptable. Anthony wished she could see the truth, and then she would understand. He didn't know if she saw the truth but refused to accept it. He felt his grandmother had no idea what the truth was.

Anthony stayed with Velma and Oscar through the weekend. On Sunday evening Velma spoke to Wanda and made arrangements for her to come and pick him up. This was not what Anthony wanted. He had no desire to go back with Walter and Wanda but he was willing to go along with the plan for now. He was pleased with what transpired over the next week.

Anthony stayed with Wanda and Walter for one week. He went to football practice but didn't talk to his friends about what had happened the weekend before. None of his new friends knew anything about his past. They knew nothing of his involvement in gangs, drugs, abuse, not anything. He did a good job of hiding his past. Velma and Oscar contacted their son Jerry and daughter Sarah about Anthony coming and staying with them. Jerry and Sarah went in together with their families and purchased a farm in middle Tennessee. The farm consisting of 600 acres was in the small town of Gordonsville.

Gordonsville had less than 2,000 people. It was 45 miles east of Nashville on Interstate 40 and 200 miles west of Johnson City. The claim to fame for the area was that several politicians came from the county. Carthage was a small town 10 miles away and in the same county as Gordonsville. Even though it was small, it was larger than Gordonsville. Ten thousand people lived in Carthage and it was critical to the large farming community. It was the home of the prominent politician, Al Gore.

Velma and Wanda agreed to let Anthony go live with Sarah and Jerry on their farm. Anthony didn't complain. He was still upset about the previous week. The only disappointment he had was leaving the football team at Unicoi County. It was obvious to Anthony that Coach Davidson liked him and he would get the chance to play if he remained in Erwin. He couldn't take it any more at home though; he had to get away from his living situation if at all possible. He had put up with all of the things at home with Wanda and her husbands for years now. He was ready to leave.

Anthony was the only one who knew of the things which had happened to him. His sister Madeline had some idea about the abuse but knew little in regards to the other sexual activity, gang activity and drug use which he was involved in. Anthony couldn't take it anymore. He blocked out periods of his life so he wouldn't remember them and he found this to be a sort of escape for his mental stress. As much as he loved playing football for Coach Davidson, he realized he needed a place where he could get a new start. He knew Gordonsville must have a football team and he could play for them, so Anthony went to Gordonsville to live with his aunt and uncle.

Anthony packed his clothes and a few other things. He left for his grandparents on a Friday after school. His uncle Leo and grandfather were driving to Gordonsville on Saturday morning and he would ride with them. Anthony went to bed that night and was up early the next morning. He packed his things in the car the night before so all he had to do was get dressed. They left that morning with Oscar driving the car.

Anthony was leaving Johnson City again. He stayed in Washington DC once before with his grandparents and Aunt Sarah for a few months, but this had the feeling of being permanent. As far as he knew, he wouldn't return to Johnson City except for short visits and hopefully he would never return to Erwin.

~ Chapter 24 ~

Gordonsville

The drive from Johnson City to Gordonsville took 6 1/2 hours. Anthony normally slept when traveling these distances but he was so excited that he was awake for the entire trip. He talked along the way with his grandfather and Uncle Leo. Leo spoke about going down and living on the farm with his family and Anthony knew he might move to the farm in the near future. Leo spoke on numerous occasions with Sarah and Jerry about this. They were both considering moving to Nashville. If Jerry or Sarah moved to Nashville, then Leo would move to the farm and take care of the cattle and raise the corn, tobacco, hay and a family garden. This would require some work but it would allow more flexibility for Leo. He drove an over the road semi-truck and was looking for a way to be around his family more.

Anthony spoke to his grandfather, whom he called Pap's, about living on the farm. Oscar spent a lot of time on the farm and he enjoyed the work that reminded him of his childhood. It was not unusual for Oscar and Velma to spend a few weeks at a time on the farm. While there Oscar stayed in one of the guest rooms. This wouldn't bother Anthony because when Jerry's son Chris wasn't there, which was most of the time, he had a room to himself even if Oscar and Velma were at the farm. If Chris was there with Oscar and Velma then Anthony roomed with Chris in one of the twin beds in the room. It was like having a brother, and Anthony and Chris got along well with each other.

No one spoke about why it was that Anthony was going to live on the farm. It was normal to have a relative around. Anthony often stayed with different people like his cousins but he was different because he was the son of their brother who had been killed. The family made the commitment to help raise him and be there for him when he needed them. Despite some of the abuse with some of the family there was a larger portion of the family that was kind and courteous to Anthony and Madeline. Anthony had spent as much time at other relatives' homes as he had with his mother.

Anthony was aware of the dysfunctional family he lived in but others would not or could not accept it. To them it was due to the fact that his father Charles was killed in a car accident when Anthony was a baby. Anthony knew this was a part of it but there was no excuse for his immediate family to be as dysfunctional as they were. He was tired of hearing excuses of why he was so different and that he needed to learn to adapt to the situations around him. To him, there was no excuse for the abuse, heartache, and hurt, and as to adapting, that was exactly what he was doing in moving away from home.

Anthony heard about how small Gordonsville was, but when he saw it for the first time he realized it was even smaller than he imagined. After exiting from the highway, they drove to the south for one mile before coming to an intersection where they turned left and went east for 4 miles. Along the way they passed the high school. Anthony was surprised at how small the school was. It contained grades Kindergarten through 12 and was smaller than many of the Junior High and Elementary Schools in Johnson City. The difference was that there were many schools in Johnson City, and the school in Gordonsville was the only one there. Oscar drove by only 5 or 6 stores in what was downtown Gordonsville.

After going 4 miles they turned right onto a gravel road. They drove 2 miles and turned left onto a gravel driveway. This was as far out in the country as Anthony had ever been, and to think he was going to be living here gave him a sense of adventure. Once turning onto the gravel road, all along the drive, up to the point of the driveway, they only passed 3 houses. The landscape consisted primarily of wooded areas and large fields which were used for hay, crops, cattle, and tobacco.

Once on the driveway Oscar drove another mile. Along this section of drive there were no houses, just fields and cattle. After a mile, the car came to the top of a small valley of rolling hills. The valley consisted of large green fields which were bordered by barbed wire fences and trees. At the bottom of the driveway was a medium sized, one story pre-fabricated ranch farm house.

Anthony saw his cousin Chris, Jerry's son, riding a motorcycle around the fields. He knew his Uncle Jerry and Aunt Sarah kept motorcycles and his Uncle Bill had a motorcycle at the farm. Anthony was excited because he enjoyed riding motorcycles and he knew he had plenty of places on the farm to ride. He knew there were other things he would enjoy on the farm. When he was smaller his mother dated a man who went out on weekend wagon train excursions. Several dozen people would go out on these trips with horses and wagons. They camped out over the weekend and had mini-rodeos. While his mother was dating this man, Anthony had the opportunity to go out on a few trips. He learned to ride horses and enjoyed the experience. The farm had horses and Anthony could ride anytime he wanted. Taking care of the horses became a chore for Anthony: feeding, watering, and brushing one horse in particular, Sandy. He brushed her and rode her around the farm checking the fence lines. He would ride Sandy; drive the tractor, or one of the motorcycles when working with the cattle.

Anthony spoke with his Uncle Leo about all of this on the drive from Johnson City to Gordonsville. Anthony looked forward to Gordonsville due to what was going to be a new experience. This lifestyle was going to be enjoyable for him. It was also one he was not used to. He lived the bulk of his life in the city which was much different than life on a farm. The ability to adapt was something he was used to, so he was excited about this new adventure ahead of him.

The car came to a stop at the bottom of the hill after pulling up next to the house. There was a large, blue Ford Tractor with a large dump scoop on the front. Everyone got out of the car and was stretching when a large Great Dane dog came from around the back of the house barking at them. Leo yelled at the dog, "Samson, settle down boy, it's just us." After yelling this, the dog ran up to Leo and Leo petted him.

Sarah and Jerry came out of the house and greeted everyone with hugs and kisses. They expressed gratitude to Anthony that he was there and was going to be living with them. Sarah told him, "Anthony, why don't you get your clothes out of the car and put up in the bedroom back there with Chris in his room. We have two beds back there and you will have one and Chris has the other when he is here. After you're done with that, go get the Yamaha motorcycle out of the garage. Then you and Chris can drive around the farm so you can see where everything is at."

Anthony was excited to drive one of the motorcycles around the farm. He responded with pleasure, "Yes, ma'am." He immediately went to the trunk of the car to get his clothes. His cousin Chris jumped in and helped. Grabbing one of the bags holding Anthony's clothes, he said, "Come on, I'll help you carry your stuff in so we can go riding quicker." They put the clothes away in less than 30 minutes. They were quickly outside and on the motorcycles. The boys rode the motorcycles until dark, getting in just in time for supper with his aunt Sarah, her husband Mark and Chris' father Jerry. It had been a great day for Anthony. If this was anything like the rest of the days were going to be like, then Gordonsville wasn't going to be a bad place at all. If anything, it was going to be a great place.

* * * * * *

"So tell me something about Gordonsville, Anthony." George said as he sat back in his chair.

"Well, I lived there throughout the year. I really enjoyed it, but there wasn't that much that went on other than learning to live on the farm and all. It was fun and different. It had to be one of the most enjoyable times of my life," Anthony responded.

"Did you make any friends?" George was trying to get information out of Anthony regarding the relationships he might have had at Gordonsville.

Anthony sat back in his chair, crossed his legs, and said, "I didn't have a lot of luck in that area. I guess it was because I was so different. Almost everyone there had grown up on farms and had never been to the city. I don't know how to really say this other than, well, most of the students, especially the boys were a bunch of rednecks. Don't get me wrong. They were good kids and all but they were cliquish and stayed to themselves quite a bit. There were several girls who where pretty nice but I wouldn't really have the chance to go out with them or anything. I guess I never really fit in."

"What do you mean that you never really fit in?" George asked, still searching, not really knowing what it was he was searching for.

"Well, I did pretty well in school when I was at Erwin, so I was excited about starting to get myself back together, but I never really got along that well with the teachers at Gordonsville. I mean I passed and everything, my grades were O.K., but it was obvious to me that I was treated like an outsider, even from the coaches on the football team, so I guess I was an outsider."

Anthony confused George because he was expressing that he did not enjoy Gordonsville that much, especially in regards to school, but Anthony did not seem upset about living there. At times it seemed like he enjoyed living there. George asked curiously, "How did your football coaches treat you, like an outsider or what?"

"It wasn't just the football coaches. The school was so small that they only had two coaches for the school in boys' sports. The coaches for football were also the coaches for basketball. I guess that since I wasn't from the area the coaches didn't give me as much playing time and acknowledgment as I felt I deserved. I played a lot and all but I wasn't one of their boys. They did things like take the other guys out on occasion, to the lake, to church, or things like that, yet I never got asked to do anything like that with them." Anthony continued, "Then there were the football play times, practice and all. I was playing as a linebacker on defense and running back on offense. I could catch better than any of the other players including the receivers, and was by far the hardest person to tackle when I was running the ball. In practices I was clearly one of the better players, yet in games I got limited play. I guess I shouldn't complain too much, after all I was only a freshman, but I still believe that as a freshman I was one of the best players on the team."

"What about the other players, how did you get along with them?" George asked.

"Pretty good I guess. I had some friends on the team but I didn't really do that much with them. In Gordonsville there really wasn't much to do unless you worked on the farm." Anthony responded.

George changed the line of questioning. "How about your home life, how were things there?"

Anthony brightened up. "It was great. I loved it. My Uncle Jerry and his boy Chris were not there much. My Aunt Sarah and Uncle Mark stayed on the farm most of the time. Sarah ran a beauty shop in Nashville and Mark was retired. They were both great. Mark worked with me at football and even came to see me play several times. That was special because it was the first time anyone had come to see me do anything. He even came to some of the basketball games. Mark had trouble with drinking but he seemed to control it better than I had seen anyone else control it. He was a scotch and soda man. He enjoyed playing golf and took me with him on weekends and throughout the summer. He played golf at least twice a week so I got to go out with him often."

Anthony continued, now speaking about his Aunt Sarah. "Sarah was great, too. She gave me money for doing chores and stuff around the house and farm. I really appreciated that for a variety of reasons. First of all, the chores were fun; they were things like feeding the horses, taking the tractor out and pitching hay to the cattle when it was cold and they needed food, stuff like that. Sarah treated me great. I'll never forget what she did for me. If I ever needed anything she was always there. It was the first time that anyone treated me like a good kid in a family situation. I hope I responded to it well. I don't know. I've often thought about it. I guess I need to get back in touch with her and thank her for all she did."

"Why don't you know if you responded to it well or not?" George asked.
"Well, we just don't see each other very much any more. We don't talk like we should either. I know I haven't thanked her like I should. She treated me as close to a son as anyone I know except for maybe my Mamaw Beechup. At the very least she was like a loving big sister. She was great."

Anthony tried to explain more of his feelings further to George. "I lived with Sarah and Mark through the year, but I ended up going back to Erwin before the start of the school year the following year. In some ways I am glad I moved back to Erwin, but in others I wish I would have made my mind up and stayed at one school instead of moving around so much." Anthony responded to George's question realizing the need for him to try and get back in touch with his Aunt Sarah to thank her for what she had done for him.

"So all in all it sounds like living in Gordonsville was something you enjoyed. Is that right?" George asked as if he already knew the answer.

Anthony answered without hesitation, knowing he had always thought that living in Gordonsville was one of the most enjoyable times of his life. "Yes, without a doubt this was one of the best times of my life. It's strange though, it wasn't from friends or anything like that. It was from living on this farm with my Aunt Sarah and her husband Mark. I was working and doing things I really enjoyed on the farm. I don't think I'll ever forget what my Aunt Sarah did for me. It was the first and one of the only times that others treated me like I was a part of the family. I enjoyed the time in Gordonsville living with them, immensely."

Anthony changed the subject, realizing his time with George was about up. "I ended up moving back to Erwin and even though I hated it, there were things that happened that made me glad I moved back. I guess that is what we talk about next week though."

George answered, smiling, "Yeah, Anthony, I guess that is what next week will be about. It sounds good, though, that we are ending this week on a good note. Let's pray together before we leave this week and then we can see each other again next week at the same time, O.K.?"

"Sure." Anthony answered.

George prayed, thanking God for giving Anthony someone like his Aunt Sarah who was there to give love, assurance, and a sense of family. Anthony realized it was a worthwhile prayer and that thanking his Aunt Sarah was something he needed to verbalize to her himself.

It was good for Anthony to have a good session with George. He remembered some of the good times in his life, and it was one of the reasons he had a good week.

~ Chapter 25 ~

Ninth Street

As much as Anthony hated it, he was spending time with his mother and Walter again. He had not seen them in the last year and enjoyed the time away from them. During the time away he did not develop any more love or respect for them. They had not visited him nor had he gone back to see them.

While in Gordonsville Anthony spoke to Wanda, Walter and his sister Madeline on the phone. He also kept in touch with his sister by writing. He did not write his mother or Walter. He also kept in touch with his grandparents. He saw them on numerous weekends when they visited the farm. There were times when Velma and Oscar spent several weeks at a time on the farm. Oscar especially liked visiting and working there.

After moving back to Erwin, Anthony got a job to save money to buy a car. He was tired of walking to football practice. He wanted a car like the rest of his friends. A car was essential for kids his age and it was something he worked hard to obtain. Looks wouldn't matter nearly as much as the ability to get him from one place to the other.

Anthony was playing football again and was now on the varsity team for the Unicoi County Blue Devils. Some of the coaches were mad at him due to him leaving the year before and he suffered the consequences of getting them upset. There was a new varsity football head coach named Anthony Smith. Coach Smith was a good man who seemed to take an interest in Anthony. The problem Anthony had with the team was with some of the assistant coaches who had been there for years. They were leftovers from the previous coaching staff and many of them had their favorite players.

Anthony hurt his knee from playing sand lot football just prior to the start of the football season. The injury was a hyper-extension and while it was painful it would heal with time and rest. He was a little slower than normal when playing. Anthony wanted to play the same positions he had at Gordonsville and he knew he was good enough to play them for Erwin. Due to his injury and being slowed down, the coaches moved Anthony to the center position on offense. He didn't like the position because there were 2 players who where bigger and better than he. He knew he would see limited play time at this position. The only condolence was he was also playing linebacker on defense.

The problem at linebacker for Anthony was the man coaching the position players. Miguel Fontez was a coach who had an attitude and opinion about everything. He was a typical jock who was reliving his playing days as a coach and took out his attitude on his players. Fontez fit the stereotype of a jock that never grew up and his players experienced both the good and bad sides of him as a result.

Anthony saw more play time in this position than at center but he still had limited play time. He was not one of coach Fontez's favorite players and it was obvious to Anthony and other players on the team. He stuck it out and played football through the season but was disappointed with the team, most of his coaches, the positions he played, and the amount of playing time.

Anthony knew he would have gotten far more play time if the coaches had given him the chance to play either tight end or fullback on offense, and would have had a different coach at linebacker. The head coach, Coach Smith, was a fair man and would've recognized his talents in those positions. Anthony knew that if he had played at tight end he would have started. He also knew there would have only been one player in front of him who was better at the fullback position. Michael Braveheart was a good guy, always friendly. As his name indicated he was part Cherokee and had a courageous attitude when playing. Michael was 6' feet tall and weighed 195 pounds. He was well built, had medium length black hair and was dark skinned.

Michael was the fullback who in Anthony's opinion was responsible for Mike Thomas gaining the yardage he did while in the tailback slot. Thomas was a junior as was Michael, and Thomas led the conference in yardage for an all purpose back. Mike Thomas was also tall, over 6' feet tall with long blonde hair. Mike weighed 180 pounds and resembled a young, long-haired Robert Redford. Thomas also ran back punts and kick-offs for the Blue Devils, and Braveheart punted for the team. Braveheart was one of the best punters in the state and later on punted for the University of Tennessee before a sledding accident ended his football career.

Anthony liked both of these players and many of the other players on the team. He realized that if given a fair chance to play the positions he was best at then he would be able to contribute more to the team, but he could also learn from both Thomas and Braveheart at the running back positions. He could learn from their talents, which he knew were better than his, but also their personalities and attitudes towards others. Both of these young men were well liked on the team and at school. Learning to respect and get along with others was something Anthony still needed to learn, and he respected both of these guys enough that he would have liked to be around them more.

Anthony saved up enough money to buy a car. A car was a means of escape from Rock Creek Road where he stayed with his mother and Walter. A car was also a way to get to practice and develop a sense of normalcy among those he hung around with. The car was one he could afford and a car which was mechanically sound. It was a late 1960's, Chevrolet Station Wagon. It was green and had some rust on it, especially around the rear tail section. It didn't look good, but ran good and provided everything he needed in a car. The car cost $125, and gas was cheap enough that Anthony could afford everything he needed for it to get around Erwin and an occasional trip to Johnson City. In Tennessee it was not required to have the car inspected or pay property tax on it, and it was put on his mother's insurance for very little. Anthony had what he wanted, and he was able to get along at home because he could leave when he wanted.

Anthony had the car throughout the football season and used it to spend his free time at his grandparents' house in Johnson City. While at his grandparents' house one weekend his attitude towards his mother and Walter came to a boiling point. He was out at a movie with one of his uncles during a break from school. Upon returning to his grandparents he noticed that his car was gone. After walking into the house he noticed his mother sitting on the couch talking to his grandmother. Shortly after entering he asked about the car and was told by his mother that she and Walter had sold it. He was surprised and angry about their decision to sell the car. He had paid for it and was taking care of it. Since Anthony was a minor he had to have the car put in his mother's name. The car was in her name so it was legally hers and she could do whatever she wanted with it, despite the fact that he was the one to pay for it and its upkeep. The decision to sell the car was something Anthony had difficulty forgiving Wanda for. It was an issue he had to deal with and let go, but it wasn't easy.

Anthony's sister, Madeline, had been trying for some time to get Anthony to go to church with her. He was committed to his decision of being a Christian but still had many of the same reservations about churches he always had. Madeline, on the other hand was active in a church called Ninth Street Baptist Church. She was a Christian and took her commitment a little more seriously than Anthony. She attended church while in Johnson City and attended and participated in their grandparents' church when visiting on the weekend.

Anthony could tell that something was different about Madeline; she always seemed happy. She wasn't having as much trouble dealing with the problems she and Anthony dealt with at home. She was calmer, not as moody, and seemed happier overall. Anthony saw this in his sister's attitude yet he didn't know it was the church involvement that was responsible for her happiness. Madeline was at church almost every time the doors were open. She was active on the youth council at church and was respected both at church and at school for the commitment to her faith. She attended church at least twice on Sunday, during special activities on Saturday, Wednesday nights, and other times through the week if special events were going on. She was responsible for getting Anthony involved in church.

While Anthony did not want anything to do with the religion practiced by most churches he realized his need to learn more about being a Christian. He still had difficulty understanding what had happened to him earlier in life. He was confused about his feelings, drug usage, and sex, all of which he was still involved with on a limited basis. It was actually his weakness for girls which got him to attend church.

It was a Sunday evening when Madeline came home from church and started talking to Anthony. She was smiling as usual, open and friendly, "Anthony, guess what happened at church tonight?" Not wanting to hear his sister talk about church again he reluctantly answered, "I don't know. What happened?"

Madeline, still smiling, got his full attention rather quickly, "Well I was at youth group tonight talking to some of the girls. We started talking about family and who had brothers and sisters, stuff like that. Then one of the girls asked me if I had any brothers and sisters and I told her about you. They where surprised that I had a brother and asked to see your picture if I had one. I pulled your picture out of my wallet and showed it around. Several of the girls started talking about how cute you where when they saw it. One of the girls, Virginia Madison, said that you were really cute and that she wouldn't mind going out with you sometime." Madeline was laughing now because she saw that Anthony was very interested.

"What did these girls look like?" Anthony asked curiously.

Madeline used a new approach on Anthony regarding getting him to try church out. "Oh, several of them were pretty cute, but Virginia is really attractive. She is also very popular at school, but I think she might be dating someone. Then again I don't know, she did say that she wouldn't mind going out with you some time. You ought to come to church sometime to meet her. She's really nice, besides, there were several other girls there who are really cute and mentioned that they thought you where cute. If you go with me sometimes I'll make sure I introduce you to them."

Anthony was now interested in going to church for the first time in his life, "Well, I'll take you up on it and go with you the next time you go."

"That sounds like you'll be going Wednesday night then. We have a youth group meeting and you'll get the chance to meet everybody. I think you'll like it." Madeline was pleased. She had found a way to get Anthony to church.

Anthony was actually excited about going to church to meet these girls. After moving from Keystone he had mellowed out quite a bit and had some difficulty making friends, especially female friends. This was an excellent opportunity to meet girls and start going out again. It wasn't just the girls though. He knew he could also develop some male friends to hang around with.

Wednesday came quickly and Anthony was nervous about going to church. He was looking forward to meeting some of the girls his sister had been talking about. Anthony and Madeline walked from Rock Creek Road to Ninth Street where the church was located. The walk was two miles but it didn't take long for them to get there. Ninth Street Baptist Church was a large two story, brick Southern Baptist Church. Anthony was surprised at how large the church was and the number of people who went there. The church averaged over 200 members each Sunday for Sunday school and sometimes over 300 for the church service. There was generally half of that at the Sunday and Wednesday night services. There were between 25 and 50 kids involved in the youth group. On week nights when the youth group met there were usually between 15 and 25 kids present.

The first person Madeline introduced Anthony to was Clinton Watkins. Clinton was a slim young man, in his twenties, around 6' feet tall, with short dark brown hair. He was the Youth Pastor and Anthony was impressed with his friendliness and kindness. Clinton did everything possible to make Anthony feel comfortable. While at the meeting, the kids in the group also went out of their way to make him feel welcome. Anthony was embarrassed when Charlotte Stevens commented to Madeline, in front of him, "He is even cuter than the picture you showed us, Madeline." His face started turning red. One of the only disappointments for Anthony was that he did not get to meet the girl he wanted to meet, Virginia Madison. She had a school activity and was unable to attend church.

Anthony asked Madeline about Virginia before leaving church because he wanted to make sure he met her. Madeline embarrassed Anthony again by asking one of her friends if she knew where Virginia was because Anthony wanted to meet her. He kidded his sister about this later on but was not upset at her. He was pleased she went out of her way to introduce him to some of the kids.

Anthony was glad he went to church. He met several people and recognized the potential to make new friends. Most of the guys were nice and he liked the youth pastor Clinton Watkins. He also recognized that some of the girls there were cute. He was so pleased with the church that he knew he would go back. He needed something to do in his spare time and this would be a good opportunity to get away from the house.

Anthony didn't intend to make church a regular part of his life but continued to go on a regular basis and became more involved. He still had difficulty in areas such as drugs and sex, but he was getting a better grasp on them and making the effort to not be involved in them as much. Something just didn't seem right and he was not as comfortable being involved with many of the activities which brought him pleasure prior to becoming a Christian. He was still fragile and he had little or no idea as to what he needed to do to grow as a Christian.

While in youth group meetings, Anthony discussed a number of things regarding his feelings on various topics, especially related to his family and past. He asked questions in such a way as to never point out his true feelings. His private and past life was something he wasn't ready to share. He didn't know if the people in the meetings would know for sure if he was talking about issues regarding his own life or if he was just asking general questions. Sometimes, he accepted the answers to the questions he asked; sometimes he didn't because it was obvious that his life had been much different than the others at church. One of the things he knew he couldn't handle right now was rejection.

* * * * * *

Football season was over and Anthony was disappointed because he knew he would not have as much to do during his free time. He didn't like the option of staying with Walter or Wanda. They were following their routine of drinking and fighting. He spent as little time as possible at home. One of the only benefits was that he now had a motorcycle to get around on.

Wanda and Anthony made arrangements to buy the motorcycle from Anthony's Uncle Billy. Anthony had driven the motorcycle in Gordonsville and he liked it. The 1972 Yamaha XL250 had power and provided all the transport he needed. He never got his driver's license for the motorcycle but he never got stopped by the police either. He knew how to drive it and that was all that mattered to him.

Anthony was driving the motorcycle around town and spending more time at church. The Yamaha 250 Enduro also enabled him get away from home when he needed to. By early winter Anthony avoided staying at home with his family. He didn't want to be away from Madeline, he loved and cared for her. He couldn't forget the things that had happened at home though, especially the time Wanda jumped on him after he tried to stand up for her against Walter.

It was around Christmas and Anthony had various places to stay through the night without going home. It was early in his sophomore year in high school, and Anthony never stayed more than one or two nights at a time at home again. He stayed 30 days or less at home from his sophomore year in high school until graduation. Moving from one place to another to survive was something Anthony was used to from the time he lived in Keystone. He was used to staying outside or finding shelter in various places when he needed to. Since he was 13 years old he had learned to live on the streets and get by. It was easier in a large city like Johnson City than it was a small town like Erwin. This is one of the reasons Ninth Street Baptist Church was so important.

Anthony spent more time with Clinton Watkins, the Youth Pastor at church. Clinton was athletic although he walked with a slight limp, probably the result of a sports injury. He reminded Anthony of a long distance runner due to his build. He had short hair although at times it did get down to his collar. He almost always had a smile and was fun to be around.

Clinton lived in a small house, behind Ninth Street Baptist Church. It was owned by the church and kept up on the outside and inside. The house had 2 bedrooms and a couch and stereo in the living room. Clinton was aware of Anthony's living situation which was why he was open to Anthony staying with him as needed. Clinton was kind and cared for the kids at church. While he cared for the kids at church, Anthony was someone he recognized needed a lot of specific help. He did not stay with Clinton every night, but he stayed with him at least four nights a week. This had certain advantages for Anthony. While at Clinton's he ate at the church when meals were served but he also figured out ways to get invited to people's homes to eat during meal time. Clinton was not one to cook much so he ate out a lot, and of course, took Anthony with him.

One of Clinton's favorite places to eat at was at a restaurant called The Elms. It was a restaurant which catered to the older crowd but that was okay with Anthony because they served home style cooking. Things like vegetables, mashed potatoes and meat-loaf. Not just hamburgers but meals that tasted like they were prepared by someone's grandmother. It was also a treat to get dessert. One of the favorites was the hot-fudge cake. They served a large portion of this fabulous desert featuring two layers of cake, with a vanilla ice cream between the cake, topped off with hot fudge, whipped topping and a cherry. Eating at The Elms and other restaurants with Clinton was fine with Anthony although he did feel guilty because Clinton spent so much money on him when eating out. Clinton never complained or said anything about it. He offered most of the time Anthony reluctantly accepted.

It wasn't long before Anthony was working his first real job. It had a weekly pay check and some things others overlooked. Things like coworkers, a time-clock to punch in and out, responsibilities and even a supervisor to help teach him the job. Anthony was working at Kentucky Fried Chicken just down the street from Ninth Street Baptist Church. This was a perfect location for Anthony to work because it was close to Clinton's house. He could keep in touch with Clinton, have many of his needs met through his friendship with Clinton, plus get to and from work easily. It was also nice having a little money so he could offer to buy Clinton's dinner on occasion.

Anthony worked at Kentucky Fried Chicken for six months before having to quit. He had an allergic reaction to the cleaning solutions and oils the restaurant used. His hands broke out and he developed a rash with sores. After quitting at Kentucky Fried Chicken he was able to pick up odd jobs from people at church to get enough money so that Clinton did not have to pay for everything. It was not like having a regular pay check and occasionally Clinton still bought meals for Anthony. Anthony still enjoyed being able to buy Clinton a meal every now and then when he had money. He was not looking for a handout and wanted to earn his own money to help pay his own way.

Anthony was resentful that he had to work for the money he got. It wasn't that he didn't appreciate that one had to work for money; he was a good worker and felt good about earning his pay. It was that his mother received a Social Security check for him due to his father being killed when he was an infant. He was upset because he had not lived at home for sometime and he was receiving no benefits from the Social Security money his mother was getting. The only money Anthony received was from his relatives and from his earnings. Oscar and Velma were great about having Anthony mow their yard or doing things they could pay him for. Unfortunately, Velma and Oscar were not the ones receiving the Social Security check to help take care of him, his mother was. This changed when he turned 18.

Anthony was involved at church throughout the year. His involvement increased due to the relationships he developed, and he enjoyed being at church. He met several girls and went out with a few of them on occasion. He developed a crush on Charlotte Stevens. She was the daughter of the pastor, David Stevens, and had a sister named Jean who was more attractive but did not have her personality. Anthony appreciated her for who she was and besides, she was rather cute. As much as Anthony had a crush on her, Charlotte saw him as a brother as opposed to seeing him as a boyfriend. This upset Anthony but he lived with it, although he did have some difficulty. He went out with Charlotte some but never kissed her. He ended up going out with her sister Jean. He tried to get Charlotte jealous but it never happened. She couldn't care less if he went out with her sister. It was upsetting to Anthony when he recognized his efforts did not work. He had fun with Jean, but she did not have quite the personality of her sister. He got kisses from her on dates but that was it. He had learned enough of his new faith to understand that the act of sex was something for those you loved and he didn't love Jean. He still had some difficulty with this area of his life but he was learning. He wasn't sure if he could maintain this attitude with Charlotte; he loved her and wanted to be with her.

Charlotte was the first person Anthony learned to love; he just didn't know what it was like to be loved. The relationship and struggle continued for several months. He had mood swings and at times became extremely depressed. He could have dated a number of girls from school or church but he had his eyes set on Charlotte Stevens. She just didn't have her sights set on him. This was another heart break for him in regards to the relationships he had with others. Anthony recognized that Charlotte was right about how she felt about him. They were more like a brother and sister than boyfriend and girlfriend. He recognized this later on when they tried to have a romantic relationship. She moved away with her parents when her father took a pastoral job in Kingsport. It was during this brief dating encounter that Anthony finally kissed Charlotte and he recognized there was nothing romantically there. He wondered if there was nothing there or if he was still upset after breaking up from a lengthy relationship he had just come out of with another girl.

Anthony dated several girls from church and school but was not serious about any of them. He had learned something important from his dating relationships. He realized his faith and involvement in church had curbed his appetite for sex. Whenever he was out with a girl and felt the urge to have sex he started hearing that voice he had heard when he got saved. A voice telling him that sex was for love and marriage and that sex was something he needed to save for the person he loved. This is not to say he was always successful at not having sex. There were times he failed. After these failures he felt guilty and recognized the need to ask God for forgiveness. The forgiveness he asked for was not an attempt to get away with the guilt. It was the realization that he had done something wrong and had hurt God. He was making the effort to turn away from what he had done wrong.

Anthony was not on a guilt trip for the things he did wrong. He was trying to follow God and do the things he was supposed to. He wanted to be a follower of Jesus in the best, most meaningful way possible. He realized what God had done for him, and he wanted to do what he could to follow God. He didn't want to do this because he felt God was a big ogre looking over him but because he realized that if he followed God, then God would bless him and he would be happier and be more fulfilled.

Some things changed for Anthony regarding him finding a serious and steady girlfriend. He finally met Virginia Madison, the girl who initially piqued his interest in coming to church by saying to his sister Madeline that she wouldn't mind going out with him. He spoke to her several times at church and felt she was very pretty but he never made a serious effort to go out with her because she was dating someone else. Virginia broke up with her boyfriend and as far as Anthony was concerned she was available. He was friendly with her whenever he saw her and she was one of the reasons he got over his crush on Charlotte.

Virginia was tall, almost as tall as Anthony. She had medium length to long strawberry blonde hair with a long slender face. She was slender and while not stunningly beautiful she was very pretty. She had a great personality and was always friendly. She was a kind person with numerous friends and was popular at school. Anthony had dated quite a few girls and while they were pretty, Virginia was someone who was not only pretty; she was an all-round girl who had the personality to match.

Anthony spent the bulk of his time with Virginia at church and they went out with each other and with other friends to various activities. They went to the movies, out to eat, concerts, church functions and numerous other events. They went out at least twice a week, not counting the time they spent together at church. They developed an extremely good relationship and friendship as a result of the time they spent together. Two of the friends Anthony and Virginia spent most of their time with were Steve Jackson and Mary Ledman. The four of them could hardly be separated. Anthony and Virginia were developing a close relationship but had not seen each other as boyfriend and girlfriend yet. He kissed Virginia on several occasions but they were kisses from the games youth sometimes play. He was excited about his relationship with Virginia though. He felt himself drawing closer to her, and he also recognized she was getting closer to him. He didn't know if this feeling for her was love or not. He had never felt it before. He knew the feelings felt good and they seemed to be feelings Virginia also felt.

The youth group at church was going to Panama City, Florida for a summer youth retreat. Anthony was excited as he received a scholarship to go on the trip, and Virginia was also going. This was the opportunity for him to find out how they really felt about each other. He was excited about the trip and others knew it. He was truly happy and fulfilled. He knew Virginia was one of the reasons, if not the primary reason for that happiness.

✶ ✶ ✶ ✶ ✶ ✶

Ninth Street Baptist Church was good for Anthony. He was starting to grow as a Christian, and the people at church were helping him when he needed help. He was developing relationships with people at the church which helped him with his growth. He did things that kept him out of trouble, and for Anthony that was good.

Anthony struggled with the memories of his past and who he thought he was as a result of the circumstances he had endured. It wasn't that he was who he was prior to becoming a Christian; he just couldn't forget or forgive himself for the things he had done to others and the things done to him. He felt those things were still within him and that at anytime he could fall back to those areas that had been so much a part of his life. The drugs, the Occult, gangs, sex, violence, loneliness and all the other things he had hoped he had left behind.

~ Chapter 26 ~

Virginia

Anthony was excited about the trip to Florida. The church was taking 2 buses of kids and some adults he respected. Among those were the Bradentons, who were Clinton's old college friends, who were slated for some of the teaching and running the cleanup detail, along with several parents to chaperon, and Beth Ann Richardson to teach and lead the music for worship.

Beth Ann was single and someone the kids appreciated and liked for the hard work she did in youth choir and Bible studies. She helped on a regular basis in many areas of ministry and was considered a co-youth pastor although she didn't get paid for it. Clinton's job would be more difficult if she was not around. Clinton and Beth Ann worked on a number of musicals with the youth which were presented at church.

Beth Ann and Clinton started a youth choir and the kids enjoyed the music they selected. The music was not what Anthony considered typical church music. It was upbeat and youth oriented. Anthony liked AC/DC, Led Zeppelin, ELO and other contemporary rock bands. As far as he knew, his kind of music was not acceptable in church and there was no such thing as 'church music', that was satisfactory and suitable for kids who liked 'rock and roll'. Prior to the trip to Panama City Anthony did not sing with the youth choir. He grew to respect Beth Ann and the direction she was taking with the music, and after returning from Florida he sang with the youth choir on a weekly basis.

Beth Ann was someone many of the youth and adults thought should develop a dating relationship with Clinton. It seemed to Anthony like Clinton and Beth Ann would make a good couple and their relationship was something he encouraged.

The trip to Panama City was better than Anthony could have dreamed of regarding his relationship with Virginia. He spent most of the time with

Virginia. The two held hands on the bus ride to Florida and from that point on, they were inseparable. Anthony realized he loved Virginia and she loved him. They recognized and accepted their love for each other, from the walks on the beach holding hands and the time they did Bible studies with each other, alone, and with others in small groups. Anthony felt something he had never felt with another person when he was with Virginia. He felt what it was like to be loved by another human being. To sit together, or be with each other holding hands was an experience which melted his heart. He cherished the experience of holding someone's hand. He knew the caressing didn't have to be sexual. To gently caress another over various parts of the body, legs, back of the neck, arms, and other places where love could be felt through soft touch was something Anthony had never felt or experienced. When they kissed Anthony felt shivers come over him. He had kissed many girls before, but kissing Virginia was an experience like no other. The kisses between the two meant something. He could not, nor would want to harm Virginia in any way. He knew the abuse he had seen in his life, towards his mother and others, was something he never wanted to administer towards Virginia. The love he had for her made it more difficult to understand the things he had experienced in his past. "Didn't everyone experience these feelings when in love? If they did how could one ever abuse another?"

Anthony gladly did anything for Virginia because he realized the extent of the love he had for her. They were not only in love with each other but they had something most couples overlook in their relationship, they were friends. The friendship they experienced was a friendship Anthony couldn't explain. They talked about everything, their dreams, the future, family, faith, their weakness, nothing was off limits. The more they spoke with each other the more they learned to admire each other for what the other had gone through and what the other believed. In many ways they were so different, yet in others so much alike.

Virginia came from a Christian family where both parents had good jobs and made a good living. She lived in a good house, had material possessions and was well taken care of. Despite the obvious differences in their life experiences, their love for each other was obvious to those who saw them together. It wasn't love at first sight for them. They often hung out together with Steve Jackson and Mary Ledman. They not only recognized the love they had for each other but felt they belonged together. The trip to Florida didn't last long enough for Anthony. He cherished the time he had with Virginia, not only the time they were alone but the times they were with their friends. He loved Florida and the Gulf Coast. He developed a love for this area that lasted a lifetime.

After the trip to Florida, any time Anthony was with Virginia they were either holding hands or had their arms around each other's shoulders and/or waist. They were inseparable, not only spiritually but physically. Anthony knew, for the first time in his life, what it was like to not only love, but to be loved. It was a feeling he cherished. Anthony didn't want to lose this feeling if at all possible. He had lost too much in is life; to lose this would be more than he could bear.

★ ★ ★ ★ ★

As the summer went on the relationship between Anthony and Virginia got more serious. Anthony spent more time with Virginia. They were together so much, many would think it would be hard to find more time. This was difficult at times for Anthony because he didn't have much money. They spent the bulk of their time together at church, and doing things which were inexpensive or free.

Anthony didn't have a car but he had his motorcycle which he drove to Virginia's house. Virginia had a small Ford Pinto which they used for dates. Anthony spent a lot of time at Virginia's house with her and her family.

Virginia lived on Ninth Street, about a half mile from the church in a nice one-story red and white brick house. The house had various bushes and flowers around it. The house was nicely manicured, the lawn well kept and trimmed. There were four bedrooms, two baths, a living room, den, library, and family room. It was the family room and library where Anthony and Virginia spent the bulk of their time, most often alone.

Anthony and Virginia spent a lot of time with each other talking or occasionally making out. As much as they loved each other they never had sex, although they came close on occasion. They always stopped, realizing the importance of saving this aspect of love for marriage. Their faith was important to them and reflected in their sexuality. They loved each other so much they truly respected the other's thoughts and feelings.

Virginia wanted to save herself until marriage for her husband. Anthony respected her for this and felt they would some day be married. He was at ease with this because he knew how strongly Virginia felt about saving herself for the man she married. He also knew how many times they struggled at not having sex with each other. Anthony felt that as much as Virginia struggled with him in this area that it was a clear indication, she loved him.

Anthony liked Virginia's family although he was never sure what they thought of him. Her mother, Lucille, was the choir director at Ninth Street Baptist Church. She was heavy set, with white hair, and was shorter than Virginia. She was always jolly and a joy to be around. Anthony enjoyed their relationship and considered her a Godly woman for the time he knew her, even up until her death some years later. She was the type of woman Anthony admired for her ability to love her family and God in the way she did. She was well respected from people at Ninth Street and from the community. If someone didn't respect and like her it was, as far as Anthony was concerned, because they didn't know her and have the joy of having the experience of being around her as he had.

Virginia's father, Thomas Madison, was a tall, balding man, with white hair. Thomas taught Sunday school at church, was a deacon, and the Sunday School Superintendent. It was obvious to Anthony that Virginia's height came from her father's side of the family; both her father and grandfather were tall. Thomas was a loving father who loved his wife and family. He showed Anthony warmth and acceptance like he had not felt before. That is not to say Thomas accepted everything about Anthony. Anthony later came to know and understand that Thomas knew how difficult Anthony and Virginia's relationship was as a result of the differences between them. That is not to say he didn't accept Anthony, he did, he simply loved his daughter and had insight that Anthony or Virginia didn't understand.

Virginia's brother Steve also lived at home. Steve was a big man, standing 6' 3" and weighing 240 pounds. Steve at one time was a standout high school football player before getting hurt. The knee injury prevented him from going to college where he was offered a number of football scholarships including one to Virginia Tech where he was intending to go when he got hurt. Steve loved his sister as only a big brother could. While he accepted Anthony, in his own way he also let Anthony know of his love for his sister, and that he expected Anthony to look out for his sister's best interest.

The Madison family was a close knit family whose members got along with each other and made every effort to support and help each other when needed. There were several times when Anthony and Virginia were making out in one of the back rooms of Virginia's house and Steve walked in on them, catching them occasionally having their hands on the other's body. He never got upset or threatened Anthony, but he cautioned them to be more careful and to respect his mother's and father's home. He made it clear that he intended for Anthony to respect his sister while at the same time allowing his sister the opportunity to make up her own mind as to the extent of growth in their relationship.

Steve had dated and been in love for sometime and understood that Anthony and Virginia loved each other. As a result of Steve's understanding he was more accepting of their behavior than Anthony would have thought. Anthony always knew that Steve knew his sister extremely well and as a result knew the two of them would not have sex with each other. Steve's faith in his sister and in her ability to make appropriate decisions was something that impressed Anthony. He was impressed with Steve's understanding and faith in his sister and in the confidence that the teachings and direction God would give her.

Anthony still got nervous when Steve walked in on them while they were making out. As nervous as he got though, he was always surprised that Virginia handled the situation as well as she did. She would speak with her brother and Steve left them together and alone. After Steve left the room they either talked or start making out again.

The seriousness of the relationship grew between Anthony and Virginia. Anthony was entering his junior year in school and Virginia was entering her senior year. They were both the same age, but Virginia was a year ahead in school because Anthony failed the 8th grade when at University School. Anthony was sure that if he hadn't failed the 8th grade and they were in the same grade, their relationship would have even been stronger. They would have more in common and would be able to go to college together.

The school year was tough on the two of them. Anthony decided to go back to University School instead of Unicoi County High School and this created some strain on their relationship. Anthony despised Unicoi County High School and wanted to go to University School where the bulk of his friends were. Virginia understood and felt it was a good idea for him to go back to school there with his friends. They saw each other during the evenings when Anthony came home, and had the weekends and times at church together, so even though they were going to different schools they saw each other just as much. Anthony and Virginia realized that seeing each other at school all of the time would hurt the other's studies. They spoke some about college and didn't want any interruption in their studies. They knew they were at the point that if they wanted to go to college they would have to maintain good grades. Virginia understood this concept longer than Anthony, but he was helped in more ways than one from the relationship with Virginia. She made him want to be a better person, as well as a better student. For the first time in his life he was making good grades and enjoying his classes. Virginia had a lot to do with this new found lease on Anthony's life.

Anthony rode to University School with one of his friends whom he spent time with at the Erwin YMCA swimming pool. Anthony worked at the YMCA as a lifeguard on weekends and evenings, and his friend was a student at East Tennessee State University in Johnson City. He rode to school with his friend on most mornings and drove his motorcycle or rode with his mother on her way to work on the other mornings.

Virginia was taking several college level courses in the spring at East Tennessee State University. She had finished her high school requirements in the fall, and she and Anthony spent time with each other in the evenings while at University School, the Erwin YMCA pool and East Tennessee State University campus. They went to numerous campus activities and concerts at East Tennessee State. Virginia liked the band Kiss so they saw them several times, and Elvis Presley three times. They also spent time at Anthony's grandparents.

Anthony's grandparents, aunts, uncles and other relatives were around Virginia a lot and liked her. They saw the change she made in Anthony's life and they respected her for her positive impact. Anthony's grandmother, Velma, and his Uncle Billy even started talking to Anthony asking if he and Virginia spoke of marriage. They gave advice such as the need for them to make sure they went to college. Most of Anthony's relatives felt they made a good couple and would end up getting married.

It wasn't long before Christmas came around. Anthony saved money to provide Virginia and her family with as good a Christmas as he could. He saved this money in several ways. He was working part-time at the YMCA as a lifeguard and he moved to the YMCA transient center where he lived in a one room unit. Once moving out of the house on Rock Creek Road, Anthony made arrangements with his mother to start receiving his Social Security check. This helped immensely; he was earning $50 a week from his part-time job at the YMCA and was getting his Social Security check of $168 a month. This was enough money to live on, pay his rent, and get Virginia and her family the things he wanted to get them for Christmas. This was important to him because he knew Virginia came from a quality family who wanted their daughter provided for. Anthony wanted to show her parents that he was a hard worker and that he would do his best to provide for her the things she needed.

The apartment at the YMCA had a bed and a dresser, and Anthony used the community shower the rest of the men at the YMCA used. He lived there with homeless people and was technically homeless himself. There were occasional transient residents who stayed for one or two nights. These people were homeless and passing through Erwin or hikers taking a break from hiking the Appalachian Trail which ran through the mountains surrounding Erwin.

Anthony fell deeper in love with Virginia and decided that one of the things he would buy her for Christmas would be a ring. He didn't have much to pay for it but he saved $200 which bought a nice little diamond ring. They were already talking about marriage and knew they were loved each other enough that as soon as Anthony graduated from High School, then marriage was an option for them.

Anthony and Virginia knew they loved each other and wanted to spend their lives together. They also knew the importance of going to college and getting good jobs. This was difficult for Anthony because he realized where he came from and for him, college was almost unthinkable. He knew he loved Virginia and wanted to provide a good life for her, and college was one of the only ways to assure the life he wanted to give her.

Anthony was anxious to get out of high school so they could start their lives together. He had wanted to experience this type of love and now that he had it, he was not patient. To him this was the best blessing God could give him and he wanted more. Trying to follow the Christian life and doing the things he needed was paying off, or as he said, it was God rewarding him for being obedient to the things he had learned about being a Christian.

Virginia accepted the ring and other gifts Anthony gave her for Christmas. It was obvious that he worked hard and saved his money to buy her the things he did for Christmas. They were not great gifts but were appreciated because of the effort Anthony had made. Others knew how hard he worked to get the money to buy things; they also knew how much it meant to him to show his love to others. Anthony also purchased Christmas gifts for Virginia's parents, Thomas and Lucille, as well as for her brother Steve.

Things were going well for Anthony, despite the abuse he had experienced, being homeless and having to find shelter wherever he could find it. He was in love, and growing as a Christian. He was happy and back at University School, the school he loved and enjoyed. He was at the school he loved and the girl he loved was spending much of her time there with him.

Anthony also spent more time with Steve Jackson. Steve and some of his friends got Anthony involved in boxing. He was excelling at the sport and doing extremely well. Anthony figured one reason he was doing so well was that he came from a good genetic pool. Two uncles on his mother's side of the family were quality, top notch boxers. His uncle Horace Oliver, called H.O., was a former, six-time National Golden Gloves Champion. H.O. fought Jimmy Ellis in the Olympic Trials Finals before losing a controversial split decision by one point. Ellis won the Olympic Gold Medal and became the Heavyweight Champion of the World. H.O. fought a number of professional fights before retiring undefeated. He didn't like the politics of professional boxing. H.O. helped develop the Job Corps in upper East Tennessee where he coached boxing for a number of years before dying of cirrhosis of the liver from alcoholism. H.O.'s brother Raymond was also a champion fighter. Raymond never fought the glory fights H.O. did but many in the family said he was a better fighter than H.O.

Raymond was paralyzed in a motorcycle accident in Florida. He rode with the motorcycle club The Outlaws. He died from a heroin overdose at his home in Kingsport, Tennessee. Anthony was impressed with Raymond's funeral. There were 400 riders from The Outlaws who rode their motorcycles in the funeral procession. It was moving as the riders from The Outlaws gave a 21 gun salute while revving up their engines before the burial. It was moving to see the leader of this group take off his leather jacket and place it in Raymond's casket.

Anthony's grandfather Oscar was a United States Naval Champion. Oscar didn't talk much about his boxing. Not because he didn't want to talk about it, but simply it was a part of his past and others didn't ask. Anthony regretted not talking to his grandfather and asking questions about his past, including his boxing.

Anthony knew he could excel in boxing because of his genetics. He fought 168 pounds and fought in fights around the Tri-Cities. Anthony fought 24 fights with a record of 23 wins and 1 loss, the loss a split decision. Anthony knocked out a number of fighters without ever being knocked down. He had his picture on the front page of the Johnson City Press Chronicle Sports Page during the preparation for one of his fights. Many of his friends and his basketball coach at University High saw the picture and were amazed that he was boxing. It was something he didn't talk much about but after the picture appeared in the newspaper it was something others asked about and gave him some praise about. It was obvious to many of his friends that Anthony had changed his life for the better. He was more serious about the sports he participated in and was not in as much trouble as when he attended University School previously. It was obvious that he was a Christian. He even participated in the Fellowship of Christian Athletes.

Anthony had difficulty and got into trouble on occasion. He ended up with friends and took pills or smoked marijuana, but it was uncomfortable for him to be in these situations. He didn't understand why he shouldn't be involved in these activities, due to them never being discussed with him. The situations where Anthony was occasionally taking drugs ended after one of his friends questioned his faith while getting high. After this experience he knew he was not being the witness he should be. He knew from the tone of his friend's voice that he was doing wrong. While he enjoyed smoking marijuana with this friend he made the effort to reduce the amount of drugs he was taking. He had reduced the amount, but had not totally quit. This was especially true with alcohol and marijuana. Virginia didn't know of the limited drug usage he was involved in and while he joked with her on occasion about his usage, he never used around her. To him, his usage was so minimal that as far as he was concerned, he wasn't using.

Anthony went to two high school proms that year. Virginia and he attended the prom at Unicoi County High, where she attended school, and the prom at University School. Anthony enjoyed both proms and his friends at University School felt he and Virginia were a perfect couple. Virginia's picture was taken by a photographer of the University High Year Book and placed in that year's edition. Under the picture was the caption, "Anthony's."

Things were going well for Anthony. Unfortunately, they changed. This should have been expected, but as usual, he was completely blind-sided. Anthony and Virginia continued to talk about their future plans and their intent to get married. It was now spring and Virginia was attending East Tennessee State University. She started changing after she started college. She talked more about the need to put hers and Anthony's marriage plans off for a short period of time. This was difficult for Anthony. He felt and took this as personal rejection.

Anthony was willing to try what Virginia wanted because they were still seeing each other. According to her, they would remain just as close as they had been before. They were just putting off getting married so soon. She felt it was best to wait until they had gone a little further in college. For her that meant a minimum of at least a year and a half. Anthony knew it could be longer because he hadn't even decided where to go to college. They continued in their relationship until the end of the school year. Virginia was in her first year of college and Anthony looked forward to his senior year in high-school. After Virginia's High School graduation they didn't spend as much time with each other as Anthony wanted. This was due to Virginia going to summer school at East Tennessee State University.

Anthony and Virginia still saw each other on a regular basis and Anthony was as much in love with her as ever. That didn't mean things were easy. He had experienced the best times of his life with Virginia. He loved her for who she was and what she had done for him. The relationship between Anthony and Virginia was about to change. Anthony would regret what he was about to do and the things he was about to say to Virginia.

They were together at church and alone when the conversation started. "Anthony, I hope you know I love you. I think the world of you but I think we need to take a break from each other and make sure of our relationship before we go any further in it." Virginia said trying to be as nice as she could but her words still hurt and confused him.

"What do you mean, Virginia? I though we had talked about this and agreed we wouldn't get married so soon. We would wait, go on to school and all that." Anthony was hurting because he was convinced she was trying to break things off.

"Well, we sort of talked about it, but we need to be sure before we get married, Anthony. I think I love you; I just want to know for sure. I don't think it would be that bad of an idea to date other people for awhile in order to make sure." She held his hand as she said this.

Anthony jerked his hand back and raised his voice, "Wait a minute Virginia, I do know. I love you. I want to marry you. I don't need to see anyone else to know that. I thought you knew that as well." He knew what was happening and had tears in his eyes.

"I do love you, Anthony. I just want to know for sure that we should be together. I'm not saying that we won't get married or anything like that. I just want to know for sure. Maybe we should even date other people to make sure of our love." She tried to be kind to Anthony but he knew this was possibly the end of the best thing that had ever happened to him.

Anthony said the words he regretted, "I don't think that is it, Virginia. You don't love me anymore and you just want to date other people. If that is the case I wish you would just say so. I'm not willing to go along with it, though. Either we are together or we're not. I love you and nothing is going to change that."

Virginia choked back her tears, "Anthony, I do love you; this is not what I wanted. I wanted us to be together, it's just that I wanted to be sure. We have our whole lives ahead of us. There is nothing wrong with being sure about the decisions we make that will affect us for the rest of our lives. I can't deal with this right now though, at least not to this extent and in this manner. I need to go, you've taken everything wrong." Virginia was crying.

She walked away from him going outside to her car. He was openly angry and he yelled at Virginia, "That's fine, Virginia, just leave. I don't care. As far as I'm concerned it's over and I don't care."

As Virginia drove off he started crying. He realized it was over. He also realized he didn't mean what he had just said. He did love Virginia. He loved her with all of his heart. She was the best thing that had ever happened to him and he didn't want to lose her. He also knew that Virginia was stubborn and he wouldn't blame her if she never came back to him after he had acted the way he did.

After about 30 minutes and some thought about what had just happened Anthony got on his motorcycle and drove to Virginia's house. She was alone in the house, crying, when he got there. He knocked on the door and she opened it with tears in her eyes. He told her upon seeing her, "I'm sorry, Virginia, I love you so much I'm afraid I'm going to lose you I don't want that to happen." He reached his arms around her and they engaged in a passionate kiss.

Virginia responded to Anthony after the kiss, "I love you too Anthony. I just want to make sure before getting married."

Anthony, hoping he had changed her mind about seeing other people asked, "Do you really think we need to see or try dating other people?"

Virginia responded making Anthony more upset, "Yes, Anthony, I do. I'm not saying we need to date seriously or even long term. Maybe just going out with someone else once will convince us that we need to stay together."

Anthony answered Virginia, still crying, "Virginia, I love you more than you will ever know, but I can't do that. I think it will just be best that we don't see each other for now if that is the case. I will say I will always be there if you change your mind. I love you Virginia." He turned to walk away, realizing that he was not going to change her mind. He was upset and needed to be alone. He felt like he wanted to end his life. He had never been this depressed. He didn't know what to do. He couldn't go back to the life he had experienced before Virginia.

She called out to him as he walked away, "I love you, too, Anthony." He heard what she said but was unable to respond as he got on his motorcycle, hurt, angry, and not wanting to live.

Anthony yelled out in the quietness of his thoughts, "God, how could you let this happen? You've taken everything from me that I ever loved. I don't care if I live anymore or not." Anthony rode his motorcycle from Virginia's house and past the church. He turned onto the back alley at the church. As he drove his motorcycle he became angrier. He knew he didn't want to live. He had had enough. Anthony was now on a road passing by a local cemetery. He was going between 50 and 60 miles an hour when he stood up on the brakes causing the motorcycle to slide out from under him. As he hit the pavement with his left leg he turned somersaults on the pavement, as the motorcycle also rolled and flipped over. He wasn't sure but the bike may have turned over twice before sliding to a rest in the grass next to the road and near where he now lay.

Anthony's leg was bleeding through the tear in his left pants leg, on his right elbow, and his back right shoulder. There was an almost unbearable burning sensation through the injuries as a result of him trying to kill himself. He looked over to his right and the motorcycle's back wheel was still spinning. He got up, limping, and feeling the pain as he walked to the motorcycle. He picked up the motorcycle, hoping it would start. He stepped over the saddle and jumped on the starter peg forcing his right leg down to give it power. The motorcycle started on the first kick. It had some scratches on it from flipping across the pavement but was still in good shape, better shape than Anthony would have imagined.

Anthony was still upset about what had just happened between him and Virginia. He drove to Ninth Street Baptist Church. He parked the motorcycle at one of the side doors of the church. He ran into the church and discovered there was no one there. He wasn't through yet. He was still wanted to die. He ran up one of the flights of stairs, after reaching the top he turned around, ran and jumped head first down the flight he had just come up. He wasn't stopping to think about what he was doing, he just did it. Anthony wanted to hit head first, maybe break his neck; hopefully this would be an easy death. Instead, he hit flat on his stomach. It was like doing a belly flop off a diving board at the swimming pool except there was no water to break his fall. He lay on the ground at the foot of the stairwell for what seemed like minutes, gasping for air from where he had just lost his breath. He was angrier than ever. As far as he was concerned, he couldn't do anything right, and his pain was an indication of how badly he had screwed up. He cursed God under his breath, "Damn it God, why don't you just let me die, let me die, please, I'm tired and can't take it any more. Let me die."

After a few minuets Anthony got up and went outside to the back side of the church. Once outside he started hitting the outside back wall of the church as hard as he could with his fist. He had boxed for some time now and hit the wall continually, right, left, left, left, and right. Anthony was throwing hooks, jabs, uppercuts one blow after another as if he were working out with a heavy bag. The punches were flush, hard, and balanced evenly across his knuckles. The difference between a heavy bag and brick wall was that as hard as he hit the wall nothing was going to give except his hands.

Anthony was crying, tears streaming down his face. He hoped the pain from the blows to the wall would cover the pain he felt in his heart. Not only did it not cover the pain, but neither did the pain of the injuries he had sustained from jumping down the flight of stairs, or the pain from the burns from the motorcycle wreck. Anthony's heart was breaking and he felt the pain of knowing he was not going to be with Virginia again. Anthony realized there must be a better way to end his life. After he finished hitting the wall for what must have been 5 minutes, he walked to his motorcycle. His hands were covered and dripping in blood. He had hit the wall so hard and for so long that he broke the skin across his knuckles on both hands down to the bone. Anthony should have been in a great deal of pain but he didn't feel it. It wasn't until he drove the motorcycle that the pain surfaced. It was all he could do to use the gas, brakes and clutch on the motorcycle, but he forced himself to do it. The more his leg and hands hurt, the more he cried out, thinking of Virginia. The crying was not a result of the injuries, it was a result of his heart hurting and the belief that the relationship with the person he loved more than life itself was over.

Anthony drove the motorcycle towards Walter and Wanda's house on Rock Creek Road. He knew they were at work so he could break in and steal Walter's 38 caliber hand gun. He ran in, took the gun, and made sure it had bullets in it. After taking the gun and leaving the house, he got back on his motorcycle and drove it to Ninth Street Baptist Church. There was no one at the church. Anthony didn't know where Clinton was, but for some reason he kept being drawn back to the church. He drove his motorcycle to Clinton Watkins' back yard behind the church. He sat in the back yard between Clinton's house and the church.

After sitting on the grass for awhile and contemplating the hard times he was going through Anthony pulled the handgun out of the back pack. He spoke to God while sitting there staring with the pistol. "I'm tired God. I love Virginia and I can't live without her. I'm ready to die. Let this end quickly." Anthony was quick but certain in his movements. He put the barrel of the gun in his mouth, pointing the end of the barrel towards the roof of his mouth. He tasted the steel and felt the cold against his mouth and across his front teeth. As he pulled back the hammer of the pistol he heard a voice in his head say, "This is going to hurt, there has to be a better way. Go to Beauty Spot."

Anthony slowly pulled the gun out of his mouth and let the trigger back slow and easy as he pointed the gun away. He didn't know where the voice came from but for some reason he listened to it. He put the gun back in the back pack while his hands shook and drops of sweat beaded up on his forehead. Anthony got on the motorcycle and drove up Rock Creek Road towards the mountains. He stopped and dropped off the pistol at Walter and Wanda's house where he had found it.

The Beauty Spot was a mountain top at the end of Rock Creek Road on the Tennessee/North Carolina state line. It was named The Beauty Spot because it broke the timber line and was barren except for grass due to its elevation. Once at the top of the mountain you could see for miles. The Beauty Spot was next to Mount Mitchell, the tallest mountain in the eastern United States. The view was spectacular with the surrounding mountains and views of Erwin and other cities.

Even though it was late spring/early summer it still got below freezing at night. Anthony felt he could freeze to death on the mountain and not feel much, if any pain. He had heard that when someone froze to death they simply fell asleep and didn't wake up. After the pain from his earlier actions he was looking for an easy out. Anthony drove his motorcycle with his blood covered hands and leg to the top of the mountain. There was no one on the mountain so he drove to a point away from the road on the grass where he could not be seen by anyone. He wore a T-shirt and blue jeans covered with blood. It was late afternoon and he lay down on the grass. He didn't have anything else except for the backpack, which he used as a pillow.

Anthony spent the rest of the evening questioning God. It was after dark now and he was hurting like he had never hurt before, not just physical pain but also emotional pain. He was hoping, even praying that he would freeze to death. He just wanted to fall asleep and not wake up, like the stories he had heard about.

Anthony dozed off and on for the duration of the night; he kept moving, tossing back and forth and waking up from it being so cold. He heard God tell him, "Don't give up Anthony, I know you're hurting but I love you and want to help you. Don't give up, live, stay awake, live. I have a purpose for you Anthony. Whether you realize it or not I have something planned for your life."

Anthony struggled through the night; he couldn't get any sleep to accomplish his purpose. He awoke at daybreak more tired and confused than ever. He didn't know what to do; he had failed at everything he tried. He had to talk to someone about everything he had gone through from the day before. He drove his motorcycle to Clinton Watkins' house.

The morning was cool and foggy but even though it was cold it wasn't as bad as the night he had just spent on Beauty Spot. He saw Clinton's car parked at the church; he knew Clinton must be home. Anthony knocked on the door, still covered in blood. It wasn't long before Clinton answered the door. "Goodness gracious Anthony, what's going on?" Clinton questioned as Anthony walked in the door crying.

"I've got to talk." Anthony answered through the tears.

* * * * * *

Anthony cried as he told the story to George at Manna House. George asked, "Well, what happened Anthony? I mean what did Clinton say to you? What did you talk about?"

"We talked about all kinds of stuff. He really helped me out. Clinton was special; he really cared for me and talked to me about things I needed to hear for a long time. As bad as this experience was for me in my life it was one of the best things to ever happen to me." Anthony answered, wiping the tears.

George reached for some tissue and while handing it to Anthony he asked, "Tell me how was it one of the best things that happened to you?"

"Well, Clinton talked to me about how I had been looking to myself for answers and all. While I had given my life to Christ I still didn't understand the full concept of that decision. I was still looking in the wrong place for the answers to my problems. No one had really talked to me about what I needed to do to grow as a Christian, and Clinton did that." Anthony showed excitement regarding the memories and lessons he learned through his discussions with Clinton.

Anthony spoke about what he had learned about the Holy Spirit. "He talked to me about the Holy Spirit and who the Holy Spirit was. We talked about the importance of reading God's Word, the Bible. Clinton told me that the Holy Spirit, while living through us allows us to experience the power of Jesus and have a better understanding of God, and the Bible. It is through that power and understanding that I am able to overcome the heartache and problems I face."

A few moments passed and after some reflection Anthony continued, "It was difficult to understand at first but Clinton really helped. He helped disciple me and helped me grow as a Christian after this terrible experience in my life. I learned more about God, His Son Jesus, and the Holy Spirit. I learned about making Jesus Christ not only my Savior but also making Him my Lord. Clinton helped me recognize and understand the importance of making Jesus my Lord. He also helped me learn about the Baptism of the Holy Spirit which was something I had not experienced or understood. It wasn't that I didn't have the Holy Spirit in my life. I did from the point of accepting Christ as my Savior back at the David Wilkerson Crusade. I just didn't understand the benefits of the Holy Spirit nor had I allowed it to work in me the way that God wanted."

Anthony spoke to George for a few moments talking about the role of the Holy Spirit in his life and the changes that had occurred in his life after his breakup with Virginia. He finally quit crying and continued his conversation with George. "I guess George, that this is the only reason I was able to deal with breaking up with Virginia at such a volatile time in my life. I mean, I love my wife immensely, but I still can't help how this thing with Virginia affected my life. If it hadn't been for Clinton helping me change the whole attitude and focus of my being, I still don't think I would have been able to deal with the breakup between Virginia and me. I loved her, and in many ways, even to this day, haven't gotten over the love we had and the way things ended. I realize that God is bigger than all of that, and that my ultimate love is in Him. God is the one who gives a perfect and lasting love and I've never forgotten that. Despite the heartache of the breakup with Virginia, it's possible that my relationship with the Lord was strengthened because of it."

Anthony felt good about sharing this story with George. Getting it off his chest for the first time was a relief. He was sharing things with George that he had needed to share with someone for a long time. For the first time Anthony experienced the importance of openly communicating with someone about his past.

"Tell me, Anthony, what is the Baptism of the Holy Spirit to you?" George asked.

"Well, like I said earlier, I had to let Jesus live through me. The way He does that is through the Holy Spirit. He allows me to know, think, feel and experience the things of God and Christ. I have been able to get into an attitude of worship since then like no other that I can explain. The worship allows me to feel close to God, understand Him more and be lifted up by the Lord when I need it. The Holy Spirit guides me and lets me know what decisions to make and what things to do." Anthony was excited about the conversation with George and the change in direction.

"I know it sounds really weird and all, but I believe it. I know how it has worked for me. I know that when I have listened to the Holy Spirit things have worked out best for me. God has taken care of me and blessed me. I'm not perfect; don't get me wrong. There are definitely times where I follow my own heart, but I recognize that is wrong and I try to always change that wrong and get back to the ways of God. I know the importance of getting back to the Holy Spirit when I do wrong. The more I listen to Him, the more He gives me the heart of God so it is not my will or my ways I follow, but my ways follow the things God wants. In many ways I develop the heart and ways of God when I am obedient to His Spirit. Does any of this make sense?" Anthony asked George.

"Yeah, in other words, when you follow God's Spirit, He blesses you and you end up doing the things He wants you to. You recognize the blessings He gives you are a result of being obedient and you feel better about this. So God's Holy Spirit helps you be more like Christ?" George asked with a smile on his face.

"That is most definitely the case! There have been times where I have sinned and turned from God, but the Holy Spirit always finds a way to bring me back. I am so grateful for Clinton Watkins allowing God's Spirit to help him instruct and disciple me." Anthony said with a smile on his face.

"Tell me, Anthony, what ever happened between you and Virginia and how do you feel now about that whole episode?" George asked, changing the subject.

"Well, we tried to get back together off and on throughout the summer, and some over the next year but it just didn't happen. She changed the more she got involved in college and we grew apart. I guess to be perfectly honest, that in many ways I still have feelings about her. It is not that I love her as much as it is I love who she was and what we had. I've gone on from there, though, and I have a wonderful wife now. I love my wife, and I know she loves me. We have two wonderful children who I wouldn't give up for anything. I know God has been good to me and one of the ways He has is that He has given me such a wonderful wife and such wonderful children. You wouldn't believe the things God has done for us."

Anthony continued about Virginia, "To be honest, though, I still think about Virginia. What is she doing? What is she like? I know that when I am ready God will answer those questions. I miss her, I miss the fun we had and I guess if I'm really honest it is like I said earlier, I still think about; What if?"

"But it is like I said earlier. God has blessed me with a good and faithful wife. He has given me a wife who I realize I don't deserve. I couldn't have asked for anyone better, and many of my friends and relatives that know her have gone as far as to tell me so."

George responded, "Well, I want to hear the story about how you got together. I'll tell you what, let's finish up today with the part up to where you get together with your future wife. I know we'll go over our time some but I really want to hear before next week about this, so is that O.K. to go over time today?"

"Sure," Anthony responded that it shouldn't take long to explain the things that happened.

"That's great. Let's stretch and get something to drink and we can start up again in about 5 minutes." George responded.

Anthony and George were feeling pretty good. Anthony was excited because he knew it wouldn't be long until he was sharing with George many of the miracles God had done for him.

~ Chapter 27 ~

Year of Confusion

George and Anthony chatted and stretched before sitting down to talk about Anthony's life again. George started back on the topic of what happened with Anthony after the breakup with Virginia Madison. "O.K., Anthony, lets get started again. Tell me what happened during that next year up to the point where things started leading up to your getting married."

"Well I made some decisions and did several things I regretted later on. I loved University School and should have stayed there but decided to do everything possible to prove Virginia wrong. I later regretted it because I would have liked to have graduated from University High. That is where my best friends were. I liked my teachers and it was a good school."

Anthony spoke about Gordonsville, "As much as I loved University High I decided to go back to school in Gordonsville. I wanted to play football in college and I felt I was good enough to play. I started to play for Erwin instead of Gordonsville but after I saw that Coach Fontez was there and was not going to give me a fair chance, I decided to go back to Gordonsville. Even though I knew the coaches were somewhat biased I felt they would give me a better chance than Fontez." Anthony gave more detail.

* * * * * *

After Anthony and Virginia broke up he decided to try and make her jealous. He started dating other girls. He dated these girls not only to try and make Virginia jealous but to see if he could develop relationships with other girls to try and get back some of the things he missed from his relationship with Virginia. One person he dated was Jean Glavine to whom he had been introduced by his uncle Leo.

Jean was the niece of professional baseball player Mark Glavine who was a pitcher for the San Francisco Giants. She was also the niece of Anthony's boxing coach Phil Glavine. She was pretty and went to several church functions with Anthony, but religion was something she was not interested in. As pretty and as nice as she was, things just didn't click between her and Anthony so they decided to break off their relationship.

Anthony also dated a girl named Julia Brooks. He turned the heads of a lot of friends while dating Julia because she was African American. They got along well and enjoyed each others' company. He met her while she worked as a cashier at one of the fast food restaurants near the Johnson City Mall. He thought she was attractive and had a fun personality. It was at their initial meeting when Anthony took the chance to see if she would go out with him. He was pleasantly surprised when she said yes. Anthony and Julia went out a number of times before they separated ways. Julia wanted to get back with an old boyfriend and her relationship with Anthony was never serious. They remained friends after the breakup. Things might have been more serious between them if it was up to Anthony, but he understood the situation and was glad they broke up before they got serious.

Anthony also dated a girl named Valerie Siemons. She lived across the street from his mother's house on Rock Creek Road. Anthony was good friends with Valerie's brother John at school and had run track with him. Valerie was a very pretty girl with long black hair. She was slim and easy to get along with. They got along well for a period of time, and they went out on a number of occasions, doing various things together including going to church functions. Anthony did not feel as close to Valerie as she did towards him, and they eventually quit seeing each other. He did not want the relationship to go to the point where he ended up hurting Valerie the same way he was hurt with Virginia. It was also during this period of time that he tried to get back with Charlotte Stevens. They also went out on several dates, and it was on those dates that he and Charlotte kissed each other on numerous occasions. He didn't have the same feelings for her that he once had, and she felt the same. They still saw each other more as brother and sister than boyfriend and girlfriend. He eventually lost touch with Charlotte, which he regretted because he recognized the friendship they had had with each other.

While Anthony adapted well with the changes in girlfriends, he hurt in other ways. He became upset, hurt, and confused at his church, Ninth Street Baptist Church. He was upset because the deacons at the church asked Clinton to resign as youth pastor. Clinton started an extensive outreach to a number of kids in the area and Anthony always felt that much of this decision by the deacons was a result of that outreach. He showed a lot of interest in the kids who lived in Unicoi, a small town near Erwin. Many of the kids were poor and appreciated the outreach. Clinton was close to a number of the kids and some of the deacons questioned the relationship he had with them, especially one of the older girls who was involved in the youth group.

Anthony felt he knew Clinton's heart and knew how innocent his heart was. Clinton cared for those kids because he wanted to see them to develop a relationship with the Lord. He wanted them to follow God, and if Clinton was close to one of the girls it was because there was not that much difference in their ages and Clinton was single. Besides, many of the kids and adults still thought Clinton would end up with Beth Ann Richardson.

Many church people fought the actions of the deacons to get Clinton to resign, but Clinton resigned under protest. It was a decision that Anthony and many within the church were upset about. They thought the actions were wrong for the church. It was wrong for Clinton to resign, and wrong for the deacons who requested it. He did a lot for the youth at Ninth Street. They had grown in numbers but more importantly, they had grown spiritually. It was shortly after Clinton left as youth pastor that the church hired a new pastor named Virgil Linzak. Anthony liked Virgil and felt that if Virgil had been at Ninth Street before Clinton's leaving, he would not have left.

Shortly after Clinton left, Anthony started working more with Beth Ann Richardson. They helped the youth group continue to grow spiritually and stay together. The youth had built a strong family core with each other and none of them wanted to see it go away. It was from this working relationship that Anthony got to know Beth Ann Richardson.

It was midsummer and Anthony still lived at the YMCA. Beth Ann had recently moved from her parent's home and was now living on Tucker Street in Erwin. Tucker Street was the street which ran parallel with the YMCA. The YMCA was on the corner of Main and Tucker. She lived less than one block from where Anthony lived and it was the closeness in proximity and their working with the youth group that they started seeing each other on a frequent basis.

Beth Ann Richardson was a short woman. She was only 5' 2" tall and weighed 130 pounds. She had medium length dark brown hair and was very attractive. She had a round face and wore glasses and at times contacts. Anthony always thought she was attractive, even when observing her work with the kids in the youth group of which he was a part. Beth Ann was older than Anthony but that didn't matter to him. Anthony was 18 and she was in her late 20's. She looked younger than her age and acted much younger to Anthony. The beginning of their relationship was entirely centered on working together. Nothing else was intended between the two other than improving the youth group at church.

The relationship continued through the summer for Beth Ann and Anthony. She had done for Anthony just as Clinton had done while he lived there. Clinton had moved back to Kingsport Tennessee, where he was originally from, and Beth Ann filled his spot by inviting Anthony to eat with her on occasion at her house, and by going out to eat and doing things together. The invitation was nothing more than friends getting together over a meal and having fun with each other. She was after all, a teacher in Unicoi County at one of the elementary schools and had taught some of Anthony's friends. To have seen each other for any other reason than friendship would have been too strange for Anthony, even though he did see her as attractive and friendly.

Anthony thought that if he was a little older or she a little younger then he would certainly make the effort to go out with her. As far as Anthony knew, she was still seeing Clinton Watkins, and he did not know the seriousness or lack thereof in their relationship. Anthony and Beth Ann continued their friendship and work with the youth group through the first of the school year.

Shortly after the school year started Anthony recognized he was not going to be treated fairly by the coaches at Unicoi County High School, especially Miguel Fontez. He made the arrangements to go live with his uncle Leo who now lived on the farm in Gordonsville. Anthony was still hurt and upset over the breakup with Virginia. He saw Virginia at church on occasion with some of her friends or someone she was dating. Anthony still spent time with her and they went out on a few dates. The kissing and touch meant just as much to Anthony but he didn't know how she felt about the relationship. He still loved Virginia and couldn't bear seeing her dating someone else. This, along with the disappointment with the football team, was more than he could handle. Anthony said his good-byes to Virginia, and Beth Ann, and the rest of his friends, then went back to Gordonsville to play football and live with his uncle Leo.

* * * * * *

The fall of the year in Gordonsville went by quickly for Anthony. Some of his friends at Gordonsville were excited about seeing him return while others did not care for him being there in the first place. He shared his faith with the team and let them know of the changes which had occurred in his life. He also shared in a few churches in Gordonsville and Carthage. Speaking at churches was not new for Anthony; he had shared at a number of churches in East Tennessee. He had changed his life and was making every effort to live for Christ. He studied his Bible and as much as he had problems, the things he had the most problems with were under control.

Anthony took control of his sexual perversions and drug usage, and was not involved in those things. He missed Virginia but much of that longing was resolved in his communication with Beth Ann over the telephone and by letter.

Anthony was proud of what he was accomplishing at Gordonsville on the football team. He was by far the best running back on the team. He could run and catch, and maintained good size and conditioning. He also did well at the linebacker position on defense. He was playing on virtually every down, on offense at fullback and on defense at linebacker. Anthony arrived back in Gordonsville midweek before the first game, but he quickly worked his way into the offensive and defensive style of play for the team.

Things were going great for Anthony. He enjoyed living on the farm with his uncle and his family, just as much now as he did before. He also enjoyed making more friends than he did the first time he attended school there. He knew his faith played a part in this but he also knew that he was easier to get along with. This was not the case with everyone because some teased him. He preferred to not respond and it took more than it used to before he would respond. There were some who wanted him to be a tough guy and while he had this attitude before, his relationship with Jesus had calmed him down.

Anthony kept in touch with Beth Ann during his stay in Gordonsville. He called her to talk every Friday night after the football games. During the conversations they spoke about a number of things which led to a deep friendship. Slowly, Anthony got over Virginia. It was difficult and he still cared for her but Beth Ann was filling the void in regards to an intimate relationship. Anthony dated one or two girls at Gordonsville but he did not take the relationships seriously. He was not ready for a serious relationship.

Things were going well for Anthony except in two specific areas. One was that he was not getting along with one of his teammates on the football team. If Anthony had known him several years prior to their present relationship, it would have been all Anthony could do to keep from killing him. It was not nearly to that point but he was ready to flatten the guy if given the opportunity. Anthony brought some boxing gloves to school one day and this boy made the mistake of challenging him to a boxing match. Anthony jumped at the opportunity; he knew this smaller and slower person had no chance. In Anthony's official boxing matches he fought as a sportsman, only looking for a knockout when the opportunity arose. This time Anthony was going to go out and make the knockout happen right away. He wanted to hurt this boy and he wanted to hurt him bad. As far as he was concerned the boy had smarted off to him one too many times. He would take advantage of the smaller, weaker, and slower chump.

Just as the boys got the gloves on, Anthony was called to the principal's office by one of the teachers who saw the two out next to the football field getting ready to box with a number of friends looking on. Upon arriving at the office, the first thing that happened was that Anthony was jumped on and yelled at by the principal for his willingness to fight. Anthony was upset because it appeared to him that this good old boy was not getting any of the blame for his actions, and it wasn't a fight, it was boxing. The next thing that the principal said is what really hurt him.

The principal told Anthony that the Tennessee High School Athletic Association had ruled that he was an ineligible player for the football team or any other athletic team at Gordonsville. The ineligibility was because he lived with an uncle who was not a legal guardian. Anthony tried to get the school to fight the decision on several grounds, one of which was that he was eighteen years of age and he had not lived at home since he was 14 years old. Since that time he had only stayed at home briefly, but for the last year and a half he had lived at the YMCA by himself, alone without a guardian.

The principal was upset over the boxing incident, and would not help Anthony fight the case. He stated, "Even if we did fight it, by the time the association made a ruling on it, the season would be over." Anthony was upset by the unwillingness of the principal and coach to fight for his eligibility. As a result, he left Gordonsville that weekend to go back to Erwin.

Anthony started receiving phone calls and letters from various colleges and universities to recruit him not only for football but also basketball. He was pleased although he wished he could have finished the season at Gordonsville.

The thing most pleasing to Anthony was that the offers showed how little coach Miguel Fontez at Erwin knew when it came to coaching football. He was the one coach at Erwin who never gave him the opportunity to excel at football. Hopefully, Coach Fontez would be the coach questioned for letting him get away from Erwin.

Anthony arrived back in Erwin where he stayed with his mother for one week. He only stayed long enough to make the arrangements needed to move back into the YMCA. He got his old job back at the YMCA where he worked as a lifeguard. He also cleaned the Downtown YMCA where he lived. This was good because it gave him extra spending money and paid his monthly rent on top of his Social Security check. Anthony was back in Erwin because he needed a place to live and he knew he had more independence while he was at the YMCA. Hopefully, things would be better than they were when he left.

✳ ✳ ✳ ✳ ✳ ✳

Back at Manna House George asked, "Were you O.K. with being back in Erwin, Anthony?"

"Yeah, I think I was. I realize now that even though I still had some hard times to overcome with Virginia, Beth Ann and I really began to hit it off. It was after coming back that I believe we began to fall in love." Anthony answered with confidence.

"How did you feel about the things that had happened in Gordonsville?" George asked curiously.

"At first not too good. I was upset and all, but looking back on it I feel pretty good. I mean, it is evidence of what all God brought me through. I wasn't dating girls because I wanted to take advantage of them. I had a principal who was unfair and while I got upset, I didn't get as upset as I had for similar incidents in the past. I had a situation happen like what had happened with James Rogers earlier in my life, and I was able to take control of it. It was almost like that last bit in Gordonsville mirrored so much of what had happened in my life prior to becoming a Christian, yet the reactions to those same types of things were so different. I've asked myself the question, 'Why?' many times. I know deep down though, that it is because God took who I was and changed that person to who I am now. Like I said earlier, I still make mistakes, sometimes huge mistakes, but I always know where to turn back to. God's Spirit gives me the guidance I need and makes it so much easier and worthwhile to follow Jesus. So when I think back on it I don't see the hurt. I see the blessings and miracles of God." Anthony responded.

It was obvious to George that Anthony believed what he was saying. "You sound confident about the power of God and his Holy Spirit, Anthony. Why is that?" George, still curious, asked anxiously, awaiting Anthony's response.

"Well, I've seen it. I saw it then although I didn't recognize it, but I really saw it over the next few years of my life and even continue to see it in my present day life. I mean, there has been so much that has happened that it is evident to me that God and His Holy Spirit were a part of it. Even my wife and children are examples of that." Anthony smiled.

The radiance on Anthony's face shined as George spoke, "I guess that gets us to the point where we were going to stop for today. The point where things start going well between you and your wife, or I guess I should say your future wife."

"Yeah, I guess it does." Anthony responded, smiling.

"We've gone over quite a bit today but I want you to know that you have blessed me, Anthony. It is obvious that God does have something planned for your life. I can't wait to hear more next week about the ways God has blessed you."

George prayed a quick prayer, thanking God for the miracles He had worked in Anthony's life. He thanked God for Anthony living and not being successful at suicide, and for what God had planned for Anthony's future. After the prayer they gave each other a firm hand shake and went their separate ways.

~ Chapter 28 ~

Beth Ann

Things were going well for Anthony. He was involved at church and active in helping coordinate the youth group activities. He was also working more with Beth Ann Richardson. After working with her he found out that she was Michael Braveheart's aunt.

Michael was the former fullback at Unicoi County that Anthony appreciated as a player and a person. It was clear to Anthony that Michael came from a good and caring family. This was one of the reasons he was so kind while he was in high school. Michael was now playing football for the University of Tennessee Volunteers. He was a walk-on, and punted and played cornerback. He was getting a lot of play time on the Junior Varsity team. Anthony was pleased for the success Michael was having. Anthony looked forward to playing college football even though he had another semester left in high school.

Anthony spent a lot of time at Beth Ann's apartment on Tucker Street. It was a small duplex that she shared with the owner, a small, elderly lady who had been single for her entire life. The elderly lady got along well with Beth Ann and was glad she had a school teacher living next to her in the other apartment.

Anthony liked the apartment. It was small, with a nice front living room which faced Tucker Street. The room had large picture windows all around the room which opened it up and kept the appearance nice and bright. Beth Ann had it decorated quite nicely with plenty of plants and comfortable furniture.

The middle room of the apartment was Beth Ann's bedroom with a single bed and dresser located in it. In the back room of the apartment there was a small kitchen and bathroom off to the side. Anthony spent so much time there it was almost like he lived there. At first he had an occasional meal with Beth Ann and they worked on church related activities. She enjoyed his company as much as he appreciated having something to do and someone to talk to.

As the fall of the year moved towards winter, Anthony started to care for Beth Ann in more ways than just a casual friendship. It wasn't long before he asked her out for a date. Initially it wasn't a date, but he knew they would have a good time if they went out to do something outside of church work. Anthony cared for her in a way that he knew was more than friendship. She was nice to him and they grew closer than many thought they should. At times, Anthony still thought of Virginia, and was dating various girls. While he dated, he limited the dating because he felt himself getting closer to Beth Ann.

Many of the kids played a game called 'Popeye' when going out in groups. It consisted of seeing cars driving down the road at night with only one headlight burning. Upon seeing the car, someone yelled, "Popeye." The first one seeing the 'Popeye,' and calling it out was allowed to request a kiss later that night from someone else in the group. 'Popeye,' was a game many of the kids liked playing and a game Anthony had played many times himself. He got kisses from numerous girls at church and school from playing this game.

The Beach Boys came to Johnson City for a concert at Freedom Hall Civic Center. Anthony knew The Beach Boys was one of Beth Ann's favorite groups and he wanted to take her to the concert. He had short notice regarding the concert and he was strapped for funds to buy tickets. After looking at his options he pawned his guitar in order to have the money to take Beth Ann to dinner and the concert.

Once discovering what Anthony did to buy the tickets Beth Ann was willing to go on the "date." The only condition was she either had to drive or let Anthony drive her car. She was willing and Anthony took her out on their first "date."

Beth Ann had a yellow 1972 Nova Super Sport. The car was a straight shift. It looked and drove nice. She purchased the car new and she was proud of it. She enjoyed it immensely and Anthony understood the importance of her letting him drive it. He drove the car to Johnson City and they went to eat before the concert. Anthony was dressed in a white leisure suit, which was unusual because he seldom dressed up for anything.

The evening started off poorly for Anthony and Beth Ann. They went to Shoney's to eat before the concert. When the waitress brought the drinks, she reached to get a drink off of her tray for Beth Ann, and when she lifted Beth Ann's drink off the tray, it tipped, and the remaining drinks on the tray fell on Anthony. Anthony was wet from all the drinks. He was disappointed, and he couldn't change clothes before the concert. He was also upset at the restaurant; they were not willing to help with the cleaning bill for the outfit. They did not apologize or offer to purchase Anthony and Beth Ann's meal.

As far as Anthony was concerned, he wouldn't eat at Shoney's again. He would go if he had to with someone else, but if it was his choice, he went somewhere else. After dinner, Anthony and Beth Ann went to The Beach Boys concert.

The Beach Boys played all of their classic hits, and outside of being a little flat on a few of their songs, they were entertaining. The concert was a sellout so the large crowd made the concert enjoyable. Anthony felt lucky with the arena being dark, the nearly 12,000 people couldn't notice his stained white leisure suit.

While driving back to Beth Ann's, Anthony observed a car with only one head light burning; he called out, "Popeye."

Beth Ann saw the kids play the game so she knew what it meant when Anthony called out "Popeye." She didn't say anything, she just grinned and carried on with the conversation they where involved in. After a few more miles Anthony saw another car with only one burning headlight; he called out again, "Popeye."

After calling it out, Anthony stated, "I guess that's two Popeye's I get to collect on."

Beth Ann simply responded, "I guess we'll have to see about that."

They went on with their conversation until they got to Beth Ann's apartment. Anthony walked Beth Ann to the door; she said, "If you want, come on in for a while before you go home."

Anthony, not thinking anything of it, responded, "O.K."

They walked in and sat on the couch to watch television. They sat on the couch for close to an hour watching television. Anthony did not sit any closer to Beth Ann than usual and they didn't talk much about anything other than the concert. It was getting late and Beth Ann got a pillow to lay down on the floor to watch television. As she lay there Anthony decided to try and collect on the two "Popeye's" he called out on the drive back from the concert. He felt uncomfortable and did not know what Beth Ann would do if he tried to collect on them. He finally mustered up enough courage and got on the floor next to her. She asked, "What are you doing here?"

She asked while smiling and Anthony did not take it as an offensive question. He felt this way because of the way she asked the question. "Oh, I think I'll try to collect on my two 'Popeyes' if that's O.K.?" Anthony was trying to be romantic but he was scared to death from not knowing how she would react. He was surprised at the answer.

"Well, if you're going to collect on them, go ahead." Beth Ann was smiling and as she had finished her response she reached to her mouth to pull out the piece of gum she was chewing. Anthony reached over to give Beth Ann the kiss from the 'Popeye.'

Most kisses collected from 'Popeye's' were short, pecking kisses unless you were kissing someone you really liked. Anthony was surprised by the kiss from Beth Ann. It was a long, drawn out, passionate kiss. He couldn't recall at the moment due to being so shocked, but he thought it was one of the best kisses he had ever received. The kiss was so good that it got Anthony sexually excited. After the kiss, he lay on the floor with Beth Ann for a few minutes before collecting on his second, 'Popeye.'

He asked, "I guess that means I can collect on my second Popeye?" Beth Ann did not answer the question with words, she reached over, put her hands behind his head, and he put his behind hers, and they engaged in another long passionate kiss. Anthony was surprised and pleased with the pay back for the 'Popeye's'.

Anthony and Beth Ann lay on the floor for the next hour kissing and making out. He was sure he would see her in a different light in the future. He didn't lose respect for her. Instead he saw her as a person he enjoyed being with and a person helping take the heartbreak away. He didn't know it for sure, but he thought he might be falling in love all over again.

✷ ✷ ✷ ✷ ✷ ✷

Erwin started being fun for Anthony. He was spending more time with Beth Ann. They started seeing each other on a regular basis. They were not spending as much time with the youth group as before because the church had hired a youth pastor.

The new youth pastor and his wife took over all aspects of the youth group from those at the church. This hurt the church more than it helped because the people who had previously been involved had felt left out and abandoned. The attendance at the youth meetings and the spiritual growth among the youth declined once this couple took over the leadership. Anthony and Beth Ann were upset and hurt as were a number of others in leadership roles. The youth group would not be the same. The church was hurt more than helped as a result of this new couple.

Anthony and Beth Ann became more romantically involved as time went by. Anthony was drawn and attracted to Beth Ann for various reasons. He enjoyed her company, her intelligence, her faith, and he was sexually attracted to her. They had not had sex but it was not because he didn't want to. Even while involved in numerous make out sessions they did not have sex.

Anthony was attracted to her for various reasons, and for some reason he was attracted to Beth Ann sexually more than he had been Virginia. He even went out with Virginia while seeing Beth Ann to see if there was a chance they could get back together. After kissing with Virginia, she confronted Anthony with the fact that it was over between them. She stated this but was just as responsible for the actions between them as Anthony was. After this encounter with Virginia in his room at the YMCA he started taking his relationship with Beth Ann more seriously. He knew what he had gone through with Virginia, and he knew what love was. He was, without question, falling in love with Beth Ann.

Things were going well for Anthony until Clinton Watkins came back into the picture and started spending time in Erwin. Neither Anthony nor Beth Ann had seen him in the months since he had left Ninth Street as youth pastor. Anthony thought of him often due to the impact he had on his life, but he was surprised when he went to Beth Ann's apartment one afternoon.

Once arriving at the apartment Anthony was upset and hurt for yet another time in his life. When he arrived at Beth Ann's he saw Clinton's car parked in her driveway. He knocked on the door and Beth Ann opened it. She asked him to come in but she was acting differently than she had over the previous months. It was obvious to him why she was behaving this way when he saw Clinton sitting on the couch.

Anthony and Beth Ann had kept their relationship as much of a secret as possible. They did this because they knew they would receive criticism, and wanted to avoid it as much as possible. Anthony assumed they were hiding what was going on between them from Clinton. Anthony sat and spoke to both of them for 30 minutes when Beth Ann said that she and Clinton were going out to eat, and she would see Anthony later. Anthony was upset because it was clear to him the two of them were going on a date and that he was not welcome.

Anthony was extremely upset by this event with Beth Ann. He walked to the YMCA but did not go to sleep. Instead, after awhile, he walked back and forth in the alleyway behind Beth Ann's apartment. He kept at a distance, waiting and watching through the window to see when Beth Ann and Clinton returned from their date. He walked back and forth, becoming angrier with each step.

Anthony still had a temper and at times hit things when he became angry. He tried to control it by doing push ups instead of hitting things. He came to the conclusion that it was better to do something that helped him physically than hurting himself. He could not control his temper this night, though. He hit a large oak tree while walking back and forth in the alley.

Anthony paced back and forth in the alleyway for almost two hours, the longest two hours of his life. He eventually saw the light come on in Beth Ann's apartment. He was in the alley, looking across a fence and from behind a large bush that helped to hide him. He saw through the back kitchen window, Beth Ann and Clinton sat in the kitchen talking. They talked for what seemed like at least an hour.

Anthony, not knowing what was being said, became more upset the more he thought about what he was seeing. He was so upset he did 200 push ups, 100 with two hands and 100 one handed, 50 with each hand. He was hurt and crying about what he was thinking and what he was seeing.

Anthony was not upset at God; he was upset at Beth Ann. "Was she leading him on?" "Exactly what was going on between her and Clinton?" and "What had gone on between them?" Anthony became more upset when he saw Clinton give Beth Ann a short kiss before going home.

* * * * * *

Beth Ann tried to be sympathetic with him, "Anthony I just don't think we should see each other for a while. I should wait and see what is going to happen between me and Clinton."

Anthony replied angrily, "Why does it have to be me that has to wait? Why don't you tell him about us and see what his response is? It's totally unfair that I am the one having to wait and see what happens, Beth Ann. There was something between us and it's not fair to throw it all away. Besides you hadn't seen him in God knows how long and now, all of a sudden, now that he's back in the picture, everything has changed. It's just not right."

Beth Ann was calm but what she said shocked him, "Anthony, Clinton asked me to marry him and it is just something that I have to think about."

Anthony recalled what he went through with Virginia Madison, the way he lost her. He knew he was not going to give up this time, not without a fight. Not that he wanted to fight anyone, especially Clinton Watkins. He was the man who was so instrumental in helping him when he needed help the most. He knew he was going to lose love in his life again, unless he made a serious effort to keep it. He responded to Beth Ann, "You can see all you want to Beth Ann, but if you think I'm going to just walk away and let Clinton have you, you're wrong. You're going to have to run me off on a regular basis because I'm going to keep coming to see you. I'm not going to let you forget how I feel about you. Things may or may not work out between us, but I'm going to do what I have to, to get the answers I need for myself and for us."

"I understand that, Anthony, but I need to find out for myself what's going on too. I need to answer the questions I have in my life." Beth Ann was still calm.

"That's fine. All I ask is that you let Clinton know about what has happened between you and me. See how he responds and see if he is any better or any more understanding than I have been. If the two of us are going to have to compete for you then it's only fair that we both play under the same rules, knowing the total truth of what is going on or has gone on. That's all I'll say. If I know about you seeing Clinton then he should know about you seeing me." Anthony was emphatic because he was confident he was right about the ground rules.

The conversation, which at times was more of an argument, between Anthony and Beth Ann continued. It went on over the next few minutes but continued over the next few weeks. Anthony was true to his word, he did not let Beth Ann forget about him and the way he felt about her. He was better prepared to handle heartbreak if it occurred, but he had learned that he needed to do whatever possible to keep the heartbreak from happening, if at all possible.

Beth Ann saw Clinton on a regular basis for several weeks. Anthony noticed the times they went out. He noticed for several reasons. First, he only lived a block from Beth Ann, and second, he made it a point to hang around as much as possible and watch what was going on.

Anthony didn't tell Clinton that he had been dating Beth Ann. He respected Clinton and Beth Ann enough that he wasn't going to be the one breaking that news. Instead, he pressured Beth Ann to be the one to share the information with him, the hurt, confusion, and relationship she had with Anthony. As far as Anthony knew, Beth Ann had not answered Clinton's marriage proposal, so his efforts must have been working in making Beth Ann think about the decision.

After some weeks, Beth Ann made her decision regarding Clinton's proposal. She realized she needed more time and that Anthony was right; Clinton needed to know about the relationship she had with Anthony. As she put it later on, "The spark was just not there with Clinton like it was with Anthony."

Beth Ann told Clinton that she was not ready to get married. She also told him that she had been seeing Anthony and that there was something between them. This upset Clinton to the point where he left and didn't see her again for sometime. During the time he stayed away, Beth Ann realized it was Anthony who she had feelings for.

Breaking up a close friendship bothered Anthony for sometime. It bothered him because Clinton was a good man who was responsible for helping him out and getting him on the right path with God. He wanted to maintain the friendship with Clinton and wanted Beth Ann to maintain her friendship with him. They had, after all, been friends for years without any type of romantic relationship; there was no reason why that should not continue.

Anthony wanted the friendship to continue, it didn't. Clinton decided not to carry on the relationship, but Anthony could not blame him after all that had transpired. Anthony regretted it and still thought highly of Clinton

Watkins. Anthony was extremely grateful for the help and discipleship he had given him.

The relationship between Anthony and Beth Ann started back up, stronger than ever. It was strained at first but got back into full swing rather quickly. They were not at the point of talking about marriage. They had just realized the relationship and romance they had with each other. They were close and enjoyed each other's company. Anthony got over Virginia more each day. Beth Ann was quickly making those feelings disappear.

✱ ✱ ✱ ✱ ✱ ✱

Anthony heard from several colleges regarding playing football and basketball. He arrived in Erwin from Gordonsville too late to play basketball for the school but he was playing for the Ninth Street Baptist Church team in one of the local church leagues. He worked out with weights and ran to keep in shape for college football. He was not boxing as much as in the past because he was keeping his focus on college to play football.

The letters and phone calls Anthony received from colleges kept his interest up. He knew he was going to play college athletics. It was another opportunity to show some of those in Erwin, especially Miguel Fontez, that they had been wrong about his abilities as an athlete.

Anthony received a letter and call about a youth conference going on in Tulsa, Oklahoma, at Oral Roberts University. They also expressed some interest in him for basketball and he knew they had a good basketball program. He was excited about the opportunity to see the campus and spend time at the youth conference taking place. There were several other schools, north of Tulsa, in Kansas, which had recruited him for both basketball and football.

Anthony did not care much about playing basketball collegiately but he did want to play football. If he could play both, he would try and do it. There was one school in particular, Tabor College, in a small town called Hillsboro, which had talked to him about both basketball and football. There were other schools in Kansas that recruited him but none as heavily as Tabor.

Anthony wanted to go into some aspect of ministry when going to college. He felt God's call into ministry, especially an area of ministry with a focus on evangelism. He realized he had a lot to work on, but he knew the background from which he came, and he wanted to work in an environment where he could give something back. This was a switch from a year earlier when he looked at going to a college to study marine biology. He applied at several schools for marine biology and was accepted but later recognized the need to help others in the ways he had been helped. He also explored the possibility of enlisting in the Navy with one of his friends on the Naval Buddy System but after his friend failed to qualify for health reasons Anthony decided on ministry studies.

Anthony purchased a car to drive to Oklahoma and Kansas. The drive went well. It was a long drive from Johnson City and Erwin but he finally arrived in Tulsa. While at Oral Roberts University he was given a tour by one of the girls the school lined up to give tours to prospective athletes. He was not surprised that Oral Roberts University had an attractive girl giving the tours and meeting the young recruits. Each of the schools he had visited did the same thing. He gave the University credit because the guide did not make the advances that many of the girls from other schools did, including some of the Christian schools he visited.

Anthony, however, was unimpressed with Oral Roberts University upon touring it. He felt it was just not the right place for him.

He knew he would not play basketball that much if he attended Oral Roberts University. He was certain he would not play his first love, football, at all since Oral Roberts University didn't have a football team. It wasn't long before he decided he would not attend this school.

After the visit at Oral Roberts University, Anthony drove to Tabor College in Hillsboro, Kansas. The drive was 4 hours long and it was late when he arrived in Hillsboro. He was surprised at how small Hillsboro and Tabor College were when he saw it, even in the dark. He was greeted by a welcoming committee and shown to his room since it was late.

The next day a young female student showed Anthony around campus. He wanted to go to a college where he could study religious aspects of the Christian faith. He also wanted a school that saw the real world and tried to reach out to that world. He was surprised how well Tabor did this. It was obvious from the conversations with those he came into contact with.

Tabor, a small Mennonite Brethren college, in a small town, intertwined ministry and "real world" reality together, which surprised Anthony. There were a number of students who were not Christians, and despite the lifestyle contract each student signed prior to acceptance, Anthony saw that there was ample opportunity to learn appropriate skills and techniques to reach people who did not know Jesus.

He met with the head basketball and football coaches and the Financial Aid Director of the school that afternoon. He was told that if he attended Tabor, with his abilities in athletics and with his financial situation, he "would never have to pay a dime to the school." He later found out this was not true.

The only reward he had on that matter was that the two coaches who made that promise were not there at the start of the school year. The year they had recruited him was the last year they had worked at Tabor. He heard later that they had left due to inappropriate promises made to recruits.

Anthony practiced with the college basketball team that afternoon and did pretty well. He was pumped up from the practice which was evidenced by the fact that while doing lay ups he touched the rim on one of his shots, one of only 2 or 3 times when he legitimately touched a basketball rim. After basketball practice Anthony met with some of the football players and some of the professors at the college.

Tabor looked good to Anthony for various reasons. It looked like the type of school he wanted to go to. He realized he needed time to think about it before making his decision, plus he needed to consider the other schools that had recruited him. It was with this understanding and discussion with the coaches at Tabor that he left for the drive back to Erwin.

The drive back to Tennessee was uneventful except for the car wreck in Memphis. No one was hurt, other than Anthony being shaken up and scared. While driving back it was raining pretty hard. The car hydroplaned when a semi-truck came over into his lane of traffic. Jerking to miss the truck, the car spun on the highway in front of traffic including another large truck behind him and he slid down a 75 foot embankment into a ditch.

Anthony was pleased when the highway patrolman called a wrecker company to have his car pulled out of the ravine it was in. The first wrecker got stuck and had to call another tow truck to pull it and Anthony's car out. The patrolman took care of the expenses and Anthony didn't have to pay anything. While he knew this wasn't an angel in a Biblical sense, he was certain the patrolman was an angel in the human sense. Anthony didn't have the money to pay for anything like this and the patrolman never asked if he did. Despite his dealings with police officers in the past this was a good and caring man as far as Anthony was concerned. After that one event, Anthony arrived back in Erwin safely.

* * * * * *

The next big event for Anthony that year, which wasn't much fun, was graduation from high school. He was resentful that he was graduating from Unicoi County High School. The only thing worse for him was what his sister was doing.

Madeline had finally had enough of living at home and left to live with their grandparents in Johnson City. Madeline went to Science Hill High School for a semester and this was the school she graduated from. Science Hill was the chief rival of not only Unicoi County High but also University High. Anthony knew Madeline never liked Science Hill, but he also knew she had put up with more at home than he ever could have.

It was a shame to Anthony that his sister was taken advantage of and abused at home like she was. As a part of the abuse at home, Anthony spent less time with his sister as they grew up through high school. He knew his sister was a much smarter student than he was and that between the two of them she was the one who really should have the opportunity to go on to college and make something of her life. Anthony prayed for his sister and the sacrifices she had to make.

Madeline was a good, smart, and attractive kid, who had her childhood and life taken from her as much as Anthony had. The difficulty for her was that it was much harder for a female to make her own way than it was for a male.

Anthony was certain that Madeline was the primary reason he developed the attitude towards women that he did later in life. He wanted to make sure that if he ever married or had a daughter he would provide as much as possible for them. This would not be from a material perspective; he knew material items only brought temporary satisfaction. Love and encouragement was the thing God could use to help women. Anthony knew God loved women as much as men and gave them gifts as much as men. Women needed the environment and atmosphere where they could blossom like a flower. Madeline didn't have that opportunity during her youth because she had been kept in the darkness of their family and never enjoyed the light of life that allows growth. Anthony prayed these opportunities would be provided his sister and that God would somehow reward her for all of the things she had to go through in her life. He wasn't the best at telling her but Anthony loved and respected Madeline more than she knew.

The night after graduation, Anthony and Beth Ann went to her apartment. He was pleased that after all he had been through; he had graduated from high school. While he was older than most other students, he realized he had done something that many in his family hadn't. He also knew that many of his friends from Keystone didn't graduate. Some died young. He was grateful for the diploma, even if it was from Unicoi County High School.

* * * * * *

Anthony spent a lot of the summer with Beth Ann. He still roomed at the YMCA but spent a lot of his time with Beth Ann. He decided to go to college and was going to go to Tabor College in Hillsboro, Kansas. Anthony and Beth Ann spoke many times about him going away. Beth Ann even said she knew Anthony "was going to be going off to college and would find a young girl to fall in love with."

The reality was, neither of them knew what the future held for them. They knew how they felt about each other, but they were both mature enough to know there were no guarantees for tomorrow. They hoped they would get back together but knew there were no guarantees this would happen.

Anthony spent a great deal of time with Beth Ann in the early summer and met many of her relatives. Living on the street behind Beth Ann was her niece, Valerie, her husband Brad and their new daughter Megan. They were around Anthony quite a bit from their visits and from Anthony and Beth Ann baby-sitting Megan. Anthony also met and spent time with Beth Ann's mother Violet, a short, heavy set lady, and her father Kenneth, a tall, slender, balding man.

Beth Ann's parents where much older than she. She had 4 older brothers and sisters. The closest sibling in age to Beth Ann was 7 years older than she. Beth Ann was the baby of her family. Anthony spent time with her family, but he didn't know what they thought of the relationship between he and Beth Ann. He was sure they were glad to see him go off to college. At least there he would be far away from Beth Ann and things would likely cease between them.

It was hard, but the day finally came for Anthony to go off to Tabor College. He loaded up his car with the things for school. The car was filled with clothes, a stereo, and a few other things. He was like most single guys, 2 or 3 boxes; a couple of trash bags filled with clothes, nothing else. Everything he had was packed up in the car.

Anthony spent the night at the YMCA before going to Beth Ann's apartment early the next morning to say bye and spend some time together. He spent a few hours with her, both of them crying. As far as he knew it was to be the start of a new life for him. He didn't know what the future held; he just knew he was leaving everything behind. The person he loved, the heart break and hurt imposed on him from the years with his family, Keystone, and Erwin was about to be left behind.

Anthony was leaving, going far away to be alone for the first time in his life. After a long drawn out kiss, Anthony told Beth Ann good-bye and that he loved her. As he drove, he cried for the first hundred miles of the trip. He thought a lot about the things he was leaving behind and the things which lay ahead of him. Things changed for Anthony that day and they changed quickly. It was another 2 years before things settled down.

~ Chapter 30 ~

Miracles of God

George asked Anthony, "Anthony, when did you start to see things were going to be O.K. for you?"

Anthony thought and answered, "I guess I've never thought that much about it. I know God always had His hand on my life in some way. I guess I really began to see over the next couple of years, though, that things might end up being O.K. There were a lot of things that happened that helped me see and understand that."

"How did you feel when things started going well for you?" George asked as he sat back in his chair and crossed his legs.

"I guess I felt pretty good. I began to believe in myself and in the things I could accomplish. My self-esteem began to develop and my confidence grew. There were several things that happened before I felt that way, though. I guess God still had a lot of things to do in my life. I know I still had to learn that God was going to take care of me. I will say this; it only took a couple of special things to happen before I realized that if I put my trust and confidence in the Lord, then He would always take care of me. After I saw this, even after I failed God, I always wanted to go back to doing things the way God wanted me to."

Anthony spoke to George in more detail about his faith. "It's like I said last week or the week before, I know that I am human. I'm not using that as an excuse; I wouldn't want to do that. It's just that I really believe that as a Christian I should strive to keep Jesus as the head of my life. That's what making Him my Lord means to me. I give Him my all, my purpose, my life, my actions, everything. I live for Jesus, not for me. If any of that makes sense? It's like the Apostle Paul said in one of his letters, "for me to die to self, is to live in Christ." I have to be willing to give God my entirety, the good, and the bad."

Anthony spoke about what some of the benefits were from following Jesus teachings. "When I was willing to do that, I realized that Christ would bless my life. He makes things better for me all the way around. I still have problems, with the dreams, the memories and all of the bad of my past. But God seems to find a way to help me realize and focus on the good, as well as the love He has for me." Anthony contemplated what he was saying.

George, thinking about what Anthony was saying, said, "It sounds like this is one of the keys for you in your life, Anthony. You think about the good and the bad. It is also important to remember, like I told you when we first started, you need to look to God as your spiritual Father. God wants to provide for you in everything and in every way what you never received from your natural family."

George told Anthony of God's love. "God loved you then, He loves you now. He wants to give you the best and He wants your life to be fulfilled. It's good that you are realizing this. God can bless you and help you more from the point where you recognize these things about yourself."

George, changing the subject, said, "Anthony, you said earlier that there were several things which happened that helped you understand God and His love for you. Do you mind talking about those things?"

Anthony was excited to share these experiences. They were some of the most miraculous events of his life and were things that convinced him of the fact that God directed him and took care of him even into adulthood.

✶ ✶ ✶ ✶ ✶ ✶

After his first year at Tabor, Anthony was back in Erwin at the YMCA. Things were going well with Beth Ann and he spent most, if not all, of his free time with her. They were in love, even though it was a love they tried to keep hidden from those around them. As time progressed they realized that if they loved each other then it didn't matter what others thought. With this attitude they talked about marriage.

Marriage was a difficult topic for Anthony. He felt an obligation to take care of his wife and family. He knew this wasn't possible because he didn't have a job. Not only did he not have a job, but most of the time when Beth Ann went to work, he stayed at her apartment. He was depressed and felt like a failure. He would not accomplish much in life unless he got a job, or went back to school. During this time of depression Anthony gained weight. Anthony gained weight in part due to the depression and what the depression brought to his life. He ate more and exercised less. His weight went from 185 pounds, which was the weight he played football at, to over 250 pounds.

Anthony and Beth Ann spoke more about marriage. Anthony started spending more time with Beth Ann's family. They both knew that at some point the family had to be involved in these discussions and unless they wanted things to be a total disaster they needed to spend more time with each others' families.

Kenneth Richardson, Beth Ann's father, was a stubborn man. He always shared his views with others, even if they didn't like what he had to say. He questioned Beth Ann as to why she was with Anthony as much as she was. He was the hardest one to talk to. He was the last one they spoke to about their relationship.

Beth Ann's mother, Violet; on the other hand was as nice a woman as Anthony ever met. He did not know it, but Beth Ann had spoken with her mother about their relationship long before. Violet was supportive of her daughter and never questioned Beth Ann about her relationship with Anthony.

Anthony fully intended on going to summer school at East Tennessee State University. It was one of the few things keeping him from being so depressed. As summer approached he knew he had to take 11 hours of classes to remain eligible for football the next season at Tabor. He enrolled at East Tennessee State University for the summer session for the full load.

Anthony enjoyed summer school and was pleased with his part time job at the University working as a lifeguard. He enjoyed the job and started to drop a few pounds. He unfortunately put them back on again after the job.

Anthony stayed with his grandparents who lived a short distance from the school, which helped with his living costs. He kept in touch with Beth Ann on the weekends and sometimes stayed with her during the week.

Things were going well and Anthony felt better about himself. He got back into shape and was confident he was going to be back at Tabor playing football in the fall. He only wished Beth Ann could go with him, but he knew they had to get married before that happened.

Things were going well for Anthony, even though he didn't have a car. He depended on walking, or others for transportation but he got everything he needed. He was at work one afternoon when Michael Braveheart, Beth Ann's nephew, came by the school to see him. Michael told Anthony that he needed to take him to Erwin. Anthony thought this was unusual, as Michael had not given him a ride to Erwin before. He questioned him about this and he told him that Beth Ann's mother had had a heart attack. Beth Ann was having a rough time and needed Anthony to be there with her.

Anthony left work early that day and went with Michael to Erwin. A couple of days after the heart attack, Violet died. Anthony knew Beth Ann was close to her mother and while he didn't understand the concept of love between a child and their parent, he understood the love between he and Beth Ann. He wanted to be with her to be the support she needed.

The next few weeks were difficult for Beth Ann and Anthony. From Violet's death, and Anthony being with Beth Ann, many in her family saw that the relationship between them was more serious than they had thought. No one said anything to Anthony about the relationship and he didn't know if they said anything to Beth Ann.

They still spoke about getting married. They discussed the possibility of getting married during the next year, possibly in the fall. Anthony could get a job, work for a year or as long as he needed, save up money and then go back to Tabor with Beth Ann. He did not know it but Beth Ann spoke to her mother about this while she was alive. Violet had recommended that they consider getting married on November 20th, which would have been her 50th wedding anniversary with Kenneth. Anthony did not speak to Beth Ann about the date of the wedding but they knew they wanted to get married. Shortly after the death of Beth Ann's mother he felt good about setting the date. They would get married on what would have been Violet and Kenneth Richardson's 50th wedding anniversary.

With the wedding happening so soon, Anthony and Beth Ann put off going to Tabor in the fall. He was O.K. with this because he was happy about getting married and he knew one year wouldn't be hard. He also knew the extra year would allow him to get into shape.

A couple of months later, Anthony, Beth Ann and her father Kenneth were going out for supper. As they were going, Beth Ann told Kenneth about the decision to get married. Anthony knew she was going to tell her dad but he was surprised at the exchange which took place. He was after all sitting in the back seat of the car.

Beth Ann spoke to her dad, which was at times difficult because he was not one for conversations, "Daddy you know Anthony and I have been seeing each other for some time now."

Kenneth, sitting in the passenger seat, quickly nodded his head and in a rough, raspy voice, replied, "Yeah."

"Well, Daddy, we've talked about it, and we've decided to get married." Anthony could tell Beth Ann was nervous about telling her father this news.

Kenneth's response was one that normally would not surprise Anthony, he had been around Kenneth for some time, but it did surprise him. He could not believe what he heard, especially since he was in the back seat of the car.

"What do you want to go and marry that bum for?" Kenneth replied. Beth Ann was more upset at her father than Anthony. Sure, Anthony was embarrassed, and in some ways hurt, but really he was more shocked than hurt.

Beth Ann responded in a way Anthony had never heard. She was short, angry, and to the point. "Because I love him, Daddy, that's why, and we're going to get married whether you want us to or not. Mom knew, and was supportive of it. She even recommended that we get married on what would have been your 50th wedding anniversary, and we're going to get married."

Kenneth gruffly responded, "Go ahead, but I won't be there. Now let's go eat"

"Well, we will get married and you can come if you want, but we're getting married." Anthony sat in the back seat, not sure, but thinking Beth Ann was going to cry.

They drove to one of the steak houses in Johnson City to eat as they often did. This trip was different though, because neither Beth Ann, her father Kenneth, nor Anthony had much to say to each other over dinner.

* * * * * *

The wedding was a couple of weeks away and there were all types of planning going on. Beth Ann's sisters, Brenda and Margaret were helping with the wedding. Brenda came home from Michigan with her family and helped with the cake and a few other things, while Margaret helped with the arrangements and the reception.

Beth Ann and Anthony were excited but he wondered if he was making the right decision in getting married. The more he thought about it the more he knew that he was doing the right thing. He loved Beth Ann and even though he still thought about Virginia Madison at times, he knew she had changed and was not the same person she was. But then again, neither was he. He saw a future with Beth Ann, one that could last a lifetime.

Anthony learned from his past experiences with Virginia. He learned something about people that he felt was a universal truth. As people get older, and as their personal experiences change, then so do they. In a relationship it is vital for those involved in the relationship to respect each other to the point to where they were willing to work together to make things work between them. Even then it is not always possible to work things out, but as far as Anthony could tell, he and Beth Ann had a good chance because of their friendship with each other and their love for each other. They had both learned lessons and were patient enough with each other, that when future problems occurred, they at least had a chance to make it.

Anthony stayed with a number of friends in Erwin after returning from Hillsboro. He stayed with his good friend Steve Jackson, and a family in the church named the Bradentons with whom he had stayed before. The Bradentons had two children named Keith and Kyle who were younger than Anthony, but Anthony got along with them and their family. The Bradenton family, Keith, Kyle and their parents, Thomas and Melanie, had adopted Anthony into their family as they had done before, and let him stay with them when he needed to while in Erwin.

Most of the people at Ninth Street Baptist Church were aware of the relationship between Anthony and Beth Ann. Many were unsupportive, while others where supportive and felt they made a good couple. Anthony and Beth Ann didn't care much about what others thought of their relationship or of them getting married. They loved each other, and wanted to share that love with each other in a Godly way.

Anthony and Beth Ann loved each other and knew that they wanted their wedding to be personal. They decided on a nontraditional church wedding. They had music from a variety of Contemporary Christian artists and wrote their own vows. Several family members and some of the wedding party didn't like the ceremony they wanted to use. This didn't bother them because it was their wedding, and they were going to share in a celebration of their love in a way that best suited them.

Rehearsal for the wedding went well. Beth Ann's sister Brenda's three boys were the ushers, and Anthony's best friend, Steve Jackson, was the best man. Anthony spent the night with Steve. They stayed up most of the night talking about the wedding, their past and anything else they could think of. They boxed against each other as they had many times, before and they listened to music.

While listening to the music, Anthony thought of all he had gone through in life. The music was a clear reminder of the help and love given to him by Clinton Watkins. It was a reminder because all he listened to now was Contemporary Christian Music.

Music was important to Anthony and he relished the chance to listen to the music he enjoyed. After he was saved and became involved in church, he quit listening to much of the music he had listened to earlier. He did this due to the severe differences in the lyrical content. He knew some of the lyrics in the music would move him away from his Christian beliefs. He wanted music to help him understand the teachings of Jesus. Anthony needed to mature spiritually, and in the early years of his Christian life he needed to surround himself in positive, good, and symbolic examples of the life he needed to live.

'Contemporary Christian Music' was a way for Anthony to find some joy in life. He heard 'Contemporary Christian Music' for the first time at Clinton Watkins's house. It was after attempting suicide and he stayed with Clinton. Clinton went into a closet and pulled out some albums to play on the stereo.

The first album Clinton pulled out was titled, 'In Another Land' by Larry Norman. Anthony was in heaven upon hearing the album the first time. It was like something important was stolen, then given back but better than when it was taken. The album was 'rock and roll,' and Anthony enjoyed it. It became one of his all time favorite albums by any artist, Christian or not.

Later in life, Anthony worked in music, especially Christian music. He cherished the opportunity to meet and talk to Larry Norman about the contribution and help he gave him through his music. He not only had this opportunity with Larry Norman but many other Christian and non Christian musicians and bands he got to know from working with them.

Many other things happened the night before his wedding. He recalled the relationships he had had with Virginia Madison, Charlotte Stevens, and other girls. He recalled the friends from University School, James Rogers, George Likens, Anthony Humphrey, Edward Collins, and others. He recalled Mr. Alexander and the help and respect he gave him. It was amazing; Anthony recalled the good things and not the bad. He wondered if it was God telling him everything was going to be O.K. Deep down he knew this was the case.

God was blessing Anthony. God gave him many wonderful things since he became a Christian. Everything Anthony received was good; he realized it came from God. He knew that one of the best gifts God could give him would be given on the following day. He was going to marry Beth Ann Richardson.

* * * * * *

The wedding went smoothly. Beth Ann was pleased because her father, Kenneth, came to the wedding after all. He did not give her away at but just being there was progress.

Kenneth was getting along with Anthony for various reasons. Anthony treated him with respect when he was around him and they did things together. They both loved baseball and Anthony went to his house to watch baseball games with him. They also went to many of the baseball games in the area. They watched the Appalachian League, a rookie league for the major leagues, in several of the cities around the Tri-City area. Baseball was a sport that not only brought out the best in competition but bridged gaps that enabled families to come together and accept each other. It was the love of the game between Anthony and Kenneth that enabled an old man to change his opinion of his future son-in-law. He no longer saw him as a bum but as a lover of the greatest and purest game on earth.

Not only was Beth Ann's father at the wedding, but two of the most important people in Anthony's life, his grandmother and grandfather came, as well as several close friends and family. Velma and Oscar were always supportive of Anthony and at this point in his life he was glad to have their love and support. It meant more to him than they realized.

Anthony and Beth Ann were disappointed in the small number of people at their wedding. They hoped for more but there was a group of about 150 present. After the wedding there was a brief reception in the fellowship hall of the church. Most everyone stayed and greeted Anthony and Beth Ann. During the reception Anthony recognized there were more people present than he originally thought. He felt better, although he hoped more of his friends, family and people from the church would have attended. The reception was short but Anthony and Beth Ann were now married and looking forward to their honeymoon trip to Gatlinburg, Tennessee.

******

Anthony lived with Beth Ann in her apartment on Tucker Street. He enjoyed living there and got along well with his new wife. One of the only things he didn't like about living there was that their landlady was getting old and senile. She accused Anthony of going over in the middle of the night and ringing her doorbell and then running off before she answered the door. Anthony and Beth Ann both knew she wasn't doing well and it wouldn't be long before she died. They tried living in the duplex for as long as they could but later decided to move out.

Anthony was still not working a regular job. He was focusing on getting ready to go back to college. Many of his relatives, especially some of the new ones from his marriage, felt that he wouldn't amount to much, and that his not working any more than he did was an indication of that. They thought Beth Ann made a mistake in marrying him, and if it would have done any good they would have told her so. Anthony knew they were wrong, but he also knew he didn't know what the future held for him.

Anthony applied to a number of places around Erwin for a job but had little luck finding one. Even though he attended college, he did not graduate nor did he have any specialized skills. As far as most employers were concerned, he was uneducated, and unskilled.

The job market and potential for employment in upper east Tennessee was poor, at best, and Anthony didn't have the credentials for consideration over others who had a higher level of education and/or experience. After looking for employment for some time he started working for his brother-in-law, J.R. Green.

J.R. was a big man, and was married to Beth Ann's sister Margaret. He was over 6' 2" and weighed 275 pounds. His hair was thinning but he was in very good physical condition. He was dark skinned as a result of his Native American heritage.

J.R. was a representative for the Wrigley Chewing Gum Company and did merchandising to the regional stores in the surrounding states. He also officiated high school and college football and it was from this activity that he had hurt his leg which prevented him from doing his job. After hurting his leg J.R. was out of action for several months on his job with Wrigley. He spoke to the Wrigley Company and talked them into hiring Anthony on a part-time basis until his leg healed.

Anthony enjoyed the job with Wrigley, even though it was a full-time temporary job. It kept him busy for several months without having to sit at home and he enjoyed the income and mileage checks he received. It was the first decent income he had earned and it felt good to contribute to the needs of his new wife.

Anthony traveled quite a bit on the job and ended up having to purchase a new used car. He purchased a 1978 Volkswagen Station Wagon. This car was used at one time as a show car and had a nice looking body and engine. The car was an automatic which made it easy to drive except for the electrical problems it had. Anthony drove the Nova most of the time while Beth Ann drove the Volkswagen.

After a few months the job with Wrigley ended and Anthony was once again unemployed. He tried to get a job at one of the local companies called Hoover Ball, which was doing some hiring. This job meant long hours and hard work. He had a few friends that worked at the company and he knew they might be able to pull a few strings for him.

Before applying for the job, Anthony started coaching a Junior High soccer team in Johnson City. He served on the board of directors for the East Tennessee Soccer Federation and gave them and the team he coached quite a bit of his time. He enjoyed everything about this activity. While he was not getting paid it was something he enjoyed and wanted to make sure he continued.

Anthony started playing soccer at Tabor and enjoyed the game. He worked at getting into better shape and at getting better. He was getting his weight down from all of the running he did on the soccer pitch.

The more he ran, the more he fell in love with running and he started running for fun and exercise in his spare time. He even ran in races in the surrounding area and did well, improving on his times in almost each race. He ran upwards of 60 to 65 miles each week. The distances for each run varied. He ran for as few as 3 miles and upwards of 12 miles at other times. There were even some days he ran twice, once in the morning and once during the evening.

Anthony enjoyed the soccer team he was coaching and didn't want to take too much time away from them. With the desire to have set working hours, he interviewed at Hoover Ball. Hoover offered him a job which he took with the conditions he wanted. He was to work 40 hours a week, generally during the midnight shift, and when he had soccer games, he didn't have to work those days but could change his schedule with other employees.

Anthony started working for Hoover Ball and it didn't take long before he started hating it. On one occasion he was working a 3rd shift and got all of his work done. He asked the floor supervisor if there was anything else he could do to help out. The supervisor took him to a wooden pallet with approximately 75 fifty pound boxes of ball bearings. The supervisor had Anthony move the boxes from one pallet onto another pallet 15 feet away. After he was finished moving the boxes from one pallet to the other he asked his supervisor if there was anything else he could do because he had finished the task. After asking the supervisor he was told, "Sure. Go ahead and move the boxes back to the pallet you just took them off of."

Anthony was angry about the response and action. He was convinced that he would not work for people like this if he could help it. This man had no respect for the people who worked under him and if this was his idea of a practical joke it was one Anthony did not think this was funny. He was convinced that he was going back to college and make something of his life. The work environment at Hoover Ball was not something he was ready for and he was not mature enough to deal with supervisors who were in positions of authority when they shouldn't be.

Anthony was convinced; God had something planned for him other than this type of work. It wasn't that the work had no value, it did. But he was convinced that there was something else to fit him. He felt God wanted him involved in some type of ministry, not that working at Hoover Ball couldn't be ministry. Anthony knew it could, but it wasn't the ministry God had for him. He didn't know the type of ministry God was calling him into, but it wasn't moving fifty pound boxes from one pallet to another.

Anthony kept the job at Hoover Ball for 4 months before he quit. He had as much as he could tolerate and knew it was time to move on. They were not cooperative with his schedule, nor did they keep the hours stable like they said they would.

At times, Anthony worked double shifts, putting in as many as 60 to 80 hours. The pay was good, but he had no time with Beth Ann. He felt this needed to change so he started looking at other job options.

Anthony and Beth Ann started talking about the possibility of children. They knew they wanted children and Anthony wanted a large family with as many as 5 or 6 children. He already had names picked out for the first 2 children. If a son, they would name him Nathaniel, and if a daughter, Marathana.

Anthony knew Marathana was a different name. He also knew no one else had heard of the name. He had accidentally made it up two years earlier. While at Ninth Street Baptist Church, he, Clinton Watkins, and Beth Ann were talking in Clinton's office. While talking Anthony read the word Maranatha and accidentally switched the word around when he was talking. When he accidentally said, "Marathana," Clinton and Beth Ann laughed, but they both agreed it sounded like it would make a beautiful name for a daughter, especially with its meaning. The word Maranatha meant, 'Behold the Lord returns quickly.' It was in reference to the fact that someday Jesus would return to the earth and take the Christians to live with him in Heaven. When

Anthony heard this he knew that someday he wanted a daughter named Marathana. He even spoke to Beth Ann about this before getting married, and she was in agreement.

In the naming of a son, Anthony had always liked the name Nathan but he did not put as much thought to it as he had the name for a daughter. He and Beth Ann did not talk about the name of a son as much as a daughter. It wasn't that they didn't want a son, they did, it was just the name didn't come about in the same way.

Having a son would be to have a child whom he could do things with. He wished he could have done things with his father. A son was important to Anthony and Beth Ann, and they knew they could love one as much as the other.

Anthony was excited that he and Beth Ann were discussing the possibility of having children, and even though he quit his job at Hoover Ball, they started trying. God had taken care of him in the past and God wasn't going to let him down now.

After a short time of being unemployed Anthony's brother in law J.R. helped him get another job. Anthony got a job working for a supply warehouse, named Smith Wholesale in Johnson City. Smith Wholesale sold tobacco products, snacks, and supplies to stock convenience stores and other types of businesses.

Anthony worked as a delivery man and salesman for the company. He traveled all over Upper East Tennessee stocking stores with various products. He enjoyed this job and the company treated their employees well. Employees were treated with respect and it was like a large family.

While working at Smith Wholesale Anthony and Beth Ann realized they needed to find another place to live, especially since they where hoping to have a baby. They took their time looking for a place to live until one day, Beth Ann returned from the doctor's office with the good news that she was pregnant. Anthony was naturally excited about the news. They had wanted a baby for some time, and after almost a year and a half of marriage, the future looked bright and they were going to be blessed with a child.

Anthony realized he had not returned to school as he had hoped, but he was pleased that he was going to be a father. The only person who wasn't positive about the news was Beth Ann's father Kenneth. When she told him the news his response was, "What do you want to go and bring another kid into this world for?"

Kenneth was not always negative. While he certainly was different, Anthony saw signs as to the kind of man he could be.

Anthony remembered seeing Kenneth over his wife Violet's casket at her funeral, thanking God for giving him such a wonderful wife. Anthony also saw him at baseball games having a good time, and when they went out to eat, flirting, in a nice way, with the waitresses. Anthony knew Kenneth was a good man and didn't take most of his comments personally. Anthony knew he was a stubborn man, who sometimes said things before thinking. Anthony knew this was the case regarding Beth Ann being pregnant. It wasn't long after these comments that Kenneth showed some excitement about Beth Ann's pregnancy.

Kenneth did this in a number of ways. One of the most common was telling Beth Ann about how to tell if the baby was a boy or girl. He told her stories about when she was young and what she was like. Beth Ann loved her father, and justifiably so. He was a good man, who had a strange way of showing love, but nonetheless told his children, grandchildren, and others, that he loved them.

As time progressed, Anthony and Beth Ann found a house. The house was a small wood frame house sitting in the woods, bordering the National Forest. Anthony liked it because he could continue his running, especially on the mountain logging trails and back roads. It was also a good place to go hiking in the mountains. The 11 mile run from their house to Beth Ann's father's house, was one Anthony frequently made.

Anthony liked where he lived and the positive things happening in his life. God had blessed him once more when he didn't deserve it. Why God continued to bless him in the way He did was something Anthony couldn't figure out. He tried to live his life as God instructed him and was reading his Bible. He knew he was imperfect. He knew it was God providing the blessings and nothing he did for himself. He knew he didn't have the ability to improve his life. He tried that in the past and was aware that he only messed things up when he put himself above God.

Beth Ann was doing okay with the pregnancy except for a few problems. She was having problems related to her eating. She was having serious heartburn due to her diet. The doctor put her on various types of medications but told her the best thing was to drink a small amount of wine. Beth Ann had never drunk alcohol so for her this was something she didn't look forward to or like. She purchased wine coolers because they hid the taste of alcohol much better than regular wine. The wine helped even though she didn't like the taste.

There was one time when Anthony became extremely concerned for Beth Ann. She was at home and in a great deal of pain in her chest and stomach. They did not know for sure but Beth Ann thought she may be having a heart attack or going into pre-labor. Anthony called the Emergency Rescue Squad; they transported her to the Emergency Room at the Medical Center in Johnson City.

On the ambulance ride to Johnson City all Anthony could think of was how much he loved Beth Ann and he didn't want anything to happen to her or the baby. When getting to the hospital they were both relieved to find out the problem was not as serious as they had thought. The doctors kept Beth Ann in the hospital for a few days, for observation and to ensure that she rested. Due to the acid reflux problems and heartburn, the doctors gave her strict orders for bed rest. She had to watch her diet by limiting acidic foods.

Smith Wholesale, where Anthony was working, was great and he could not imagine them being any more considerate. They allowed him to be off work to spend as much time with her as needed while she was in the hospital. They also provided food, and helped with shopping and other errands. His experience at Smith Wholesale was much different than it had been at Hoover Ball. He enjoyed working for a company that actually cared about their employees. There was only one thing about working there that bothered him and that was selling and marketing tobacco products. He overlooked that because of the appreciation they showed their employees.

* * * * * *

The house Anthony and Beth Ann lived in was small. They had a lot in the house due to the gifts from baby showers and house gifts. The house was decorated for the new baby who would arrive soon. While the house was small it was cozy and nicely decorated.

Anthony and Beth Ann took Lamaze classes and were excited about the opportunity for Anthony to be present and help with the baby's birth. The birth of the baby was constantly on Anthony's mind. He talked about it everywhere, telling people he was going to be a Papa. He was excited and everyone around him knew it.

One day Anthony was talking to Pam, the lady who cut his hair about having the baby. Pam asked, "Well, tell me Anthony, what is it you want, a little boy?"

Anthony answered, "No not really, I'd really like to have a daughter for my first child. I don't know why. I guess because she could be such a witness for the Lord with the name her mother and I want to give her."

Pam asked the next logical question, "What name would you give a daughter?"

"Marathana," Anthony answered. He went on to explain in the same sentence what the name meant. He'd been asked many times before and anticipated the next question from Pam. "It comes from the word 'Maranatha'. I just kind of came up with it one day while with some friends. It means..."

Pam interrupted, "Oh, I know what Maranatha means; it means the Lord is coming back quickly."

Anthony knew Pam was a Christian. She heard him speak at one of the local churches and he saw her at one of the Charismatic churches in the area where he worshipped on occasion. Knowing she was a Christian, he opened up about wanting a daughter. "Yeah, I'd like to have a daughter for this reason but I know it's not going to happen. Everyone in my family has boys, all dark headed little boys. I wouldn't mind a son either though. I know that one day, I really want one, but if I had my druthers, for my first child, I'd like a blonde headed little girl that I could name Marathana." He truly believed there was no way he was having a daughter.

Pam surprised Anthony; she told him something she was convinced of. "Now, Anthony Beechup, you need to understand that you can always ask God for what you want. It doesn't mean He will give it to you, but you can still ask. Have you prayed and told the Lord what you want?"

"Yeah, but I know we're going to have a boy. The doctors have even told us that. They think it is pretty obvious that we're having a boy because of the heart rate of the baby." Anthony knew what the doctors had said; he also knew that no ultrasound had been taken that showed it to be a boy.

Anthony liked Pam's response, "Now listen here, doctors have been wrong before, and they can be wrong again. If you want that baby girl, you need to ask, and keep asking God for it. If you get it, you know God has given you a special gift, especially since so much seems to be going against your getting a daughter. If you don't get it, you can feel confident that there is a special reason God decided to give you a son."

Pam smiled, and let Anthony know of the seriousness of her thoughts. He always appreciated the conversations with Pam. He saw the quality of this lady's faith. Her actions were a witness for Anthony. He appreciated and respected that she had maintained her own faith and love for God even after tragedy in her own life.

Pam's small son was accidentally run over by a car and killed shortly after this conversation. Anthony saw the irony of her sharing with him about obtaining a gift from God, and then experiencing the loss of what had been given to her by God. To Anthony, Pam was one of those people who had a tremendous impact on others, even when they didn't realize it. She certainly had a lasting impact on his life that he never forgot. He was convinced she enabled him to understand in an important way regarding the ways God can bless his children.

******

Beth Ann was several weeks past due and Anthony was concerned regarding her pregnancy. It was kind of funny being around Beth Ann's family, she was pregnant, and her two nieces, Jennifer and Valerie, were also pregnant. To be with them for a Sunday dinner was comical for almost everyone around. It was like being at a pregnancy convention for expectant mothers. These three very pregnant women also had fun with it. They kidded everyone around them about, "If you're not careful we could all have these babies at the same time."

One July summer evening after being at Margaret's house with all of the pregnant moms, Anthony and Beth Ann went home. They had had a busy day and were tired. It was July 8th and late. It was not that big of a deal to be home so late because it was summer and Beth Ann was out of school for the summer.

Anthony was surprised in the middle of the night when Beth Ann woke him up. "Anthony, get up my water broke and I'm getting ready to have this baby. We've got to go to the hospital."

Anthony jumped out of bed now wide awake. It was 2 o'clock in the morning with a full moon outside. He was excited to the point that he was instantly alert and ready for action. He ran to the car, started it and put Beth Ann's prepacked overnight bag in it. He knew that when the water breaks, the birth process is not far away. He was ready to go and would drive from Erwin to Johnson City, not stopping until he got to the hospital. He drove quite a bit over the speed limit for most of the 15 mile trip.

The next 14 plus hours were excruciating, long, and painful for Beth Ann. Anthony may have said they were painful for him but if he had, Beth Ann may have killed him. At this point, she understood pain and knew as most mothers did, there was no way the father had any idea about what pain was like.

The labor was long and hard for Beth Ann. To go through 14 hours of hard labor was something that not even the doctors or nurses were used to. They had experienced long labors before, but in situations like Beth Ann's where the water had broken it was not common. The medical staff planned for a cesarean.

Neither Beth Ann nor Anthony cared if this was the route the doctors used. They wanted to get out of the long, drawn out process and pain as quickly as possible. They were at the hospital, in the labor room, for over 14 hours now. It came as a surprise for them when the doctors inspected Beth Ann and said they thought it was time to go to the delivery room for, "this little baby boy you are about to bring into the world."

Beth Ann, after being in labor for so long, was relieved and hopeful the pain would soon be over. As far as she was concerned, the delivery couldn't be as bad as what she had already experienced. She was ready for the process to be over and to see her child. She wasn't bitter like many mothers were towards their husbands. She wanted Anthony there to help with what they had learned through Lamaze. This was an important event in their lives and a moment they wanted to share together.

Anthony was helping Beth Ann breathe, helping her stay calm. The doctors and nurses did their part, and Anthony was doing what he had been trained to do from the Lamaze classes. He was telling her; "blow short breaths, fff, fff, fff, come on now Beth Ann, fff, fff, fff."

Beth and responded, "fff, fff, fff" She was helped to focus her thoughts.

"That's good, now don't push, hold on. The doctors will let you know when to push." Anthony told her.

Beth Ann responded again, "fff, fff, fff"

"Good," Anthony replied, "Now rest and keep focusing on your breathing."

After 30 minutes in the delivery room, Beth Ann started trying to push the baby out, "The baby is coming, its, coming, aghh." She yelled in a loud voice.

The doctors and nurses tried to stop her, "It's not time yet Mrs. Beechup, don't push."

"It is time. I feel the baby coming out." Beth Ann responded.

"Come on, honey, don't push. The doctors know," Anthony tried to reassure her.

"I feel it. I know it's time. Check and see. Please check and see," Beth Ann told the nurses.

After Beth Ann's insistence the nurses checked. "She's right, doctor. The baby is ready." The nurse said with a surprised expression.

The doctor checked some of the instruments and tools in the delivery room and checked Beth Ann, "Sure enough nurse, she's ready. Let's deliver this baby boy."

The doctor turned to Beth Ann, "Mrs. Beechup, are you ready?"

As Beth Ann shook her head yes, Anthony helped her know when to push and breathe. Anthony held Beth Ann's hand the whole time. It was strange, they had been up since 2 a.m. and here it was 4:17 p.m. and both of them were awake and excited.

They both heard the doctor say, "Your baby boy is almost here, Mr. and Mrs. Beechup. Its head is out now. It is almost over. Hang in there, one last push and you're going to have a new son."

Beth Ann made one last push with the help of Anthony. She was screaming in excruciating pain while holding Anthony's hand and blowing at the same time, "Fff, fff, aghh, fff."

"Here he comes." The doctor said.

Anthony and Beth Ann were surprised at what the doctor said next. He was shocked and amazed, "Well, I'll be, Mr. and Mrs. Beechup. It's not a boy. You have a new baby daughter."

They were both crying. God had given them the child they wanted. Anthony was pleasantly surprised. After the doctor cleaned the baby up he said, "Look at the head of blonde hair on this child." Anthony knew his prayers were answered.

There was no question as to the name of the child. Her name was Marathana Gwen Beechup. Beth Ann wanted Gwen as a middle name. It was the middle name of her mother Violet. Anthony agreed to it, especially since Violet was such a Godly woman and Beth Ann loved her so much.

After cleaning the baby off, the doctor took Marathana to Anthony. "Mr. Beechup, I'm proud to present to you your new baby daughter."

Anthony, still crying, held Marathana for the first time. He held her before Beth Ann as she lay on the delivery gurney. It didn't make sense to him and seemed unfair that he was the first to hold Marathana. He walked over to Beth Ann with Marathana in his arms. His new little girl had a round chubby face with squinty eyes. She had scratches on her face from where her fingernails had grown due to her lengthy development in the womb. She was over a month overdue.

Anthony hadn't been around many newborns. He was honest about his feelings, thoughts and perceptions. With this attitude he took Marathana to Beth Ann to hold. As he bent down to kiss Beth Ann he said, "Well, honey, she's not the prettiest baby in the world, but she's ours."

Beth Ann didn't respond to what Anthony had said except to smile. She was still crying when she looked up and told Anthony, "I love you, honey."

* * * * * *

Anthony waited to find Beth Ann's room assignment. He took his grandparents, in-laws, mother, and others who showed up at the hospital to see Marathana. She was 9 pounds 4 ounces, and 21" long. She was a chubby little baby who was more beautiful every time Anthony looked at her, despite what he said to Beth Ann as he handed Marathana to her earlier. Anthony was convinced; the more a father is around a child the quicker his perception is changed. He was excited about his daughter and more so when he was with Beth Ann in the room where she was staying.

Johnson City Medical Center was a new hospital with top notch facilities. The staff was extremely nice and treated Anthony and Beth Ann with the utmost kindness. Anthony was excited because he got to stay with his 'two girls'. He slept on a cot and was able to hold his new daughter anytime he wanted.

Anthony was amazed at how small she was. Everyone told him that she was a big baby, but to him, she was tiny and fragile. She held onto Anthony's finger and her whole hand barely wrapped around it. He couldn't imagine a baby being any smaller. He realized the gift of love his wife gave him. It wasn't just her gift, though. They both knew that Marathana was a gift of God.

✴ ✴ ✴ ✴ ✴ ✴

Anthony worked at Smith Wholesale after Marathana was born. It was only a few weeks after her birth when he started having feelings of guilt about working at Smith Wholesale. He was distributing and selling tobacco products. He asked himself questions like, "Is this something that I should be doing with my life?"

Anthony knew how he felt about tobacco and was often critical of those who used it with frequency. This was somewhat hypocritical; he used chewing tobacco and occasionally smoked a cigar. He knew what cigarettes did though. He also knew he needed to question and find out what God's plan was for his life.

Less than 2 weeks after Marathana's birth Anthony decided he needed to quit at Smith Wholesale and go back to college. He knew that he had left Tabor under bad circumstances and he needed to go back, finish school, prepare for ministry and live a life that would hopefully be a witness to others in a positive way.

Anthony never forgot where he came from, nor what God had done for him. He wanted to be a messenger of that love. He wanted to share God's Son, Jesus Christ, with others. After discussion with Beth Ann, they decided on a plan. Beth Ann was teaching school and they felt God would have Anthony go back to finish college at Tabor. It was disturbing for them that among most all of their relatives, it seemed as if no one supported this decision.

To Anthony's amazement, the only relative on either side of the family who supported their decision was Beth Ann's father, Kenneth. He told them, "If this is what the Lord wants you to do, then you had better do it. He has a way of taking care of you and blessing you if you follow Him. So make up your minds and follow God's direction. Even if others think it's wrong, the Lord will take care of you."

Anthony was surprised but pleased with the support Kenneth gave them. Beth Ann and Marathana would move and live with her father. Anthony would go back to Tabor College in Hillsboro, get enrolled in school, look for a job and they would save enough money to move Beth Ann and Marathana to Kansas as soon as possible. Anthony would get Beth Ann on the substitute teaching list for the Hillsboro school system. She could eventually get a full-time teaching job. With this plan, they followed what they thought was God's direction.

Anthony, Beth Ann and Marathana were together on the day Anthony was to drive to Hillsboro. They sold the Nova, which was hard on Beth Ann because it was her first car and such a good car. Anthony used the money to help get started in Hillsboro. He had to find a house, make the required payments, and take care of himself until he found a job. Beth Ann would use her father's car to get to work, and to do the things she needed to around town.

Leaving Beth Ann and Marathana was the hardest thing Anthony had ever done. He loved his wife and daughter more than anything outside of his God. He felt God wanted him to leave Erwin and finish school. That was why he was willing to leave them, despite the disagreements with many in his family.

Marathana was less than 5 weeks old and Anthony was leaving for college. He knew he was following God's direction even though the decision made no sense. He could not explain it other than knowing there were times in his life the Holy Spirit told him to do something. They happened at important moments including the night he invited Jesus into his life, the day he attempted suicide and visited Clinton, and now.

They were sharing hugs and kisses, telling each other good-bye. Anthony knew the family should be together and God wouldn't give him a daughter only to separate them like this. He also knew he could not deny what he and Beth Ann felt the Lord telling them to do.

As Anthony drove to Hillsboro Kansas, neither he nor Beth Ann knew how long it would be until they were together again as a family. What was happening could not be explained and did not make sense. Less than 5 weeks ago he was in the delivery room helping his wife deliver a baby. Yet, here he was in his car driving down Interstate 40, going west without his daughter and wife. It seemed as if he was leaving everything that was important to him behind. He didn't know when they would be together again. He thought it would be at least 6 months before he saw his family again. Due to his past, he was paranoid about something happening which would prevent him from seeing them. He knew God was better than that though. He knew God had something planned for him and his family. Since he made the decision to listen to the Holy Spirit, he had not been let down yet.

* * * * * *

It was strange driving back into Hillsboro from Tennessee. It was almost 3 years since he had been there and he wondered how many of his old friends were still there. Could he find a house? What was going to happen? He didn't even know if he would be allowed back into Tabor because it was a private school with limited enrollment.

It was a 20 plus hour drive and Anthony drove it straight through in the little green Volkswagen. He carried 2 car batteries in case he accidentally turned the car off. The car had an electrical problem that for some reason would not allow it to start once it was turned off unless you hooked up another battery. He couldn't explain it because there was nothing wrong with the battery. It was the way it was so he knew better than to stop or turn the car off.

After the long drive Anthony arrived in Hillsboro at 2 PM. The first place he went was a Realtor on Main Street. His first responsibility was to find a house or apartment. He knew he didn't want to be homeless. He experienced that lifestyle when he was younger and he knew Hillsboro was not a place to be homeless.

Anthony didn't know how fortunate he was. He later realized that he should have had more faith in God. It was no more than 30 minutes after entering the Realtor's office that he was driving to a house 8 miles away from Hillsboro, in a town named Lehigh.

Lehigh was a small town, with less than 500 people. The house was a 2 story wooden framed house on Main Street. Main Street was a hybrid blend of gravel and pavement and it was obvious there was not a large tax base to provide the needs for the town. The rent was surprisingly low at $125 a month. Anthony had to pay a month in advance for a deposit and the first month's rent for a total of $250.

Anthony knew God was already looking out for him. He left Erwin on a Sunday, arrived in Hillsboro the next day and by 3 o'clock had a house to live in for his family when they arrived. He didn't know when they would arrive but if God was looking out for him this quickly, he knew God would bring them there.

That first night in Lehigh was not very eventful for Anthony other than being in an empty house. He had no electricity, furniture, food, nothing. It would be the next day before the power was turned on, but the only benefit of power was that he would have heat. He still had no furniture or necessities needed when moving into a home.

Anthony brought from Erwin a small piece of foam rubber to sleep on, blankets, clothes and a pillow. He could get by for now. He could eat out or buy things that would not spoil without refrigeration.

The other eventful thing that night was that one of the neighbors was giving away puppies. Anthony picked one out to take to his new house in Lehigh. It provided the company Anthony needed to keep him from being so lonely. The puppy was a small, long haired, black and white dog with spots all over it. He named the dog Spot. Anthony called Beth Ann from a pay phone, shared the good news, and went to bed with Spot at his feet.

Anthony got up early the next morning. He was going to the school system in Hillsboro and have Beth Ann's name put on the substitute teaching list. He was also going to look for a job, and enroll at Tabor. He had a full day but he hadn't driven from Tennessee and left his family just to wait around. He had read 'Where the Red Fern Grows' as a boy and knew the importance meeting God half-way.

The first stop Tuesday morning was at the school offices. The building was new and doubled as an elementary school. It was a one story brick building and upon entering, it was clear to Anthony that the school system was one which took pride in its schools. He walked into the office and sitting behind the desk was a nice looking blonde headed lady in her early 40's. "Can I help you, sir?" She asked.

"Yes, ma'am, I just moved back to Hillsboro yesterday and am going back to school at Tabor. I'm married and have a daughter that was born a few weeks ago and my wife and daughter are going to be moving to Hillsboro as soon as they can. I was wondering; what do I need to do to get my wife put on the substitute teaching list?" It was obvious Anthony was nervous.

The lady asked, "Is your wife certified as a teacher?"

"Yes ma'am," Anthony responded, "She is currently teaching school back in Tennessee but will come out as soon as she gets a job or as soon as I save up enough money to get her here. If I can get her on the substitute list then she will move out here as soon as possible."

"I'll have to take her name and get a phone number where I can reach you. I'll give her name to Dr. White, our Superintendent of Schools. I think we have an opening for a position but we have over 60 applicants for that job and I think Dr. White has already interviewed someone for the position. If I'm not mistaken he has already made his mind up about who he wants for the job and is going to hire them in the next day or so. To be honest with you, we have so many applicants for the teaching job who are willing to substitute that I don't even think we can fit her in."

The lady while pleasant wasn't hopeful. She wasn't saying what Anthony needed to hear for him to have the confidence about his family moving out soon.

"Would you just take her name and give it to Dr. White and tell him I came by? I'll have a phone number I can bring you later today. Then if you need to get in touch with me, you can," Anthony responded.

She agreed and as Anthony left he had little hope that Beth Ann would get to teach. Hopefully they could find room on the substitute list. Hillsboro was a small town in the middle of a large school area. Beth Ann would not be able to teach in another school system. She would have to drive such a long distance that it would not pay for her to teach or substitute someplace else. Anthony and Beth Ann knew school there started in less than two weeks and they had little hope of securing a position. Even their hope of getting on a substitute list did not look promising.

After leaving the school Anthony visited the Tabor College admissions office. After a great deal of discussion and coming up with a payment plan, he would start his full-time studies at the start of the fall semester. He was working hard at running and lifting weights, and was in the best shape of his life. He had lost the weight he had gained, and was stronger and faster than he had ever been. The news that he was going to start school again was exciting and he was going to play football.

With the good news, Anthony would take what was left of the day and look for a job. Things were going well and he got a jump start on the search. He knew he had a chance because many of the college students were not in town yet and some of the employers were looking for help.

Anthony did not take into consideration that Hillsboro was a small town with very few businesses. He was hopeful to find a job but was surprised that few businesses had positions available to hire. He didn't see any help wanted signs and thought it might be harder to find a job than he had anticipated.

Anthony went to the grocery store to buy he and his dog some food. While making his purchase he asked the man waiting on him for the manager of the store. This was the first person he spoke to and knew it wouldn't hurt to at least ask for an application.

The man operating the cash register was a small man, around 5' tall, balding, wearing glasses, and he had a round figure. He was nice to Anthony and stuck out his hand to shake Anthony's when he asked him for the manager. "We don't really have a manager," the little man said, "but my name is Dennis Funk, I'm one of the owners. How can I help you?"

The little man was pleasant and friendly. After introducing himself, Anthony told him his story of coming to back to Tabor, about Beth Ann and Marathana and how he was looking for a job. Mr. Funk asked him, "Do you have anyone in Hillsboro that remembers you from when you were here before?"

Anthony responded that he did and gave him the names of several people he knew from his freshman year. Mr. Funk went to his desk near the entrance of the store to get an application. Giving it to Anthony he said, "If you can go over there and fill this out then I'll get back with you in a few minutes." The little man responded in a nice and courteous way as he walked to his desk to make some phone calls.

Anthony was surprised that Mr. Funk offered him the application as soon as he had. He was working on it when Mr. Funk returned to talk to him. "Well, Anthony, I've called some of the people you told me about and they remember you. They said that you had played football. They even shared some things about you, that you worked hard, and were a pretty good student. I also spoke to one of your teachers who shared about your having some difficulty keeping your college payments up but that you always made the effort to send something and keep in touch if you were going to be late. I also spoke to Sally at the superintendent's office and she verified your story about trying to get your wife a job. I'll tell you what; if you can be here tomorrow morning I'll start you on a job here at the store. You can work full-time, 40 hours a week until school starts. After school starts I don't want you working more than 20 hours a week, especially if you're playing football, and if you are involved in athletics I expect you to give the school and athletics priority over your work here in the store. I expect you to be here everyday you are scheduled. If something at school comes up to where you can't be here that's O.K., give that priority, just make sure you let me know in advance if possible."

Mr. Funk continued speaking to a surprised Anthony, "I'll start you out at $4.35 an hour. Minimum wage is only $3.50 per hour but I'm starting you out for a little more so you can get that wife and daughter of yours out here as soon as possible. Is that O.K.?" It was obvious to Anthony, Mr. Funk was extremely nice. He was more than a good man, he was a great man.

"Yes Sir, Mr. Funk." Anthony responded with a big smile on his face.

"Oh Lord, don't call me Mr. Funk. That makes me sound like an old man or something," He responded, "just call me Dennis. By the way Anthony, take this phone number back to the school and give it to the secretary over there. Tell her that if they decide they need to call you, they can reach you here. Also tell her that if you're not here then we'll hunt you down or take the message to you in Lehigh." Mr. Funk stuck out his hand for a nice, firm handshake.

"Thank you, Mr., I mean Dennis." Anthony responded.

"Oh no, thank you. You're going to be working for me starting tomorrow. I'm the one that should be thanking you for coming to work. Now go home and get some rest. You start tomorrow morning bright and early at 7:30. I'll see you then," Dennis said as he shook Anthony's hand.

"See you tomorrow," Anthony responded as he walked out the door with a big smile almost ready to break out into joyous laughter.

Anthony went directly to a pay phone to call Beth Ann. It was 3 PM and this had been a near perfect day. He called her to let her know how the day had gone. She was already at school getting ready for the students' arrival in 2 weeks. The schools in Erwin started at virtually the same time as those in Hillsboro, but the teachers in Erwin started 2 weeks earlier to get their classrooms set up.

Once reaching Beth Ann he shared the good news of starting at Tabor and his job. He also shared the bad news, that it didn't look good for her working as a substitute in Hillsboro. He was sure Mr. Funk wouldn't just let him and his family be separated without any chance of being together. The people of Hillsboro were caring and friendly. That was one of the reasons he wanted to come back to this town.

* * * * * *

It was Monday of the following week. Anthony was in Hillsboro for one week and worked at 'Jack and Dennis' Thriftway' during that time. He had received his first paycheck and was excited because between what he and Beth Ann were earning, they would be able to save enough money so she could be there by Christmas. Things looked good for Anthony, even better than what he imagined would be happening.

Early that afternoon while at work Anthony received a phone call from the Hillsboro school system. He was helping carry out groceries for a customer when Dennis called him to the back of the store. "Anthony, come back here right away. Get Jack to help up front. You need to take this call."

"Yes sir." Anthony responded as he walked to the back of the store to take the call. Along the way he saw Dennis's son, Jack, and told him what his father had said regarding covering the front of the store.

Dennis was smiling as he handed the receiver to Anthony. "Here you go son, you'll want this phone call."

On the phone was Dr. White, the Superintendent of Schools for Hillsboro. "Is this Mr. Beechup?" Dr. White asked as Anthony said, "Hello."

"Yes sir. Can I help you?" he responded.

"Ah, yes you can. You see I was given your wife's name last week for a substitute teaching position here in our schools and, well, to be honest with you, son, I've had over 60 applications for a position I'm supposed to hire this week and I thought I had made my mind up, but I can't get your wife's name out of my head. Do you have a phone number or something that I can have to try and reach her? I've tried calling her home phone number in Tennessee that you left my secretary but I can't get an answer. Do you have the number of the school she is working at now, or even the name of it so I can call information to get it?" Dr. White spoke in an almost distressed tone, but one which reassured Anthony.

"Yes, sir," Anthony said with a big smile on his face as Dennis Funk was looking on, watching, with a big smile on his face. He was listening to the conversation, but Anthony didn't care. Mr. Funk was one of the kindest and most Godly men he had ever met. He knew this after knowing the man for only one week. He was confident this man went out of his way to help he and Beth Ann and prayed for them since their initial meeting.

Anthony pulled the phone number out of his wallet. "The number is 615-743-7782 and the name of the school is Rock Creek Elementary School."

"Thank you very much, Mr. Beechup. I'll try to reach her there. Goodbye." Dr. White said as Anthony said, "Goodbye and you're welcome," back.

That afternoon Anthony got a call from Beth Ann while at the store. Dennis was just as excited as Anthony and acted like a small child. He stood around again, getting some idea of what the call was about. "Let me know if it is good news or bad news?" Dennis asked right away before Anthony picked up the receiver.

He and a number of other employees at the store were praying for Anthony and his family to get together again as soon as possible. Dennis was among the finest Christian men as Anthony had ever met, as nice as Mr. Alexander back at University School even though he was not sure if Mr. Alexander was a Christian.

"Hey, Anthony, guess what!" Beth Ann asked.

"I don't know. Do you have a job working as a substitute?" Anthony asked not expecting any thing more than that.

"No, it's much better than that." Beth Ann responded. "Dr. White just talked to me. He also asked to talk to my principal who was here with me, and then he asked to talk to one of the teachers here. After he spoke to the two of them he spoke with me again. After he spoke to everyone he told me that if I could be there on Thursday morning of this week, then I have a teaching job starting that day. The only condition is I have to be there to start Thursday morning."

Anthony was tearing up as he listened to Beth Ann. "I've already called and made reservations for airplane tickets to arrive in Wichita on Wednesday morning. Can you get off work to pick me up at the airport in Wichita?" She asked through tears.

Anthony, now crying with Dennis looking on, responded, "I don't know. Let me ask Dennis." Turning towards him, not fully in control he asked, "Dennis, can I have Wednesday off to pick Beth Ann and Marathana up at the airport? Dr. White offered her a teaching job if she..."

Anthony did not have time to finish the comment before Dennis jumped in. "Don't even finish that statement. You get to that airport to get your wife and daughter. You just better be back to work on Friday after you pick her up on Wednesday."

Dennis was smiling and acting even more like a kid, "Just make sure you bring her by here on Thursday so we can meet her and your daughter, though." Dennis was almost laughing, as he walked out to tell the other employees what was going on.

"Yeah, I can get off." Anthony said as he heard everyone in the front of the store start clapping and yelling for him. "Did you hear that?" Anthony asked.

Beth Ann responded, "Yeah, I heard everything. Tell Dennis I wouldn't miss meeting him and everyone else for anything in the world. I'll see you Wednesday Anthony. Oh yeah, Anthony, I love you."

Anthony got a few more details regarding the flight Beth Ann was coming in on. Then before hanging up he told her "I love you, too, Beth Ann. Give Marathana a kiss for me."

******

Anthony was excited about getting to see his wife and daughter. Seeing them was a reminder of what God had done for him. He hoped to never forget about where he came from, or of the blessings God had given him. He came through a lot in life and every good thing God had promised, he delivered. There were times that Anthony wanted things that were outside the will of God or things he misunderstood God's Word about but God still came through.

For Anthony, seeing his wife was a reminder of how God had taken care of him and had kept his promises. How his wife and daughter got to Hillsboro and how God had worked the miracles was a great moment. This wasn't the only miracle. There were many more in the months and years ahead.

God had a way of displaying his love in Anthony's life. It was a love Anthony was forever grateful for. God continued to work miracles for Anthony, Beth Ann, and Marathana. Even over the next weeks, it was evident that God wanted them there. There were struggles and difficulties but God provided.

When arriving in Lehigh, all Anthony had were the things he had brought with him from Erwin, and the new family addition, Spot. Within a week the people of Hillsboro, Lehigh, and Jack and Dennis' Thriftway supplied the family with everything they needed. They no longer had to heat their food on top of the car on the hot summer days. They now had, pots, pans, beds, baby items, a stove, and a refrigerator. They had everything they needed to make a new home. Things were given by people they didn't know or had never seen. People showed up on their door steps with gifts. There were times they came home and found items on their front porch with notes taped on them, welcoming them to Kansas.

Several months later Anthony rented a truck to go get their things in Erwin. Until then the people of the area gave them everything they needed. Anthony and Beth Ann realized those gifts and blessings were really from God. The people allowed God to use them to bless someone else. With this type of love over the next years, Anthony started and finished college in Hillsboro, Kansas.

* * * * * *

Anthony was crying in George's office. He was reminded of how God had blessed his life. He spoke with George over the next weeks and George helped him understand the events of his life. For the first time, Anthony understood and accepted what had happened in his life. Those events made him the person he was. God didn't cause them, but he found a way to use them.

Later on Anthony occasionally got help for various struggles, but he understood his life now. He was on the road to a new and better life. A life which was fulfilling and rewarding for him and the many he came in contact with.

~ Chapter 31 ~

Epilogue from the Author

Writing this book has been a unique, and at times, difficult task. Unique and difficult because as best as I can remember, the story you have just read is absolutely true. Most of the names were changed because many of the people who impacted my life with the abuse are still alive. As hard as it may be to believe, I the author, Michael Furches, am Anthony and I experienced God's love in my life. As a result of His love, I am able to love those responsible for the abuse in my life. That is not to say I have forgotten.

When sharing my story with many of my friends and my first counselor I was told I needed to write a book about my life. I quickly realized; the more I told my story, the better I felt. Telling my story is about much more than helping me though.

I cannot recall the number of times I have spoken at various events and had people come up to me after my presentation to share their stories which were similar to mine. Many sharing their stories of abuse are oftentimes sharing that aspect of their lives for the first time, often with tears in their eyes.

From these events I realized God could use my story to help others, and thus, 'The Keystone Kid.' I know some who read the book will be skeptical. I hope not. The things that happened to me happen to thousands across America. If you don't believe me, take the time to visit a homeless shelter or drive to a housing project, get out and walk around. While you are walking around, talk to the people who live there.

While I may have forgotten some dates or specific events, I have written things as close to memory and research as possible. They were so close to reality that I had difficulty writing about much of the story. Some things were very hard to write about, it is one of the reasons a great deal of detail was left out. I have also cried over the reminders of the joys God brought into my life.

One of the aspects of Post Traumatic Stress Disorder, (PTSD) is that people suffering with it often forget or try to block out parts of their past. As much as one tries to do this, they are continually haunted by nightmares, memories and flashbacks. While this is true for many, the Lord brought back vivid memories and I never forgot about much of my past. That doesn't mean I don't suffer from the nightmares and memories. I do, but as time goes on, it is less. I realize the importance of the Holy Spirit in my life and he has given me the ability to talk about my past. My talking about my past has helped me deal with my own PTSD.

It was through counseling and help from many friends that I realized the abuses in my life were not my fault. I have done everything possible to deal with those events and am assured that if any of the events were questioned; many of those who experienced the events with me would be witnesses of those events. I will also say, many in my family are opposed to my telling the story, not because there is a denial of the facts, but because we should 'let the past be the past' and 'bygones be bygones' and 'we do after all need to forgive and forget.' Those individuals to my knowledge have never seen or heard the stories I have from the individuals who have been helped because of this story.

I am aware of the abuse that was rendered on me but I want to be clear about something else. I do not want to make excuses for the abuses I inflicted on others. While my reasoning and thought process regarding violence and sex were affected by the abuse on me, I take full responsibility for my actions on others. I had the choice to do or not do the things I did in my life. I know God has forgiven me for my actions and I hope and pray that those I took advantage of can forgive me. I also understand that for many who have helped the abused, and who have been abused, it was impossible to develop an appropriate attitude towards sex and relationship with others.

It was during my freshman year in college I thought of writing this book. It was then I started journaling many of the events. I never got around to putting it in book form until I was 36 years old. I don't know about God's timing, I just know His timing has always been best. I will remind you, there were a number of years of struggle between my freshman year in college and the time I actually sought out help. My wife and children were recipients of much of that unfortunate behavior and experience from me. There was a lot of misunderstanding and the strength of my family to endure is more than admirable and appreciated.

Hopefully this book is a reminder to the power of the Gospel of Jesus Christ. For me, being born again and changing my life around would not have been possible without the power of God. Jesus rose from the dead, and he raised me from death. He has that kind of power. I know from personal experiences, and from witnessing the miracles in the lives of others.

Many question the reality, truth, and message of Jesus. For those people, I challenge you to read of C.S. Lewis, or Josh McDowell's books, 'Evidence That Demands a Verdict,' 'More Evidence That Demands a Verdict,' and 'More Than a Carpenter.' Other books could include Lee Strobel's, 'A Case for Faith,' and 'A Case for Christ.' Each of these individuals wanted to disprove Jesus. In their research to disprove him they proved his reality.

C.S. Lewis, Josh McDowell and Lee Strobel are only a few of the many who came to believe during their attempts to disprove. If you don't want to read and prove to yourself the reality of Jesus Christ, then ask yourself, why do you put the date down every time you date something, whether on a check or beside your signature on a document? The date is symbolic of the date someone was born. That someone was Jesus Christ.

Why has our world given Jesus Christ this type of recognition? Maybe, just maybe, Jesus is who he said he was, the Son of God, the Savior of mankind. It is quite simple. If Jesus is who he said, then there is a decision you must make in your own life. Jesus said, "I am the way the truth and the life. No one comes to the Father but by me." This is a simple statement. What will you do with this statement from Jesus?

Listen to your inner voice while asking the question. I am confident you will experience the same Holy Spirit I experienced when I asked the question. Jesus came to earth from heaven to die for the sins of the world. It is only his sacrifice on the cross that can save us, and give us the full, eventful, everlasting life God intended for us.

While I am a Christian, I am also a realist. I believe God, his son Jesus Christ and the Bible can be proven. I also believe that if others are open to listening to logical thought and debate they will be convinced. People often find reasons to deny the existence and truth of God and the Bible. There are others who accept many religions as being expressions of God. They might say, "Well I'm glad you found God in your own way." Or, "That is truth for you." That is not what Jesus said about himself.

While each religion may have some component of truth, only the Christian faith has a risen Savior and an empty tomb. In looking at what Jesus said about himself; was he a madman? Was he delusional? If looking at historical facts one must come to the conclusion, Jesus was exactly who he said he was. Jesus is the Son of God, the Savior of the world. It is up to you. What will you do with Jesus Christ? Accept Him or reject Him?

I will tell you from personal experiences, as you have read in this book, there is a dark force led and controlled by Satan. Jesus wants the best for you, but he will let you choose whom to follow and what life to lead. There are only two decisions one can make. You either serve God, or serve Satan. You need to understand that when you put off the decision and decide to serve self, others, or no one, you are in reality, serving Satan. It is Satan's goal to take as many away from God as he can. This breaks Gods' heart. Satan wants to hurt God as much as possible.

How does God respond when you give him your life and make Jesus your Forgiver and Leader or Savior and Lord? The Bible says that, "All the Angels in Heaven rejoice." In other words, God throws a party because he is excited about having a meaningful relationship with you.

If this is a decision you make, please get in touch with me so I can send you materials and help. I want you to get the help I missed out on. I will also help you find a good church that loves God, follows the Bible, and loves people. You can also take advantage of my web site The Virtual Pew until that time. We will do everything possible to locate a church for you. Start reading the Bible. Find a translation that is easy to understand. There are many good translations and some good paraphrases available, from the New International Version, (NIV), to New King James Version and the Contemporary English Version to The Message, there are many Bibles that can help you. I am reminded of the comment by the late J. Vernon McGee; 'the best translation is the one you will read.' Ask God to help you understand what you read when you read it. It is amazing, but I know from personal experience, God's Holy Spirit will help you understand what you are reading.

There are four simple steps once you have made the decision to follow Jesus, I have made mention of one of them, reading the Bible, but those four steps, or foundations of your faith will be:

1) Read your Bible, it is Gods ultimate love letter and instruction manual for you.

2) Pray, prayer is simply talking to God like you would anyone else. You can do it in your small inner voice or at times, even out loud.

3) Find a church; spend time with other followers of Jesus. Being with other followers of Jesus will help you in the times you need. It is one of the reasons to find a good church, which we will help you with.

4) Share your faith; tell others about your decision to follow Jesus. Some say this is witnessing and that it is difficult because others will challenge you about the things you do wrong. That is okay; use that as a challenge to do better. You want to become as much like Jesus as possible, and that means you will be concerned about telling others about your love for him so they can receive what you have received.

✱ ✱ ✱ ✱ ✱ ✱

Post Traumatic Stress Disorder is something I will have to deal with for the rest of my life. While I love those who abused me in my childhood, I still suffer as a result of that abuse. I still have nightmares and sometimes have difficulty sleeping. I also have difficulty going back to the area where the abuse took place, when there; my emotions and temperament change. It is not as bad as in the past, but it is still noticeable.

I realize God heals and takes care of those who love Him. I also realize this does not always occur overnight or to the extent some want us to believe. I have studied many concepts of healing.

I hate to say this but there are many false healers who take advantage of others for various reasons, including profit. I personally know of 'ministries' who have misled people, and some who are involved in not only moral deficiencies but also criminal activities. Integrity is a critical component of ministry, and there are many ministries who have virtually no integrity. There are some healings which need documentation to verify. There are unfortunately, many who have had harm come to them under the pretext of being healed at a healing service. I have personally preached the funerals of people who thought they were healed from Mental Illness. They quit taking their medication as a result of being told to come off their medication. They would still be alive if they had continued their medication. There is excellent research on this subject.

Two excellent authors, both Christians, are Denny Koren and André Kole. They have done extensive research and presentations in regards to the concepts of psychic healings and false Spiritual or Christian healings. In the area of mental illnesses, diabetes, and other chemical imbalances, it is entirely possible that God's choice for healing the person is the medication used to help restore the body's chemical imbalance. I am not taking away from authentic miracles. I have experienced miracles from God, and will experience more, but why limit the methods of the Holy Spirit?

For my Post Traumatic Stress Disorder I have an occasional counseling session, supplements and people I have developed relationships with. My communication with the Creator through prayer and Bible study is also a way to get the relief and comfort I need. These things give me, by far, the greatest healing.

The evidence of the healing for me is the ability to love my family. I do not have the same types of relationships with my relatives that others do, but it is miraculous that I have the love I do for them. There are some in my family I probably have a better relationship with than some do with their family. Of course there is also the miracle of my family including my wife, and children. The love for them is exceptional.

This does not mean that everyone who has experienced abuse should make the effort to get back in good standings with their abusers. What it means is that you should seek out help from appropriate therapists and counselors.

I went to a good organization to get help, but I can not guarantee the appropriateness of all counselors and therapists. I encourage you to seek out, study and find good, appropriate, therapists and helpers. While I'm not willing to go to just any doctor for help with my physical well being, neither would I be willing to go to just anyone for my psychological well being. Find someone you can relate to and you know can help. They should have an understanding of what is important to you. For example, if your faith is important, the person you are seeing must have an understanding of that faith. If they don't, how can they really help you?

I will also state that the ministries I lead, The Virtual Pew, and Mosaic Church have worked at developing a program to provide help in this area for whatever the person can afford. I challenge churches to provide this type of help, at either a free, or whatever a person can afford basis. It is a shame that the primary reason people don't get help is because they can't afford it. Mosaic ARC (Abuse Recovery Center) mentions money one time. In the first meeting a sliding scale is presented. We never obtain financial information, or mention money or payment again. It is our hope and belief that God is still Jehovah Jireh and will provide our needs. I am convinced through these services and meetings with abuse victims, that we are not alone.

Psychology is a legitimate science with provable components to certain aspects of illness. The sooner pastors quit comparing mental illness to Demon possession, the better off their congregations will be. This is not to deny Demon possession. I believe it exists; however, mental illness is not Demon possession. Study the facts about mental illness and legitimate brain diseases and the causes.

Do pastors realize that 1 out of every 4 persons is affected by mental illness? Do they realize that 1 out of every 100 persons has a diagnosable mental illness such as schizophrenia, and that in many places around the world it is a higher ratio than that? Do pastors know that MRI's, CAT scans, or brain scrapings can verify the mental illness or imbalance? With these diseases affecting so many, we should learn more.

Churches should make as much of an effort to learn about mental illness as they do the second coming of Christ. The Bible tells us not to worry about the second coming, but to live each day as if it were our last. No one knows when Jesus is returning. Contrast this to when Jesus said loving God, and loving others are the two greatest commandments, and that the way we show love to God is by loving others.

Jesus told us to live by his example, and his example was, "What you do for the least of these you did for me." Physical and sexual abuses are areas affecting our society. The only ones denying this are those who have their heads hidden in the sand.

Since becoming a Christian, I have come to believe that sex is for marriage. It is God's gift to two people in sharing their love for each other. Unfortunately, many in our churches and congregations are victims of abuse.

The abuse includes, physical, emotional and yes, sexual. It is oftentimes overlooked, especially by those in churches. It is a subject I have spoken on in churches, only to have individuals walk out because they didn't want for themselves or their children to be subjected to the reality of its existence. I have prayed for God to protect the children of those families from the reality of this evil. We even hear of pastors arrested for sexual molestation. In a former church where I served, we had a person responsible for the organization of our bus ministry arrested and convicted of statutory rape and sexual molestation on numerous counts. I know first hand from the abuse I received as a child, some 'Christians' are the perpetrators of abuse.

Why do we tolerate and refuse to address these problems? It affects the lives of so many innocent victims, in such a destructive way. Yet, many churches and Christians are too embarrassed to address these areas with those who need the help. We must ask the question, "Would Jesus allow this type of abuse to take place without saying or doing something about it?" The answer has to be, "Absolutely not!" Hear this statement from one who has lived with this painful memory. "A person who does nothing about the abuse is just as guilty as the person committing the abuse in the eyes and mind of the abused."

I want to say something to the abused. I've been there with you, and you need to realize, as I have, the appropriate place, purpose and nature of sex. God has given sexuality to us as an expression of love. I would also tell you, there are people who will listen to you. You have done nothing wrong. "No," means "No" and any time a minor is involved in an act of sex or someone says no and sexual activity takes place, both incidents are violations of the law.

Society often makes the victims of these crimes feel like they are in the wrong. Don't let that happen. God does not want that for you. He loves you and it hurts him to see anyone hurt and abused. For those who have been abused, I would say, tell someone, the authorities, teachers, someone at church, the police, social services, tell someone. After you tell, stick it out until the appropriate actions are taken. If the people you tell don't act, tell someone else. Don't let anyone make you another victim by letting the abuser get away with the abuse.

To the abuser I say, 'Look out!' I, and others in society, am not putting up with it any more. There are places you can get help without continuing the cycle of abuse. Get the help you need. I realize you may be someone who was abused yourself. This does not excuse you from the abuse you inflict on others. If you are abusing, you are in sin, and in violation of the law. There are severe consequences for both.

I encourage churches, pastors, schools, clubs, families, anyone in our society who is aware of an abuser to turn that abuser in to the authorities.

They need help, but that doesn't mean they shouldn't suffer the consequences of their crime. Why should we insist on the consequences of their actions? For 2 reasons: To keep them from abusing someone else, and to give the victim a sense of security in knowing the abuser paid for their actions. Sexual abuse, physical abuse and mental abuse have to be stopped.

* * * * * *

Writing this book was 'a dream come true' for me. I love to write, but to think it is possible that God may use my story to help others is rewarding. I know the language and content has likely offended some. I want to assure you, much of the content, including the language was toned down from what my life was actually like. I did this to make the book more accessible to both Christians and youth. I also did it because it was hard to relive certain events. It is who I was, though, and it was the environment I grew up in.

I believe that if adults take the information in this book and discuss it with their families they can benefit their family and society. I also hope for people to see the miracle of change which took place in my life. My life continues to be blessed. I am amazed, almost daily, how God shows me his love. He continues to work miracles in my life and family.

Since the ending in this book, I graduated from Tabor College and have done various jobs from working in the music industry, to the mental health industry, and even as a writer, pastor and more. I have a wonderful son who was given to us in a miraculous way through adoption, and more regarding my family. There is a movie in the planning stages for the Keystone Kid, and much more. There are many other stories consisting of both real events in my life, as well as teachings and stories that are fictional. But those are other stories and other books. This story though, if I have learned anything about Anthony's journey, (at least this part of the journey because the story continues beyond this), it is that this isn't just my story, but in many ways, it is the story of thousands. Hopefully, it is also a story of the hope that exists. How do I know there is hope, I know because I live.

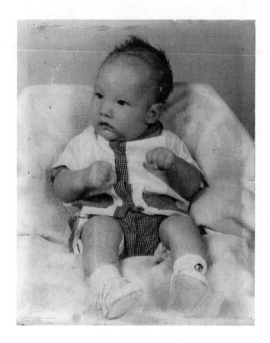

Anthony as a baby.

Anthony on the basketball team at University School.
Mr. Alexander was the coach.

Anthony's father, Charles.

Anthony's dog General.

Anthony and his uncle Mark on the farm in Gordonsville.

Anthony and some of the guys he ran with in Keystone.

Anthony and his grandparents, Oscar and Velma.

Beth Ann while Anthony was at Tabor the first time.

Anthony and Gerald.

Anthony prior to moving to Erwin

Anthony as a child.

Anthony on the football team at Tabor College.

Anthony and Beth Ann shortly prior to getting married.

Anthony's mother Wanda shortly after his birth.

Wanda and Walter shortly before they were married.

Anthony's mother Wanda.

Unsure but one of these is Wanda's 2nd Husband William Smith.

Madeline and Anthony.

Beth Ann and Anthony's Wedding Day.

Anthony, (Mike) and his family today.